CRITICAL INSIGHTS

Dracula

CRITICAL INSIGHTS

Dracula

by Bram Stoker

Editor
Jack Lynch
Rutgers University

Salem Press
Pasadena, California   Hackensack, New Jersey

Cover photo: The Granger Collection, New York

Published by Salem Press

© 2010 by EBSCO Publishing
Editor's text © 2010 by Jack Lynch
"The *Paris Review* Perspective" © 2010 by Juliet Lapidos for *The Paris Review*

∞ The paper used in these volumes conforms to the American National Standard for Permanence of Paper for Printed Library Materials, Z39.48-1992 (R1997).

Library of Congress Cataloging-in-Publication Data
Dracula, by Bram Stoker / editor, Jack Lynch.
     p. cm. — (Critical insights)
Includes bibliographical references and index.
ISBN 978-1-58765-612-5 (alk. paper)
     1. Stoker, Bram, 1847-1912. Dracula. 2. Horror tales, English--History and criticism. 3. Dracula, Count (Fictitious character) 4. Vampires in literature. I. Lynch, Jack (John T.)
     PR6037.T617D7824 2009
     823'.8—dc22

                                                                        2009026314

PRINTED IN CANADA

Contents

The Book and Author

Critical Contexts

Critical Readings

Resources

About This Volume_____

Jack Lynch

Dracula is ubiquitous. As I type this prefatory note, September is changing into October; by month's end, Dracula masks and vampire decorations will be everywhere. Bram Stoker, the Irish civil servant-turned-theatrical manager, gave the world one of the great myths of the modern era. But while the cultural myth is omnipresent, the original novel has too often been ignored. This contribution to the *Critical Insights* series collects a number of critical studies with the aim of correcting the long neglect of the novel.

Unlike most other canonical works of literature, *Dracula* was nearly a century old before it was taken seriously by literary critics. The novel was successful enough on its original publication in 1897, and with each passing decade the Transylvanian Count became more familiar to the world at large. Still, scholars paid little attention to the world's most famous vampire. This critical oversight is clear in the most comprehensive survey of literary criticism published in the last century, the *MLA International Bibliography*. If we compare the number of articles on Bram Stoker to those of other major authors, we see increases between the 1950s and the 1990s across the board—the amount of literary criticism on virtually all authors has increased—but the rise in studies of Stoker is truly remarkable. Not every published study appears in the *Bibliography*, so these numbers are not definitive; they do, however, give us a sense of the relative rise in critical interest over time. Between 1950 and 1959, for instance, Charles Dickens was the subject of 312 items indexed in the *Bibliography*. Between 1990 and 1999, it had grown to 1,270; four times as many articles on Dickens, that is to say, were published in the 1990s as in the 1950s. The increase in Jane Austen scholarship has been even steeper: it went from 64 studies in the 1950s to 869 in the 1990s, an increase of 13.6 times. Another major nineteenth-century Gothic writer, Mary Shelley, went from a mere 12 articles in the 1950s to 443 in the 1990s, an increase of 37 times. But Stoker criticism virtually exploded over that same period, starting nearly at nothing: only two articles discussed him in the 1950s, compared to 208 in the 1990s, for an increase of 104 times. This means that most of the best criticism of *Dracula* has come in the last two decades, and the essays in this collection draw on that recent scholarship.

The volume opens with several introductory essays before moving on to a section headed "Critical Contexts," on *Dracula*'s context and reception, containing a series of wide-ranging overviews of the author's works and career. A longer section, "Critical Readings," follows, with samples of critical close readings from a number of schools of thought. The volume is rounded out by a chronology of the important events in Stoker's life, a list of his works, and a bibliography with suggestions for further reading.

THE BOOK
AND
AUTHOR

On *Dracula*

Jack Lynch

Bram Stoker's *Dracula* (1897) now seems to be everywhere, but it did not come out of nowhere. It is one of the nineteenth century's most lasting and influential examples of the Gothic novel, a genre that blends two distinct strains of fiction. One is the old-fashioned romance, with its fondness for the supernatural and the miraculous; the other is the realistic novel, with its painstaking detail of actual people living ordinary lives. The Gothic novel—created in the eighteenth century, only to flower in the nineteenth—brings together the fantastic elements of the romance with the plausible psychology of real people. Bridget M. Marshall's "Stoker's *Dracula* and the Vampire's Literary History," the first contribution in the "Contexts" section of this volume, sets Stoker's most famous achievement in the context of that developing literary genre.

The world's folklore and mythology are filled with monstrosities of every conceivable variety: man-eating dragons, mermaids, zombies, gargoyles, demons. And vampires have been a recurring feature in many of the world's belief systems: the Un-Dead, feasting on the blood of the living, have shown up in ancient Persia, Greece, Babylon, Israel, and India, as well as in virtually every country in medieval Europe. Before the nineteenth century, though, despite their popularity in orally transmitted folktales, vampires made few appearances in serious literature. The early English novel—the form developed in the first half of the eighteenth century, most famously by Daniel Defoe, Samuel Richardson, and Henry Fielding—declared its allegiance to the realistic depiction of everyday life. As far as sophisticated eighteenth-century readers were concerned, the supernatural was fit only for the nursery. Serious grown-ups did not bother with stories of giants, dragons, and devils.

But the supernatural could not be excluded from serious fiction forever. On Christmas Day, 1764, Horace Walpole published a small book called *The Castle of Otranto*, a tale of haunted castles, hidden dungeons, maidens in distress, and animated skeletons. He called his work "an attempt to blend the two kinds of romance, the ancient and the modern. In the former all was imagination and improbability; in the latter, nature is always intended to be, and sometimes has been, copied with success." This attempt "to reconcile the two kinds" of fiction resulted in what we now call the Gothic novel, a hybrid of the old-fashioned supernatural tale and the new realistic novel.

For several decades, Walpole's *Castle of Otranto* had the Gothic genre almost entirely to itself. In the 1790s, though, British culture rediscovered the attraction of the fantastic. That decade gave us dozens of examples of the Gothic, including Ann Radcliffe's *The Mysteries of Udolpho* (1794) and Matthew Lewis's *The Monk* (1796). From our vantage point in the twenty-first century, though, the eighteenth century's Gothic experiments seem to be little more than warm-ups for the Victorian masterpieces that were to follow. Some of the nineteenth century's monsters are still with us: Robert Louis Stevenson's *The Strange Case of Dr. Jekyll and Mr. Hyde* (1886), Oscar Wilde's *The Picture of Dorian Gray* (1891), H. G. Wells's *The Invisible Man* (1897), as well as less obviously monstrous figures like Heathcliff in Emily Brontë's *Wuthering Heights* (1847).

Count Dracula, though, stands at the head of the list of nineteenth-century creatures of the night, with only a single rival. And, as it happens, the two figures, English literature's most famous monstrosities, were conceived at the same time, at what may be the most famous single gathering in English literary history. In the "wet, ungenial summer" summer of 1816, Percy Bysshe Shelley, his lover Mary Wollstonecraft Godwin, and her sister Claire Clairmont visited Lord Byron and his friend John Polidori in Switzerland, in the Villa Diodati on the banks of Lake Geneva. After passing some hours with a book of German horror tales, Mary (now Mary Shelley) recalled in 1831, "'We will each write a ghost story,' said Lord Byron; and his proposition was acceded to"— Percy, Mary, Byron, and Polidori all set to work on their own terrifying narratives.

Only one of those tales is familiar today: Mary Shelley's depiction of the man of science who creates a living being and pays for his presumption has been famous since it was published in 1818 as *Frankenstein: Or, The Modern Prometheus*. But another member of the circle of friends, John Polidori, did complete his story; "The Vampyre" published in 1819, became the first work of vampire fiction in English prose. Polidori's tale, with its portrait of the horrific Lord Ruthven, has few fans today, but it made the figure of the vampire available to later authors. Victorian fiction made much of Polidori's vampire, including, most famously, the anonymous *Varney the Vampire: Or, The Feast of Blood* in 1847 and Sheridan Le Fanu's *Carmilla* in 1872. Marshall's survey of the Gothic genre places Stoker's *Dracula* squarely in this tradition.

Marshall looks forward as well as backward from 1897, glancing at the long tradition of film versions of Stoker's story—for most of us, of course, the conduit through which the literary creation became a cultural archetype. The vampire and Frankenstein's monster were conceived together on the banks of Lake Geneva; it is fitting, then, that they were even more famously brought together in 1931, the year in which Universal Studios produced a pair of movies that have taught us to imagine our most notorious monsters.

Camille-Yvette Welsch's "A Look at the Critical Reception of *Dracula*" addresses not the creative legacy of *Dracula* but the novel's critical fate after its publication in 1897, including both the immediate reactions to it in the press and its longer life as a cultural archetype. The history of *Dracula* criticism, as noted in the headnote to this volume, is comparatively short; only in the 1960s and 1970s did literary critics begin paying serious attention to it. But in the last few decades it has been the subject of intense analysis. Welsch therefore helpfully explains the way critics of various schools—psychoanalysis, New Historicism, postcolonial studies—have tried to make sense of Stoker's achievement.

Monsters, it goes without saying, are unsettling. A pair of essays—Allan Johnson's "Modernity and Anxiety in Bram Stoker's *Dra-*

cula" and Matthew J. Bolton's "*Dracula* and Victorian Anxieties"—examine some of the many ways in which monsters can stand in for other things that we find unsettling. As Bolton puts it, "*Dracula* is important less for any timeless literary merit that it may possess than for the glimpse it offers a modern reader into the anxieties that preoccupied the Victorian mind." (He adds that, since we share many of the same anxieties today, "the book may reveal as much about our own culture as it does that of the Victorians.") "Every age," Bolton observes, "gets the monster it deserves," and the late Victorians deserved Count Dracula. Dracula is threatening because he is foreign, because he questions Victorian bromides about progress and science, but above all because of his perverse sexuality. Bolton calls the vampire figure "a distinctly Victorian monster in part because it represents the dangerous return of repressed sexual desire," and Count Dracula in particular "an embodiment of the repressed sexuality of the Victorian era." The novel is all about "vanquish[ing] abnormal sexual desire, restoring a 'normal' order." Repression, vanquishing—these were much in the air, as Bolton recalls, at the end of the nineteenth century when Sigmund Freud was formulating his theories of the subconscious.

The next section of this volume moves from broad surveys and overviews to more focused readings of Stoker's novel. *Dracula*'s transmutation from literature to myth makes it appropriate that many critics have approached it with the same tools they would use to decode other mythologies. In "Recreating the World: The Sacred and the Profane in Bram Stoker's *Dracula*," Beth E. McDonald uses the insights of one of the twentieth century's most influential theorists of religion, Mircea Eliade (1907–86), to "illuminate the mythic patterns in the text and demonstrat[e] why it is important that Dracula be destroyed."

McDonald reads the novel as a series of struggles between two varieties of "sacred" power. On one hand is the "numinous" vampire—the "wholly other," the uncanny figure with his connections to the world of spirits and devils; on the other is the strictly secular worldview of the English characters—"their own established secular power, which they perceive as sacred." For McDonald, *Dracula* is about the attempts to preserve Victorian English identity as it was threatened with the numinous. "Perpetuating the sacredness of their own cultural world view, when that view is threatened," she writes, the characters "seek to fortify its crumbling foundations through the reestablishment of its secular sacredness, rather than through an actual reunion with the divine." And yet it is impossible for them to forsake the numinous altogether; in resorting to the host and the crucifix, they must "engage in mythic rituals in order to establish their relationship with the divine." Only by destroying the vampire can they avoid a confrontation with "their own apathetic faith in God."

Eliade's brand of criticism, though it once flourished in literature departments, has in recent years fallen on hard times, but the attention to archetypes and universal myths of the sacred has not disappeared entirely. Mythology today, though, is more often explored through the lens of the sciences, especially evolutionary psychology and sociobiology. What once were universal archetypes mysteriously rooted in our psyches have since been reconsidered as the product of evolutionary forces. In "The New Naturalism: Primal Screams in Abraham Stoker's *Dracula*," Carrol L. Fry and Carla Edwards apply some of the insights of these developing sciences to the novel. Their account of *Dracula* explores the "primordial power of the story" and emphasizes the way it plays on our deepest fears. The authors argue that "Stoker's novel seems founded on four narratives: fear of the predator, territoriality, male bonding and cooperation, and protection of the female." All of these impulses can be explained in terms of evolutionary advantages. We fear the dark and monsters under the bed, the sociobiologists teach us, because such fears served our ancestors well: those who feared monsters were less likely to be eaten by them, and they therefore lived to pass their genes on to us. It is no surprise that questions of evolutionary fitness were prominent in the 1890s; this was the era, as Fry and Edwards point out, when "Darwin's findings caused spiritual indigestion" in the Victorian public.

Another late Victorian context for the novel is Stoker's own life, one aspect of which is explored in Samuel Lyndon Gladden's essay, *"Dracula*'s Earnestness: Stoker's Debt to Wilde." Stoker and Oscar Wilde had once been close. They had much in common—both promising young Irishmen, both making their way in London, both fascinated by the theater. They even shared a lover, albeit in an exceedingly complicated set of relationships: Wilde, though homosexual, had been engaged to Florence Balcombe; it was Stoker, though, who married her. Things grew unbearable after Wilde's conviction on charges of "gross indecency" for his affair with Lord Alfred Douglas, and Stoker abandoned and disavowed his former friend. Gladden usefully summarizes the criticism on Stoker and Wilde to date and, while he observes that other critics have noted the frequent occurrence of the word "wild" in *Dracula*, Gladden goes further. He examines the appearance of the word "earnest," which would have resonated in the aftermath of Wilde's most famous play, *The Importance of Being Earnest* (1895, just two years before *Dracula*). "'Earnestness' figures throughout *Dracula*," Gladden writes, "in both its adjective and adverb forms to denote the seriousness and importance of the gestures, work, and attitudes of a variety of characters."

It is also in Gladden's essay that, for the first time in this section of the volume, we see serious concern with Victorian anxieties—"anxiety" being a word that haunts *Dracula* criticism. Gladden dwells on Stoker's distaste for the "new sort of figure emerging in that particular fin de siècle: the male homosexual." Perverse eroticism—what Stoker saw as perverse—is one of the novel's recurring concerns and is central to Dracula's monstrosity, along with "degeneracy, Jewishness, and non-capitalist models of economy"; in using his onetime friend's unconventional sexuality as a model for Dracula, Stoker seems to have been exorcizing his personal demons in literary form.

Myths generally take place outside history, in an undefined once-upon-a-time. Stoker's *Dracula*, though, is very much the product of its age. Those who know the *Dracula* story only through the movies can be excused for failing to place *Dracula* in its historical context, but readers of Stoker's original text can hardly miss its setting at the end of the nineteenth century. Newfangled technology is highlighted on nearly every page; the novel thrusts its modernity in readers' faces. *Dracula* is filled with many specifically nineteenth-century artifacts: railway timetables (locomotives began traveling across Britain in the 1820s), typewriters (first sold commercially in the 1870s), phonographs (patented by Thomas Edison in 1878), and Kodak cameras (the Eastman Kodak Company was founded in 1892).

Dracula's late Victorian contexts were not only technological and personal; they were also political. In "*Dracula*: Righting Old Wrongs and Displacing New Fears," Jimmie E. Cain, Jr., relates Stoker's novel to anti-Russian sentiment, which was running high in Britain in the 1890s, in the wake of the Crimean War of the 1850s. "Russia and her Slavic client states in the Balkans," Cain observes, "posed political, social, military, economic, and racial threats to Victorian middle class stability," and *Dracula* figures England's enemy as an Eastern European with a Slavic ancestry.

But politics can also be domestic. In "Vampires, Mummies, and Liberals: Questions of Character and Modernity," David Glover situates Stoker's novel on the fault lines dividing various conceptions of character at the end of the nineteenth century. Political theory had given the Victorians the liberal individual, the man—usually conceived specifically as a man—in charge of his destiny, and the existence of such an autonomous subject was cherished. And yet other fields of thought were challenging the tenability of this conception of character. Darwinian selection viewed human beings not as free moral agents but as animals locked in a struggle for survival; the nascent discipline of criminology began looking at the way environment influenced the choices of the supposedly free individual; phrenology and physiognomy suggested that character was literally imprinted on our bodies; and mesmerism was beginning to reveal the strata of the mind that could work against one another as easily as they could work together.

Glover makes the case that "one of the remarkable features of Stoker's work lies in the way in which he attempts to hold on to the older notion of character, while being completely transfixed by the findings of the modern sciences and parasciences."

The struggles between the individual and society, between freedom and limitation, also feature prominently, as is evident in "Feminism, Fiction, and the Utopian Promise of *Dracula*." Nancy Armstrong, one of the leading feminist critics of the novel genre, offers a reading of *Dracula* that is as much about the early twenty-first century as the late nineteenth. She offers a survey of feminist readings of the novel in general and *Dracula* in particular, and then takes up "the question of when and by what cultural means people came to be soft-wired with [a] compulsion to imagine utopia in terms of expanding possibilities for individual fulfillment, only, it would seem, so that those same people would feel conversely compelled to limit those utopian possibilities." The novel is all about the autonomous individual—the genre, she writes, "was born as authors gave narrative form to this wish for a social order sufficiently elastic to accommodate individual ambition." But this conception of the novel results in undeniable tensions between novelistic heroes who get to make their own fortunes, and novelistic heroines, for whom such self-invention is closed off. With the help of critics like Judith Butler and Georg Lukács, Armstrong describes how the novel takes an "inward turn" around the middle of the nineteenth century: utopia will be found not out there in the real world, but in the individual. As Armstrong puts it, "The novel performed its own version of the inward turn, as it used a class-specific model of the household to displace the ideal of civil society as the collective body on which one depended for care and protection. In so doing, the novel made that household *the* model for imagining social relations." How does *Dracula* fit into the picture? "Victorian fiction," Armstrong argues, "offers its readership a glimpse of alternative kinship practices only to demonstrate spectacularly that such alternatives dissolve gender differences and so produce monsters." The nineteenth-century

Gothic works "to turn any formation that challenges the nuclear family into a form of degeneracy so hostile to modern selfhood as to negate emphatically its very being."

One of the most sophisticated and demanding readings of the novel comes from Patricia McKee, whose "Racialization, Capitalism, and Aesthetics in Stoker's *Dracula*" brings together many of the elements discussed in the other essays in the volume. Her essay synthesizes Marxist, postcolonialist, and feminist approaches into a single reading of the novel, an expression of "the capitalist dimensions of racialization" in the British Empire of the 1890s. McKee begins with a meditation on "a construction of modernized whiteness" and "the productivity of late capitalism," and on how the connection between these two "allows whiteness to claim regenerative powers." She argues that the English heroes and heroines are in fact "characterized by unsettled behavior," just like Dracula himself; they "comprise a group of Western citizens who belong within no single nation or social class and who are experienced travellers." They derive their strength, however, from "their power to capitalize upon mobility, to convert changes of place into opportunities for investment." The novel dramatizes the "disciplinary formations" that "expand power through productions of both difference and identity."

This paradoxical argument—that the novel progresses through both the expansions of freedom and the limitations of control—is uncommonly well suited to Stoker's *Dracula*, for the novel itself is riddled with paradoxes. Bram Stoker is morally conservative, reactionary even. Like many of his contemporary readers he distrusted social change and fretted about the breakdown of the social order. Most readings of *Dracula* to date have focused on the ways the novel tries to ward off instability of every kind. But Stoker's focus on the forbidden, his attempt to keep chaos under control, serves only to bring that chaos to our attention. As Matthew J. Bolton puts it in his contribution to this volume, "[P]rudishness is itself a form of sexual hyperawareness." *Dracula* is an erotic novel by a prude, a journey to the exotic East by a man who clung to Western values, an exploration of homoerotic attraction by a man who disavowed his homosexual friend, a meditation on the "New Woman" that wants nothing more than to restore everyone to their proper gender roles. Such is the function of the monster—it embodies our deepest fears, and puts before our eyes the very things we are afraid to see.

Biography of Bram Stoker

Richard Means

Background and Early Life

Although he was best known among his contemporaries as the co-manager of the Lyceum Theatre in London, England, Irish author Bram Stoker's lasting fame is as the author of *Dracula* (1897). Stoker wrote seventeen other novels, none of which equaled the fame and influence of his expertly crafted vampire tale. *Dracula* was compared favorably to Mary Shelley's *Frankenstein* (1818) upon its publication, and it is still considered one of the definitive works of the horror genre.

Abraham Stoker was born on November 8, 1847, in Dublin, Ireland. His father, also named Abraham, was a civil servant, and his mother, Charlotte, was the daughter of a lieutenant in the Irish army. Bram had four brothers and two sisters.

Young Bram was often sick and very weak as a child; he did not walk until he was seven years old. During adolescence he began growing rapidly, and soon he was one of the tallest and strongest students at his school. He was shy, and the other children teased him about his size. However, Stoker was quite intelligent, and his teachers recognized that he had a photographic memory.

At the age of seventeen, Stoker enrolled at Trinity College in Dublin. He excelled as a student and became more confident and outgoing. During his years at Trinity, he was president of the Philosophical Society, belonged to the Historical Society, and became one of the university's best athletes.

Though he was intent on making a career in the arts, Stoker graduated from Trinity with a degree in law in 1870. For several years, he followed his father's career path and worked as a civil servant. During this period, he wrote literary and theatrical criticism. He also finished his first novel, *The Primrose Path*, published in 1875.

In 1876, Stoker left Ireland to live in London, where he met the actor Sir Henry Irving, who was well known for his lead performance in

Shakespeare's *Hamlet*. Stoker was a fan of Irving's work and wrote numerous favorable reviews of him. When Stoker began working at Irving's Lyceum Theatre in 1878, he found that it was poorly managed and had large debts. However, the popularity of the Lyceum began to grow as Irving's performances became more famous. The plays staged by the group included *The Bells*, *Coriolanus*, *Hamlet*, *King Arthur*, and *Madam Sans-Gêne*. After several seasons, the Lyceum was known throughout Europe and America as one of London's most successful theaters.

Early Literary Career

Irish poet Oscar Wilde was a key figure in Stoker's life. Wilde's mother, a writer who used the pen name "Speranza," invited Stoker into her exclusive circle of artistic and literary figures. This began an acquaintance between Wilde and Stoker that would last several years.

Wilde's lover, Florence Balcombe, fell in love with Stoker. The two married on December 4, 1878. Their only child, Noel, was born on December 31, 1879. Even after her marriage to Stoker, Florence received letters from Wilde, who claimed that he would never forget his love for her.

During this period, Stoker wrote *The Duties of Clerks of Petty Sessions in Ireland* (1879), which was based on his experiences as a civil servant. He also published a children's book titled *Under the Sunset* (1882). He published his third novel, *The Snake's Pass*, in 1890.

In 1883 Irving and Stoker traveled to the United States for a tour of the Lyceum's plays, staging numerous performances in New York City. At this time, the Lyceum had become world-renowned and was generating large profits. The 1883 American tour was so successful that Irving and Stoker returned on a yearly basis until their farewell tour in 1904. Stoker first met the American poet Walt Whitman in a Philadelphia café during the 1884 tour. The two writers met several more times, and each wrote accounts of their friendship.

Although he was working long hours at the Lyceum, Stoker continued to study law and in 1890 was called to the bar. Stoker's legal degrees meant little to his writing career, but they helped the author earn his father's approval.

In 1898, after performing the lead in *Richard III* at the Lyceum, Irving suffered a severe knee sprain and was unable to finish the remaining performances of the winter season. Ellen Terry was also unavailable for performances during those months, causing a large decline in the theater's profits. Stoker was left to manage everything while Irving was injured and closed the Lyceum for the season after incurring a debt of more than £6,000.

Stoker continued writing throughout the Lyceum's period of financial difficulty, and in 1897 *Dracula* was published. Early reviews of the novel ranged from excessive praise to contempt. It was extremely popular, especially after a dramatized version was produced at the Lyceum. Irving hated the stage version of *Dracula* and voiced his opinion publicly. The play was a great success, despite the fact that it horrified its audience and on one night caused many theatergoers to faint.

Writing *"Dracula"*

Dracula is the story of the Transylvanian Count Dracula, a vampire who terrorizes a group of friends, led by Dr. Abraham Van Helsing, in his search for victims in London. The novel uses letters, journal entries, newspaper articles, and other invented sources to structure its narrative; this technique heightens the sense of mystery surrounding the story's events.

Apart from its impact as a horror novel and comparisons to Mary Shelley's *Frankenstein*, *Dracula* surprised literary critics, who had generally disregarded Stoker's abilities as an author. Like his early novels, his more recent works, including *The Watter's Mou'* (1895) and *The Shoulder of Shasta* (1895), were not very successful.

The Dracula character was based on Prince Vlad V of Wallachia, a fifteenth-century Romanian tyrant better known as Vlad the Impaler. An infamous torturer and murderer, Vlad was known as "Dracula," because his father belonged to a society called the Order Draconis. As this made his father a "dragon," it made Vlad "Dracula," which means "son of the dragon." Stoker learned details of Vlad's life from a Hungarian professor named Arminius Vambery, who greatly influenced the novel's central ideas.

Dracula was also influenced by *Carmilla*, a horror novel by Irish author Sheridan Le Fanu. Although Stoker was known for writing vivid descriptions of landscapes he had seen, the writer had never visited Romania, and only imagined the Transylvania in which Dracula lived.

In 1898 a large fire destroyed the storage areas of the Lyceum Theatre. All of the props, costumes, promotional materials, and sets were lost, causing setbacks from which Stoker and Irving could not recover. The theater staged several more performances but never reestablished its momentum. By 1899 the Lyceum was undergoing conversion into a music hall.

Irving, having been diagnosed with pneumonia and pleurisy, died in 1905. Stoker eulogized his business partner in the memoir *Personal Reminiscences of Henry Irving* (1906). Soon after, the author suffered from a stroke. Doctors did not recognize the cause of Stoker's condition until seven years later, however.

Later Life

Stoker's later novels, most of which were either unnoticed or panned by critics, include romances such as *Miss Betty* (1898), *The Man* (1905), and *Lady Athlyne* (1908) and horror novels such as *The Lady of the Shroud* (1909) and *The Jewel of Seven Stars* (1903), the story of a resurrected Egyptian queen. His last novel, *The Lair of the White Worm*, was published in 1911.

Shortly after the birth of his son in 1879, Stoker's sexual relationship with his wife ended. In the years following, during which he visited prostitutes, Stoker contracted syphilis, which was later identified as the cause of his mysterious stroke. At the time of his death, he had lived with the disease for roughly fifteen years, in addition to suffering from gout and a kidney condition known as Bright's disease. Stoker died on April 20, 1912.

Dracula remains a classic literary horror novel that has been adapted for the stage and screen countless times, and its main character has firmly entered into the popular culture lexicon. Notable film adaptations of Stoker's novel include the silent film *Nosferatu* (1922); the Universal Studios production of *Dracula* (1931), starring Bela Lugosi; a series of British films produced by Hammer Film Productions during the 1960s and 1970s, in which the title character was often portrayed by Christopher Lee; and *Bram Stoker's Dracula* (1992), which was directed by Francis Ford Coppola.

From "Bram Stoker: Background and Early Life," "Bram Stoker: Early Literary Career," and "Bram Stoker: Writing Dracula" in EBSCO Online Database *Literary Reference Center*. Copyright © 2006 by Great Neck Publishing. Reprinted by permission of Great Neck Publishing.

The *Paris Review* Perspective_____

Juliet Lapidos for *The Paris Review*

Dracula was not literature's first vampire—John Polidori's Lord Ruthven, Théophile Gautier's Clarimond, and Sheridan Le Fanu's Carmilla all predate the Transylvanian Count—but he is undoubtedly the most famous. Although Irish writer Bram Stoker never reaped significant financial rewards from his creation, *Dracula* was called "the sensation of the season" when it was published in 1897. The *Christian World* said it was "one of the most enthralling and unique romances ever written," while the *Daily Mail* compared it favorably to Mary Shelley's *Frankenstein* (1818). Reviewers commended the theme of good triumphing over evil and cheered the "Crew of Light" members: everyman hero Jonathan Harker, his loyal wife Mina, two kindhearted doctors, a down-to-earth aristocrat, and a Texan who adds a little comic relief. Something beyond familiar themes and familiar characters, however, propelled the novel to lasting celebrity.

What made *Dracula* immortal? One source of its appeal was the deft way it exposed the anxieties of the late Victorian age. When Dracula, an eastern noble, travels to London, Stoker was gesturing toward a fear of invasion—of the British Empire finally getting a bit of what it had been giving for centuries. Just as the British gained power in India by controlling trade there, Dracula lays the groundwork for his blood-sucking empire by mastering property law and buying up real estate.

Dracula's attacks likewise played with Victorian attitudes toward women. The role-reversing scene in which Mina sucks blood from Dracula's bare breast is both a paranormal encounter and an adultery set piece. Recording the incident in his diary, Dr. Seward refuses to allow Mina an active role, stripping her of both control and desire: he says that "the attitude of the two had a terrible resemblance to a child forcing a kitten's nose into a saucer of milk to compel it to drink." But Mina's account is more ambiguous; she says, "I was bewildered, and, strangely enough, I did not want to hinder him. I suppose it is part of the horrible curse that this happens when his touch is on his victim." The vampire's power lies not in his physical strength but in his ability to persuade.

In addition to needling Victorian mores, the novel tapped into contemporary unease over the rapid pace of modernization. To defeat the Count, the crew must embrace technology (the telegraph), but they also must put their faith in Catholic traditions. When the crew confronts Dracula at his house in Piccadilly, Dr. Seward flashes a crucifix and feels "a mighty power fly along [his] arm." Dr. Seward, who most embodies modern thinking in *Dracula*, is forced to acknowledge that the cross is not just a symbol but a still-powerful tool.

Dracula got right to the heart of Victorian angst, but it remains relevant—and still read—to this day. Compared with other adventure novels, *Dracula* contains few action sequences, but these are the most frightening and memorable moments in the novel. Stoker manipulates tension and suspense expertly as the novel unfolds. He never provides Dracula's perspective: the monster remains mysterious throughout, and the reader stays almost as much in the dark as the characters. At the same time, the crew members are constantly racing against the clock. At Castle Dracula, Jonathan knows he must escape before the date of the last predated letter; in the final pages, the crew members must get to the vampire before the sun sets.

Dracula is a remarkably flexible text. The title character has been adapted into various media, and as one reads this collection of essays, it is clear that the Count has been subjected to nearly every school of interpretation—Freudian, Marxist, postcolonial, and feminist, to name just a few. The word "monster" comes from the Latin noun *monstrum*, which means a sign, a warning, a divine portent, or a wonder. Dracula manages to encapsulate all four of these meanings in the course of the novel: he is a symptom of greater social and psychological anxieties, a warning to readers about foreign invaders and sexual predators, a portent of modernity, and a wonder to behold as he flits through London and Transylvania.

Bibliography

Belford, Barbara. *Bram Stoker: A Biography of the Author of Dracula*. New York: Knopf, 1996.

Moretti, Franco. "The Dialectic of Fear." *New Left Review* 135, November-December 1982.

Murray, Paul. *From the Shadow of Dracula: A Life of Bram Stoker*. London: Jonathan Cape, 2004.

Stoker, Bram. *Dracula*. Maud Ellmann, ed. New York: Oxford University Press, 1996.

Sullivan, Jack, ed. *The Penguin Encyclopedia of Horror and the Supernatural*. New York: Viking, 1986.

CRITICAL
CONTEXTS

Stoker's *Dracula* and the Vampire's Literary History

Bridget M. Marshall

Although Bram Stoker's Count Dracula is perhaps the best-known vampire in popular culture, he is not the first vampire to haunt literary history. Stoker borrowed from a wide variety of vampire folklore, tales, and stories to create his masterpiece. Published in 1897, Stoker's *Dracula* went on to become a model for other vampire tales; few modern film or book versions of the vampire can avoid calling upon a connection to Stoker's work. The changes Stoker made, and those made by the vampire-writers after him, indicate that the Un-Dead have quite a varied literary life and that the public has an insatiable appetite for vampires.

Stoker's Research into Folklore and Legend

Within the novel, we see Count Dracula reading maps and guidebooks to learn about England, and Jonathan Harker reading travelogues and dictionaries to prepare for his visit to Transylvania. Like his characters, Stoker himself did considerable research before undertaking his project. In recent years, scholars have discovered a wealth of information on Stoker's sources for *Dracula*, particularly through research at the Rosenbach Foundation in Philadelphia, which holds Stoker's notes. From Stoker's own notes, we know that one essential resource he turned to was the work of Emily Gerard, a Scottish novelist who briefly lived in Transylvania; she published an article, "Transylvanian Superstitions," in 1885, which she later expanded and published as *The Land Beyond the Forest* (1888). Gerard's guide is specifically his source for the term "nosferatu." Stoker also used *Transylvania: Its Products and Its People* (1865), by Charles Boner, and E. C. Johnson's *On the Track of the Crescent: Erratic Notes from the Piraeus to Pesth* (1885) for additional information on geography and customs of the area. In fact, it is clear that parts of Stoker's description of Transylvania are "almost word for word" from these sources (Gelder 3). Although Stoker himself never visited Transylvania, these sources served him well for his detailed descriptions of Harker's trip to Dracula's castle.

While Stoker may have borrowed details of travels to Transylvania, he is in fact responsible for the widespread connection that we make between Transylvania and vampires. As Stephen D. Arata explains, "the 'natural' association of vampires with Transylvania begins with, rather than predates, *Dracula*" (164). Stoker's vampire borrowed from a variety of legends, mythologies, and stories, but his particular mix of characteristics became an iconic figure that would be a standard against which all others—before and after—would be compared.

Stoker's Literary Predecessors

Long before Stoker's Dracula, vampires were frequent visitors in classic French stories. The particular features and powers of these vampires vary considerably. Charles Nodier's "Smarra" (1821), features a demon that has "fingers armed with nails of a metal finer than steel, which penetrate the flesh without rending it, and suck the blood from it like the insidiously pumping leech" (45). Stoker's Dracula has "nails that were long and fine, and cut to a sharp point" (165); however, they do not appear to be made of metal, nor are they the primary means of the vampire's bloodletting. In Théophile Gautier's "The Beautiful Dead" (1836), the vampire (a female) observes her non-vampire lover accidentally cut himself: "The blood immediately gushed forth in a little purple jet, and a few drops spurted upon Clarimonde [the vampire]. Her eyes flashed, her face suddenly assumed an expression of savage joy such as I had never before observed in her" (67). In a remarkably similar scene in *Dracula*, Harker accidentally cuts himself while shaving, and the Count's "eyes blazed with a sort of demoniac fury and he suddenly made a grab at my throat" (172). The vampire also appears in English Romantic-era poems, such as Lord Byron's "The Giaour"

(1812) and Samuel Taylor Coleridge's "Christabel" (1816). Vampire tales became increasingly popular throughout the nineteenth century.

The vampire's first appearance in English fiction came with the publication of John Polidori's "The Vampyre" in 1819. Polidori, a young doctor and personal physician to Lord Byron, penned his initial notes for the story in the summer of 1816 while staying with Byron, Percy Shelley, and Mary Shelley (who began writing *Frankenstein* at the same time). Polidori's story brought him nothing but trouble; it was first published under the name of Lord Byron, who disavowed it and separated himself completely from Polidori. Byron did, it seems, write a vampire tale from which Polidori may or may not have borrowed while he was writing his own (Gelder 26). Polidori's vampire is named Lord Ruthven and bears a more than passing resemblance to Lord Byron, which presumably further enraged the poet. Ruthven's character features several traits that are now well-known signals of vampirism, in particular, the "deadly hue of his face" (69). The face of Stoker's Dracula is similarly described as "deathly pale" (182). Polidori's vampire is not a repellent monster; rather, he is attractive and seductive: "his form and outline were beautiful, any of the female hunters after notoriety attempted to win his attentions" (69). Although Stoker's Dracula is repellent when Harker first encounters him in his castle, upon his arrival in London he is a very different creature. When Mina spies him in London, she describes his face as "sensual" (292). Both Polidori's Ruthven and Stoker's Dracula (after his arrival in London) are attractive versions of the vampire; part of the danger they pose is that they are able to walk among us undetected and entice their victims because of their particular appearance.

Polidori's story is somewhat odd in the canon of vampire tales in that it shows no graphic scenes of biting; we never see the classic fangs that we expect in a vampire's mouth. We do see the aftermath of the biting: when a victim is discovered, "upon her neck and breast was blood, and upon her throat were the marks of teeth having opened the vein" (77). Like most vampires, including Stoker's, Polidori's Ruthven has "strength [that] seemed superhuman" (76); he can take a man and "lift [him] from his feet and hurl [him] with enormous force against the ground" (76). The vampire's brutality and physical power make him an unstoppable force; even aside from their blood-sucking, vampires strike fear into their mere human enemies, who generally cannot compete physically with vampiric strength.

In both Polidori's "Vampyre" and Stoker's *Dracula*, the vampire first makes contact with an innocent young man; in Polidori's story, this is Aubrey, while in Stoker's his name is Jonathan Harker. Polidori's Aubrey might be seen as an ur-Harker, unable to read the signs of vampirism. Rather than having a lover like Harker, Aubrey has an innocent sister, who becomes another of Ruthven's victims. And like Harker, who cannot seem to put together the rapidly mounting evidence that the Count is not human, Aubrey likewise seems to know that there is something very wrong with his companion, "yet still he wished to disbelieve" (80). Both men fail to identify the vampire and take action, and it is the women in their lives who pay the price for their failures. Aubrey himself goes mad, and his sister comes to her end at the hands of the vampire; we do not see the act, but we are told that she "had glutted the thirst of a Vampyre!" (85). Thus the novels show how both men and women are ruined by the vampire.

Both Harker and Aubrey are terrified when the vampire leaves their home territories (in Transylvania and Greece, respectively) to join them in England. Aubrey leaves Greece, believing Ruthven to be dead, much as Harker leaves Transylvania attempting to forget the horrors he has seen there. Spying Ruthven at a party, Aubrey "gazed till his limbs almost refusing to bear their weight, he was obliged to take the arm of a friend, and forcing a passage through the crowd, he threw himself into his carriage, and was driven home" (81). Similarly, the first time Jonathan spies Dracula on the streets of London, he is "very greatly terrified; I do believe that if he had not had me [Mina] to lean on and to support him he would have sunk down"; shortly thereafter, his "eyes closed, and he went quietly into a sleep" from which he awakes with no memory of what has happened (292). Both men are physically incapacitated by the mere sight of the vampire, and they are unable to protect themselves or their loved ones from his menace. Both flee the scene and try to forget the threat, and both are ultimately hurt by their inaction.

Despite some similarities between Polidori's and Stoker's basic characters, overall the stories are quite different. In Polidori's version, the vampire legend and threat come from Greece, but we get very little insight into the history of the creature, and the rather short story is quite underdeveloped, particularly lacking any scenes of actual vampirism. In form, Polidori's version has little of the Gothic trappings of found narratives and inserted stories that Stoker uses. However, the notion of the vampire as an attractive, mesmerizing figure (as opposed to simply a repellent demon) was an idea that Stoker may have found in Polidori's model.

Polidori's novel also left its mark on another terrifically long and well-known vampire story, *Varney the Vampire: Or, The Feast of Blood*, which was published as a series of pamphlets between 1845 and 1847, appearing in book form in 1847. *Varney*'s authorship remains somewhat contested, with some arguing for James Malcolm Rhymer and others for Thomas Preskett Prest. It is clear that *Varney*'s author knew Polidori's Ruthven, since some of the descriptions of Varney and some elements of the plot seem to be similar to those portrayed by Polidori. Like Ruthven, Varney attempts to marry (and ruin) innocent young women; also, both men have their powers revived by moonlight. But Varney also departs from Polidori and sets numerous new standards for vampires. According to Margaret Carter, "The seeds of later vampire convention—the black and clammy touch, the religious overtones, the stake and the funeral pyre, the eternal fascination of the Undead—are all buried in the pages of *Varney*" (xxxix). Varney's first appearance (in the bedroom of his soon-to-be victim) is classic vampire: his face "is perfectly white—perfectly bloodless. The eyes look like polished tin; the lips are drawn back, and the principal feature next to those dreadful eyes is the teeth—the fearful looking teeth—projecting like those of some wild animal, hideously, glaringly white, and fang-like" (3). Polidori's quite short work hardly compares to Rhymer/Prest's expansive three-volume work, and indeed, *Varney*, which was sold cheaply in small sections, was far more popular in its day than Polidori's story. However, while Polidori's novel is frequently anthologized with other vampire tales, *Varney* today is read infrequently.

Another relevant precursor to Stoker's *Dracula* is Sheridan Le Fanu's long story *Carmilla* (1872), which appeared in Le Fanu's collection *In a Glass Darkly*. Le Fanu's *Carmilla* is important to Stoker's *Dracula* in particular because of the portrayal of the female vampire. Stoker was no doubt familiar with the female vampire. In one source or another, he would have read of Elizabeth Báthory (1560–1614), known as the Blood Countess for her habit of bathing in the blood of virgins. Le Fanu's portrayal of the female vampire in *Carmilla* may have provided some useful information for Stoker's research. *Carmilla* is set in Styria, "an older designation of Slovenia—also the setting, incidentally, for Stoker's short story, 'Dracula's Guest' (1914)" (Gelder 44). Carmilla is the vampire; her victim is the narrator, named Laura, a young woman whose father takes in the mysterious Carmilla. *Carmilla* does involve a frame narrative of sorts, with a Dr. Hesselius introducing Laura's narrative of the strange events, and also, a few short, inserted stories within Laura's story that corroborate her tale. Nonetheless, the form of *Carmilla* is still far from the elaborate series of letters, clippings, and telegrams that Stoker used.

Early on, Laura details an event she remembers from when she was six years old that strongly affected her: she awoke alone in her room and

> saw a solemn, but very pretty face looking at me from the side of the bed. It was that of a young lady who was kneeling, with her hands under the coverlet. . . . She caressed me with her hands, and lay down beside me on the bed, and drew me towards her, smiling; I felt immediately delightfully soothed, and fell asleep again. I was wakened by a sensation as if two nee-

dles ran into my breast very deep at the same moment, and I cried loudly. The lady started back, with her eyes fixed on me, and then slipped down upon the floor, and, as I thought, hid herself under the bed (90).

Although her family tries to tell her that she must have dreamt the encounter, she is convinced it was real. Carmilla's encounter with the vampire lady in her bedroom is echoed in Jonathan Harker's encounter with the three vampire ladies in Dracula's castle. He, too, insists that he "cannot in the least believe that it was all sleep" (181). He recalls that three beautiful women appeared to him in the night, and explains: "I lay quiet, looking out under my eyelashes in an agony of delightful anticipation. The fair girl advanced and bent over me till I could feel the movement of her breath upon me. . . . I was afraid to raise my eyelids, but looked out and saw perfectly under the lashes. The girl went on her knees, and bent over me, simply gloating. There was a deliberate voluptuousness which was both thrilling and repulsive" (181–182). Both Laura and Harker are attracted to the vampires, and both are clearly sexually aroused by their attentions. Laura describes how Carmilla "drew me to her, and her hot lips traveled along my cheek in kisses . . . leaving me trembling" (104–105). Harker can "feel the hot breath on my neck" and finds himself in a "languorous ecstasy" (182). Stoker's vampire victims, like other literary models, find themselves both fearful and aroused; as Franco Moretti explains, "Fear and attraction are one and the same: and not just in Stoker. Much of nineteenth-century bourgeois high culture had already treated eros and sex as ambivalent phenomena" (154). While the explicitly sexualized image of the vampire might not have been portrayed on film until many years later, the sexual threat of the vampire was a feature of the creature from its earliest versions.

While some of Stoker's descriptions of Dracula portray him as creepy and revolting, Le Fanu's Carmilla is consistently described as quite beautiful: "she was slender, and wonderfully graceful. Except that her movements were languid—very languid— . . . Her complexion was rich and brilliant; her features were small and beautifully formed; her eyes large, dark, and lustrous; her hair was quite wonderful, I never saw hair so magnificently thick and long" (102–103). The beautiful female vampire also appears in Stoker, not only in the form of the three vampire ladies but also in the form of Lucy Westenra, once Dracula has turned her into a vampire. Appearing as the "bloofer [beautiful] lady" (296) and feeding on children, Lucy uses her attractive looks to help her to gain her prey. When the vampire hunters attempt to kill her, they are nearly stopped by her beautiful appearance: "more radiantly beautiful than ever . . . the lips were red, nay redder than before; and on the cheeks was a delicate bloom" (315). Vampire women prove to be particularly dangerous to their victims because they use physical beauty, rather than physical brutality, to overpower their victims. In both *Dracula* and *Carmilla*, the early death of a beautiful young woman inspires the men in the stories to take action against the vampires. In *Carmilla*, one of Laura's friends, Bertha, dies in mysterious circumstances. Her father vows, "I devote my remaining days to tracking and extinguishing a monster" (93). The deaths of Bertha and Lucy galvanize the strength and dedication of the men, who redeem themselves by saving Laura and Mina later in the stories.

In both *Dracula* and *Carmilla*, the narrators are anxious about whether their readers will believe them. Laura indicates that she is writing her story ten years after the events unfolded (104), but she insists that she is reliable: "I am now going to tell you something so strange that it will require all your faith in my veracity to believe my story. It is not only true, nevertheless, but truth of which I have been an eye-witness" (91). Mina places a similar address to her reader at the end of her collection of documents. When the band of vampire hunters gathers years after their adventures, they are shocked to realize that "there is hardly one authentic document; nothing but a mass of typewriting . . . we could hardly ask any one, even did we wish to, to accept these as proofs of so wild a story" (460). These narrators acknowledge that their stories will shock their readers and perhaps leave them in disbelief. Van Helsing claims, "We want no proofs; we ask none to believe us" (460). Despite what the reader may think, the characters themselves fully believe their own wild tales.

Class distinctions, particularly between the nobility and the peasantry, are important lines of demarcation in the vampire worlds of Stoker, Polidori, and Le Fanu. Carmilla explains to her new acquaintances that she is from a family "very ancient and noble" (103), Dracula claims to be "of an old family" (170) with "a right to be proud" (174), and Polidori's Ruthven is called "a nobleman" (69). While the role of the "old blood" nobility is frequently aligned with that of the evil vampire, it is people from the lowest classes who are typically most informed and aware of the true nature of the vampires. In Polidori's "Vampyre," Stoker's *Dracula*, and Le Fanu's *Carmilla*, the peasantry and uneducated classes have knowledge of the vampire that the upper classes refuse to believe or fail to understand. Aubrey's beloved, Ianthe, described as an "uneducated Greek girl" (75) and an "infantile being" (75), displays "her earnestness and apparent belief" (74) in telling tales of vampires, although he "persisted in persuading her, that there could be no truth in her fears" (74–75). When he talks to her family, he "mock[s] the belief of those horrible fiends" (75), which only increases the family's concerns. Likewise, Laura's father declares that the local peasants who keep dying mysteriously have a fever rather than vampire bites; he insists that their strange medical condition "is strictly referable to natural causes. These poor people infect one another with their superstitions" (109). Jonathan is likewise dismissive of the concerns of the locals. He calls the worrying and praying of the innkeeper "very ridiculous," and when she begs him to delay his trip to a less dangerous time, he insists that "there was business to be done" (154). Indeed, Harker's dismissal of the peasants is alarmingly aligned with that of Dracula himself, who says "your peasant is at heart a coward and a fool!" (168). Stoker's characters show the same kind of ignorance as those of Polidori and Le Fanu, and they eventually pay for their disbelief and unwillingness to heed the ample warnings of the peasants.

Stoker's *Dracula* Adapted for Stage and Screen

Stoker himself created the first dramatic version of his novel, staging *Dracula: Or, The Undead*, his own five-act play, at the Lyceum Theatre, where he worked. It played for only one night, and Stoker himself called the performance "Dreadful!" ("Drama, Vampire" 195). In 1923, Hamilton Deane wrote a script based on *Dracula*, which was staged in 1924 with great success; it ran for almost four hundred performances in its initial run in London, followed by three touring companies that ran it well into the 1930s ("Drama, Vampire" 195). Meanwhile, in America, John L. Balderston bought the American rights to the novel and extensively rewrote Deane's version. The New York and touring versions of the show featured Bela Lugosi in the lead role. This play version was also the source of the "domesticated" version of Dracula, wearing formal clothes and a cape and looking particularly aristocratic instead of demonic. Numerous stage versions and revivals of the original stagings have been mounted over the years.

Film adaptations of *Dracula* have continued to revise the appearance of the vampire. As Ken Gelder explains, "Each new vampire film engages in a process of familiarisation and defamiliarisation, both interpellating viewers who already 'know' about vampires from the movies (and elsewhere), and providing enough points of difference (in the narrative, in the 'look' of the vampire, and so on) for newness to maintain itself" (86). The reinventing of the vampire on film began with the first vampire film production, F. W. Murnau's 1922 masterpiece of black-and-white silent film, *Nosferatu, eine Symphonie des Grauens* (*Nosferatu, a Symphony of Horror*). Murnau was unable to secure the rights to film the novel, so the film makes a variety of changes; for instance, "Count Dracula" becomes "Count Orlok," the film is set in 1838 rather than the novel's 1890s, most of the characters' names are altered, and their home country is Germany, not England. But the changes were few enough that Stoker's estate successfully sued for copyright infringement, winning a court order to have all copies of the film destroyed. Fortunately, a few copies were saved; however, most prints available today are of poor quality. Murnau's Count Orlok is possibly one of the most frightening versions of the vampire on screen. Played by Max Schreck, Orlok is rodent-like, with pointy ears, a bald head, and extremely long nails. He is barely able to keep up anything resembling a human appearance, and his creepy movements on screen make him a truly believable vampire. Elements of Schreck's portrayal of the vampire come from Stoker's portrayal of Dracula when Harker first encounters him, when he describes him having a "high bridge of the thin nose and peculiarly arched nostrils," "a lofty domed forehead," and "ears [that] were pale, and the tops extremely pointed" (165). But Schreck's Orlok is never transformed into the magnetically attractive Count; he remains the hideous creature throughout the film.

Murnau's film directly spawned other vampire films as well. In 1979, another German director, Werner Herzog, remade Murnau's *Nosferatu*, titling it *Nosferatu: Phantom der Nacht* and starring Klaus Kinski. The making of Murnau's *Nosferatu* became the subject of yet another film, *Shadow of the Vampire* (2000), featuring Willem Dafoe in the character of Max Schreck/Count Orlok. In *Shadow of the Vampire*, the character of Count Orlok (Dracula) explains that he has in fact read Stoker's novel, and that it made him sad. He explains:

> Dracula hasn't had servants in 400 years and then a man comes to his ancestral home, and he must convince him that he—that he is like the man. He has to feed him, when he himself hasn't eaten food in centuries. Can he even remember how to buy bread? How to select cheese and wine? And then he remembers the rest of it. How to prepare a meal, how to make a bed. He remembers his first glory, his armies, his retainers, and what he is reduced to. The loneliest part of the book comes when the man accidentally sees Dracula setting his table.

The idea that "Dracula" is a "real" being in the world, capable of commenting upon Stoker's apparently inferior portrayal of him, adds life to the character. The fact that Schreck comments upon the most mundane elements of Stoker's novel further adds to the irony of the scene.

While Murnau's vampire (and those that followed his vision) portrayed the vampire as a filthy, horrifying creature, other films portrayed a far more suave, attractive vampire. The 1931 Universal Pictures black-and-white film, directed by Tod Browning and featuring Bela Lugosi as Dracula, was the first licensed film version of the novel. Lugosi had previously portrayed Dracula in the stage version in New York. His film version, with aristocratic black cape and a thick (and exaggerated) Hungarian accent, became the standard image of Dracula for years to come.

In 1958, Hammer Films, a British production company, released their version of *Dracula*, featuring Christopher Lee and Peter Cushing; it was the first time the *Dracula* story would be filmed in color. In the American release, the film was titled *Horror of Dracula* to distinguish it from the Browning/Lugosi version of 1931. Christopher Lee also tried to make his Dracula different from that of the well-known Lugosi; although he "adopted the Lugosi Dracula's elegance and charm, the sleek, back-brushed hair, the arched eyebrows," he "dropped the foreign accent and underscored Dracula's sexual attractiveness and ferocity" (Gelder 91–92). Hammer Films made eight *Dracula* sequels, giving the series life until the mid-1970s; the series was wildly popular in both England and the United States.

The most recent big-budget *Dracula* is that directed by Francis Ford Coppola in 1992 and titled *Bram Stoker's Dracula*. Despite its title, the film is no more dedicated to Stoker's original story line than previous film adaptations, which is to say, it takes many digressions from its source. The film provides a backstory for Dracula, linking him explicitly to Vlad the Impaler. Another notable departure is having Mina be a reincarnation of the original (pre-vampire) Dracula's wife. The ending has Mina preventing the men from killing the vampire so that, at his request, she can do it herself. Following the release of the movie, the novel *Bram Stoker's Dracula* was published, based on the film, and written not by Stoker but by Fred Saberhagen (Gelder 90). While the film does maintain some elements of the original, including portraying Harker's trip to Transylvania and Dracula's travels to London, the serious departures, particularly from the ending of the novel, left many critics cold. The reincarnation story was an attempt to make the vampire sympathetic, implying that the man had turned un-dead and done his evil deeds because of the tragic loss of his beloved wife. At the end of Stoker's story, Mina does admit that she "shall be glad as long as I live that even in that moment of final dissolution, there was in the face [of the Count] a look of peace" (459). It is perhaps this note of sympathy that Coppola attempts to portray in his revision of the ending.

Seeing the character of the vampire as a sympathetic figure is a trope that appears in many of the film versions, and is also a central issue for Anne Rice's *Interview with the Vampire*, a novel she published in 1976 that was made into a film in 1994. While Stoker's novel features multiple narrators, with nearly every character speaking in his or her own voice for at least some portion of the novel through letters, diaries, and telegrams, one voice is notably missing: we hear from Dracula only as he is explained by other, non-vampire characters. Rice's novel then turns the tables, finally giving the vampire himself a chance to speak. Rice's vampire has many of the classic features; he "was utterly white and smooth, as if he were sculpted from bleached bone, and his face was as seemingly inanimate as a statue, except for two brilliant green eyes that looked down at the boy intently like flames in a skull" (4). Rice's version of the vampire is clearly related to Stoker's, but she makes the vampires—Louis, Lestat, and Claudia—the main characters, rather than the vampire hunters.

While many stories of vampires came before and after *Dracula*, Stoker's novel has had an unmatched and ongoing popularity; the novel has "been in print continuously since it was first published" (Riccardo xvi). Ken Gelder estimates that more than three thousand "vampire or vampire-related films have been made" (86). Stoker's

Dracula lives on, in a wide variety of media, each with its own particular take on the appearance and powers of the vampire. An episode of the television program *Buffy the Vampire Slayer* features a vampire character named Dracula who claims he was the model for Stoker's novel. At the end of the episode, Buffy is unable to turn the vampire to dust, despite repeated attempts with her stake. While the character never appears on the show again, it seems that Dracula is alive and well in the popular imagination and in our cultural productions.

Works Cited

Arata, Stephen D. "The Occidental Tourist: *Dracula* and the Anxiety of Reverse Colonization (Extract)." *The Horror Reader*. Ed. Ken Gelder. New York: Routledge, 2000. 161–171.

Bram Stoker's Dracula. Dir. Frances Ford Coppola. Perf. Gary Oldman, Winona Ryder, Anthony Hopkins, Keanu Reeves. DVD. Columbia Pictures, 1992.

"Buffy vs. Dracula." Created by Joss Whedon. Dir. David Solomon. *Buffy the Vampire Slayer*. Season 5, Episode 1. 26 September 2000.

Carter, Margaret. "A Preface from Polidori to the Present." *Varney the Vampire or the Feast of Blood*. Ed. Devendra P. Varma. New York: Arno Press, 1970. Volume I. xxxi–xlii.

"Drama, Vampire." *The Vampire Book: The Encyclopedia of the Undead*. Ed. J. Gordon Melton. Detroit: Visible Ink Press, 1994. 193–198.

Gautier, Théophile. "The Beautiful Dead." Trans. Lafcadio Hearn. *Blood & Roses: The Vampire in 19th Century Literature*. Ed. Adele Olivia Gladwell and James Havoc. London: Creation Press, 1992. 47–70.

Gelder, Ken. *Reading the Vampire*. New York: Routledge, 1994.

Le Fanu, Sheridan. *Carmilla*, 1872. *Three Vampire Tales*, ed. Anne Williams. Boston: Houghton Mifflin, 2003. 86–148.

Moretti, Franco. "The Dialectic of Fear (extract)." *The Horror Reader*. Ed. Ken Gelder. New York: Routledge, 2000. 148–160.

Nodier, Charles. "Smarra." Trans. Judith Landry. *Blood & Roses: The Vampire in 19th Century Literature*. 1821. Reprint. Ed. Adele Olivia Gladwell and James Havoc. London: Creation Press, 1992. 44–45.

Polidori, John. "The Vampyre." 1819. *Three Vampire Tales*, ed. Anne Williams. Boston: Houghton Mifflin, 2003. 68–85.

Riccardo, Martin V. "A Brief Cultural History of the Vampire." *The Vampire Book: The Encyclopedia of the Undead*. Ed. J. Gordon Melton. Detroit: Visible Ink Press, 1994. xiii–xx.

Rice, Anne. *Interview with the Vampire*. New York: Ballantine, 1976.

Shadow of the Vampire. Dir. E. Elias Merhige. Perf. Willem Dafoe, John Malkovich. DVD. Lion's Gate Home Entertainment, 2000.

Stoker, Bram. *Dracula*. 1897. *Three Vampire Tales*, ed. Anne Williams. Boston: Houghton Mifflin, 2003. 149–460.

Varma, Devendra P., ed. *Varney the Vampire or the Feast of Blood*. New York: Arno Press, 1970.

A Look at the Critical Reception of *Dracula*_____

Camille-Yvette Welsch

In 1897, one of the best known characters in English literature crept into the Western imagination, where he lurks even today. *Dracula* became the standard for all vampires. Though he had precursors, like Sheridan Le Fanu's Carmilla, Dracula became synonymous with "vampire." Most of the rules and regulations attributed to vampires—from garlic to bats, neck bites, and crypts—were made famous by Stoker's version. In the century-plus since its publication, it has never been out of print, attesting to the lasting appeal of the immortal fiend at the story's heart.

Stoker was born in Ireland on November 8, 1847. His father worked as a civil servant and his mother tended to her seven children. During his early childhood, Stoker was a sickly child, rarely rising from his bed until he was seven or eight. His mother, Charlotte, a proponent for women's rights, stayed by his side, telling him supernatural tales culled from Irish folklore. Despite the fact that much of Ireland was Catholic, the Stoker family maintained their Protestant affiliation. According to Clive Leatherdale, the Catholic faith brought many stories with it, one of them being the tale of vampires. Stoker recovered to grow into a vigorous adult and followed in his father's footsteps, becoming a junior clerk. However, he had a great passion for the theater, and that passion led to his meeting Henry Irving, with whom he shared a lifelong friendship. Irving had impressed the young Irishman with his performance in Richard Sheridan's *The Rivals*. He saw the actor in a few more plays and wrote favorable reviews of Irving's performances, which led Irving to initiate a meeting. The two became friends, and in 1878 Stoker began to work for Irving, serving as business manager for the London Lyceum, Irving's theater company. During the partnership, Stoker traveled with the company across Europe and to the United States. He helped Irving to research his characters and attended social gatherings with the company. Both the research and the new acquaintances helped

Stoker in his writing; he often used the names of acquaintances and the details of visited places and researched stories in creating characters and settings in his novels, and *Dracula* is no exception.

The partnership lasted into the early 1900s, when the Lyceum was sold to a syndicate. Irving introduced Stoker to many of the most influential people and writers of the time, including Alfred, Lord Tennyson, Mark Twain, and Thomas Hardy. Stoker was also friendly with Sir William and Lady Wilde, the parents of Oscar Wilde. The two were authorities on Irish folklore, and Sir William was a noted Egyptologist. Stoker is known to have consulted with them in writing his stories.

Irving himself continued to fascinate Stoker, and Clive Leatherdale suggests that portions of the actor's character helped to shape *Dracula*. During his tenure with the theater, Stoker worked continuously, maintaining an impressive publishing record. In 1895, his novel *The Shoulder of Shasta* was published but met with poor reviews, which complained that the novel was haphazardly executed. Stoker changed his tactics for *Dracula*, conducting extensive research for a period of more than six years, beginning in 1890.

Contemporary Responses

Initially, the novel met with enthusiastic reviews that placed the book with other sensational Gothic literature, such as Ann Radcliffe's *The Mysteries of Udolpho*, Robert Louis Stevenson's *The Strange Case of Dr. Jekyll and Mr. Hyde*, Mary Shelley's *Frankenstein*, and Emily Brontë's *Wuthering Heights*. Contemporary critics enjoyed the titillating, supernatural tale but were unwilling to consider it literature in the canonical sense. Rather, *The Daily Mail* suggested, "Persons of small courage and weak nerves should confine their reading of these gruesome pages strictly to the hours between dawn and sunset" (Auerbach and Skal 363). It was considered an inventive piece of pop-Gothic fiction. The *Athenaeum* review was somewhat more damning: "'Dracula' is highly sensational, but it is wanting in the constructive art as well as in the higher literary sense. It reads at times like a mere series of grotesquely incredible events, but there are better moments that show more power, though even these are never productive of the tremor such subjects evoke under the hand of a master" (Auerbach and Skal 364). The reviewer also took the novel to task for one-dimensional characterizations (a critique that plagues the book even today). The *San Francisco Chronicle*, unlike the English papers, was more positive, calling the book, "One of the most powerful novels of the day, and one set apart by its originality of plot and treatment" (Auerbach and Skal 366).

Perhaps the most prescient review came from home. Stoker's mother, Charlotte, wrote to her son, ". . . it is splendid, a thousand miles beyond anything you have written before, and I feel certain it will place you very high in the writers of the day. . . . No book since Mrs. Shelley's 'Frankenstein' or indeed any other at all has come near yours in originality, or terror—Poe is nowhere. I have read much but I have never met a book like it at all. In its terrible excitement it should make a widespread reputation and much money for you" (Farson 162). Mrs. Stoker's linkage to *Frankenstein* is a connection of great merit, as both are considered among the best "monster" books in the English language. In fact, critic Franco Moretti called them two sides of the same coin, "the disfigured wretch and the ruthless proprietor" (43). Unfortunately for Stoker, his mother's prophecy would not come true until after his death. Prior to Francis Ford Coppola's 1992 movie *Bram Stoker's Dracula*, most people did not know the name of the author who had created the mythic figure, and the book did not create significant funds for Stoker (although the film rights may well have, had he lived another century).

Despite scattered earlier studies, the novel went largely unnoticed by literary critics until the 1970s, when it was rediscovered. Part of its new life lay in its appeal for burgeoning fields of literary theory: Marxist, poststructuralist, feminist, psychoanalytic, historicist. With its homoerotic undertones, Freudian sexual tensions, discussion of the "New Woman" and setting in the fin de siècle, there was much to mine from the story.

In 1959, Maurice Richardson began a Freudian analysis of the story, using Stoker's childhood to further many of his claims. Richardson likens Dracula to an "evil father who wants to keep all the women to himself." It then becomes the job of Good Father Van Helsing to coach the Crew of Light into directing their desires toward more socially acceptable modes. In 1966, Richard Wasson introduced the notion that *Dracula* was a deeply political novel, built on the tensions of Imperialist England and its great and varied power and holdings. Dracula came to represent the encroaching East and Britain's fears of collapse. Wasson suggests that the book highlights the British struggle between modern technology and tradition that marked the fin de siècle. Bacil Kirtley researched the many mythic references in the novel, such as the Scholomance and St. George. His work was continued ten years later in 1966, when Grigore Nandris investigated the myth behind the monster by explaining Stoker's use of Vlad the Impaler as an historical precedent. The early work of these critics set up three of the primary strains of *Dracula* criticism: psychoanalytic, historical, and textual.

Psychoanalytic Criticism

Dracula criticism boomed in the 1970s. With the advent of psychoanalytic theory, critics were ready to undertake an analysis of the popular novel, as it seemed to embody so many of the suppressed fears of the Victorian fin de siècle. The psychoanalytic strain often explores issues of sexuality, homoeroticism, and desire, with marked differences between male and female sexual desire. Critics often use the historical framework of the Victorian era to help make sense of their arguments. At the turn of the century, women were finally attaining long-sought rights. Mary Wollstonecraft's *A Vindication of the Rights of Woman* (1792) had begun a movement that was strengthening among women across the United Kingdom. The New Woman was a manifestation of some of Wollstonecraft's ideas. Women wanted education, freedom to marry when and whom they pleased, the freedom to determine when and how many children they would have, and the freedom to pursue their own interests and goals independent of the men in their lives and their government. The New Woman was also associated, although the women who actually espoused it were in the minority, with sexual freedom—often thought to be manifested in the more comfortable modes of dress these women adopted. Stoker himself makes mention and offers both criticism and praise of the New Woman model in *Dracula*. Mina Harker makes contradictory remarks in the pages of her letters and journal, and the men in the story also make glancing references to changing gender relations. In his personal life, Stoker appeared to be of a mixed mind regarding the New Woman. His mother firmly believed in women's rights and he was very close to her. Leatherdale notes, though, that Stoker firmly believed in chivalry and that a woman who was without fear was not feminine. According to Daniel Farson, Stoker's wife, Florence Balcombe, became frigid after the birth of their son, and Stoker turned to women of the evening for satisfaction. This may have ultimately resulted in his death, as many believe that Stoker died of syphilis.

In addition, Stoker's acquaintance Oscar Wilde, a former suitor of Stoker's wife, was suing another gentleman for libel while Stoker was working on the novel. The gentleman in question had left a calling card, naming Wilde a sodomite. Wilde accused him of libel. Unfortunately, the trial unearthed Wilde's homosexual lifestyle and resulted in his sentence of two years' hard labor for "obscene acts." Wilde was portrayed as a sexual predator spreading the "contagion" of homosexuality among young men. The newspapers and the court vilified the writer. While Stoker distanced himself from his fellow Irishman (some suggest due to his own homosexual tendencies), Stoker's employer, Sir Henry Irving, was extremely supportive of the beleaguered Wilde. Still, the tide against homosexuals was running high, and many people of the time felt that the seeming rise in homosexuality correlated with the unbecoming moral and sexual conduct of the New Woman.

Critics in the psychoanalytic tradition paid particularly close attention to gender relations and what they revealed about the characters and the society in which they are set. They place their criticism firmly in the context of Victorian social mores. In 1972, Carrol L. Fry linked the treatment of women to an earlier tradition in English literature, from Samuel Richardson to Hardy. Fry posits Dracula as the traditional rake who seduces the innocent young lady, in this case both Mina and Lucy. She also linked the novel to popular melodramas of the end of the nineteenth century. In the same year, Christopher Bentley examined Stoker's creation of metaphorical sexual acts. Perhaps because of the Wilde trial, the censors were particularly vigorous at this point. None of Dracula's attacks are overtly sexual. Instead, Dracula enacts sexual congress via the drinking of blood. Dracula, unlike the proper Victorian men of the novel, need not wait to have his desire fulfilled; instead, he can sate his "hunger" at will and thus represents desire unchecked, which, if the obscenity trials are any indication, was unacceptable in popular society. Additionally, Bentley examined the ways in which Stoker introduces metaphoric castration, rape, and oral sex into the text without alerting the censors.

In 1977, Phyllis A. Roth built her commentary on the work of Maurice Richardson, referring to his assertions about the Oedipal myth in the work. In Roth's reading, the men are enacting their ambivalence and terror toward the woman figure. As long as the woman is pure, chaste, and innocent, she is good. Once she becomes sexualized, she becomes terrifying, and consequently a threat to the social order, a kind of "new woman." The men then feel compelled to eliminate the threat of the sexual woman—thus Lucy's "death." Roth also notes that the "stabbing" and beheading of Lucy are rich with overtones of sexual conquest and satisfaction bordering on orgiastic. Roth shows the ways in which this desire to kill the "mother" speaks to the rivalry for Lucy's affections. She rejects three suitors and must pay for it. Also in this reading, Dracula is the father who acts out the fantasies that the Crew of Light cannot bring themselves to acknowledge, much less enact.

That same year, 1977, Judith Weissman also examined sexual and gender roles in the light of Victorian mores. She links man's terror of the sexual woman with the treatment and fear of Bertha in Charlotte Brontë's *Jane Eyre*. In both Victorian novels, the sexual woman is construed as flirting with madness and very dangerous. Weissman also suggests that vampirism for men is about power, whereas for women it is about sexuality and desire, making both genders worthy of fear. The male vampire has the power to control others and to create sexual women. The sexual woman has the power to seek satisfaction of her own desires. Weissman asserts, like Roth, that the act of sexualizing and destroying women plays out the gender struggles of the era.

James Twichell addresses "The Vampire Myth," claiming that the novel reinforces gender roles, with the man as dominant and the woman as submissive. He adds the Electra myth as a lens to view Dracula's seductions of young women, a typical structure with the older man sexually initiating the younger woman. The exploration of the intersection of Victorian mores and sexual identity in the novel continues in Gail B. Griffin's examination of vampirism. She views vampirism as a way to make the danger of the New Woman clear. The New Woman is sexual, she is tainted not only by the blood of victims but also by metaphorical menstrual blood, and she is indifferent to children. These characteristics make her completely unacceptable as a lady, and completely dangerous to society. Unlike Dracula, who remains a faceless threat for the majority of the book, Lucy and Mina are present in the company of men and therefore are dangerous. Leila S. May broadens the notion of the "body" in suggesting that Dracula epitomizes the Victorian fear of contagion and prostitutes. Dracula has the potential to assault both the actual body and the social body, thereby destroying society.

Christopher Craft offers yet another view, exploring the novel in terms of gender roles and queer theory. Craft asserts that part of Dracula's danger is his inversion of seemingly static dualities like life and death, male and female, penetration and reception, good and evil. Dracula can essentially negate death by living forever. Jonathan Harker, in his episode with the three female vampires, longs for penetration from them, thereby reversing gender roles and sexual roles. Similarly, Lucy becomes the sexual aggressor, and there is the suggestion that Dracula attacks the women only so that he might ultimately make his way to the men, again intimating homoerotic overtones. Finally, the "good" characters in the book behead people, stake them through the heart, and hunt a man down. Their actions, on the surface at the very least, suggest some serious wrongdoing. Finally, Craft claims a three-part tradition in monster stories where the monster is invited in, entertained, then suddenly disowned. This analysis brings Stoker back together with other authors such as Edgar Allan Poe, H. G. Wells, Mary Shelley, and Robert Louis Stevenson.

Like Craft, Talia Schaffer finds ambiguity in the sexuality of the characters. She suggests that Stoker found an outlet for his conflicted feelings about his own alleged homosexual nature and the trials suffered by Oscar Wilde during his very public court appearances. Schaffer sees the character of Dracula as representing the public view of the homosexual man, one who emerges from a liminal space and is monstrous in appearance, action, and odor (the Wilde trial linked odor to anal sex). However, Dracula is only one side of a duality. Wilde and Stoker himself are also Jonathan Harker, imprisoned and terrified at this view of homosexuality, with a hatred and fascination that is often self-directed. Ultimately, Schaffer believes that the novel represents "Stoker's attempt to transform homosexual 'infection' into heterosexual 'procreation'" via the birth of Quincey Harker. Allan Johnson continues this by looking at doubling in the novel. He contends that Swales and Renfield are meant to be doubles to Mina and Lucy, respectively. This interest in Stoker's doubling technique appears in later criticism as well.

Comparative Analysis

Kirtley's 1956 essay began a long exploration into Stoker's use of myth, history, and literature in his novel. Devendra Varma continued the tradition with articles in the 1970s and 1980s examining the biographical, literary, and folkloric origins of the story. Varma makes links to Samuel Taylor Coleridge's "The Rime of the Ancient Mariner" as well as Shakespeare and Greek myth. Joseph S. Bierman added a textual reading with his examination of Stoker's research notes for the novel. David Seed contends that the structure of the story aids in creating suspenseful pacing and reinforces meaning, keeping the novel from devolving into mere romance. Instead, as the narrative accounts become more uniform and the writers more involved and tightly knit, Dracula becomes more endangered and seeks to destroy the newly woven explanation of his past and habits.

In contextualizing the work, Gwenyth Hood broadens the discussion of *Dracula* to include other literary works. She compares Tolkien's Sauron with Stoker's Dracula. Both characters utilize the Un-Dead and the dark; both have the power not only to enter the minds of their victims but also to control them. John Paul Riquelme places *Dracula* in the context of the Gothic oeuvre. Benson Saler and Charles A. Ziegler try to answer one of the most compelling questions about the novel: Why does it endure? The authors note other vampire tales that are arguably better written, particularly Le Fanu's *Carmilla*, but they isolate two major reasons that Dracula became the prototypical vampire. First, Stoker's novel follows a three-pronged approach that audiences associate with monsters. These monsters emerge from some mysterious dark depths; they prey on humans; and then, they are vanquished by the native intelligence and strength of a human being. In addition, Dracula possesses many of the traits made famous by monsters of folklore and myth. Saler and Ziegler suggest that viewing the monster through the lens of anthropology will help to make sense of the continued shared response of audiences.

The use of anthropology as opposed to historical context to view the novel is a newer one, begun late in the 1980s. Some critics felt that defining the book solely by its historical context was to ignore many potentially productive veins of criticism. John Allen Stevenson contends that vampires might be considered another race entirely, subject to their own societal rules in terms of sexual relations, family structure, food, and taboos. In order for the vampire family to survive, they must seek "marriage" or new blood with which to strengthen the fold, as cultures have for generations. In addition, the typical rules of incest do not apply to vampires, as the family structure is more fluid than that of the typical Victorian. The abject fear of Dracula might be considered a fear of deracination as the women selected by Dracula become vampires at the expense of their human lives.

Textual and Technical Analysis

In 1979, Carol A. Senf began to examine Stoker's narrative technique, with his use of many letters, diaries, and newspapers. The gathered papers suggested to Senf the unreliability of the multiple narrators. Rather than proving their own virtue, the Crew of Light eventually proves how very close they are to the evil they fight. Senf also looks at the means used to tell the story: shorthand, a typewriter, a phonograph—all very modern devices. Senf suggests that these devices are meant to distance the characters from the myth they fight, creating a dichotomy between the old myths and traditions and the new technology and modernity of the day.

In addition to a concern with science and modernity, critics have demanded that the text itself be given more attention. Christine Ferguson examines the use of standard and non-standard English in the text. Contradicting many Victorian protestations to the contrary, Ferguson posits that it is the very fluid nature of English, with its slang and dialect, that kept the Crew of Light and, by natural association, England from being conquered by the rigidly structured vampire, or outsider. Unlike native speakers, Dracula cannot understand the deviations in standard English. Just as he is subject to the rules of the supernatural, he is subject to the rules of the language. Without the ability to change and adapt, the vampire is ultimately ruined and the use of language reinforces this ruin throughout the novel.

New Historicism

New Historicism invites readers to make sense of the text in terms of the society in which it was written, acknowledging the social, political, and economic climate. Critics of this strain believe that in so doing, the reader will gain a richer understanding of the text. Thomas B. Byers examined the family structure suggested in *Dracula*. He sees Dracula as the head of the family, the father figure, with his four brides, the three female vampires and eventually Lucy. In keeping with family structure of the day, the father ministered to the needs of the women. He was the sole provider. In trying to satisfy the needs of his women, he offers them a child in the hope of shifting their emotional need away from him. Dracula makes mothers, and Mina becomes a mother of sorts. Each of the mothers is meant to satisfy the emotional needs of men, who later assuage their own feelings of weakness by destroying the mother figure. Again, the mores of the time feed the structure of the novel.

Ernest Fontana examines Stoker's use of the ideas of criminologist Cesare Lombroso, who believed that criminality was hereditary and that inherited physical characteristics could be used to identify criminals. He claimed that criminals were evolutionary anomalies, throwbacks to other, less evolved incarnations of man. Fontana uses these theories, and Stoker's knowledge of them, to suggest that Dracula identified his victims by these traits and hoped to reawaken them after biting his victims, thereby creating a "new" race of human beings. This reading suggests, as have many others, that part of *Dracula*'s particular terror is that the potential for evil is to be found within. Judith Halberstam sees *Dracula* as taking advantage of other forms of stereotypical fear-mongering. She suggests that Stoker used the nineteenth-century conception of the "monstrous Jew" as a way of making the vampire into a dangerous other. Like Lombroso's criminal, the Jew, a reviled figure in England at the time, made for an easy association for audiences. Part of what intrigues Halberstam is the ways in which race, class, and gender coincide to create a character who is subsequently made to be the "other."

Other historical readings have reflected on the use of science and technology within the book. While an early review claimed that it was the up-to-date technology that marred the story, critics in the twentieth century have embraced the novel as useful reportage of life and science at the turn of the century. Martin Willis looked at germ theory and disease in the novel. His careful analysis shows Stoker's early interest in germ theory and miasmatic contamination in his story "The Invisible Giant." His use of the theories matured in *Dracula* to include ruminations on property and the site of contamination. Building on this kind of commentary, Nina Auerbach suggests that this interest in modernity makes Dracula a true member of the twentieth century. As a character, the vampire is fascinated by new technology and reinvention. He plans to move, after centuries of habitation, away from Transylvania to England, the site of industry and technology. This ability to adapt may also account for the popularity of the vampire myth, according to David Glover's reading of the novel, which includes a very contemporary link to new diseases, such as AIDS. John Rider examines the phonograph in the novel and the ways in which certain characters mimic its qualities by becoming human recorders of sound, capable of replay and transmission. Mina and Jonathan Harker are of particular interest here as they transcribe sound via shorthand, speak of the contents of Dracula's mind, and knit together the divergent tales of the various narrators.

Dracula also tests the boundaries of religion with a number of readings derived from a comparative analysis of Christian myth, folklore, and the novel itself. Christopher Gist Raible sees Stoker's telling of *Dracula* as an inversion of Christian myths. David Punter furthers this reading by considering the myth of Christ's blood, which is meant to give life. For Dracula, blood is life. This reduction of needs to only blood makes Dracula the ultimate aristocrat. He has phased out the bourgeois need for food, fancy dress, and servants and, like the ancient lords to their vassals, seems never to die. Though the lord is replaced by his progeny, the change never affects the lives of the vassals—thus the sense of immortality. Ultimately, Dracula comes to stand for lineage as surely as he stands for the breaking of Victorian taboos.

The novel also has spurred a number of Marxist critics. The novel's status as popular fiction makes it ripe for examination according to the Marxist theory of romance posited by Northrop Frye. In 1980, Burton Hatlen considered Dracula as an outsider to the bourgeois Crew of Light. He acknowledges that even within that group, there are outsiders by birth—an American, a Dutchman, and men in trade. However, for the most part, they are united by their bourgeois morals and ideals, thus affirming their status as the English ruling class. According to Hatlen, they also share a repressed desire to submit to the exotic other. Franco Moretti offers a reading wherein Dracula represents capital. He amasses capital with absolutely no need to spend it. He never reinvests it in society; instead the money is an end in itself. What makes him even more terrifying is that his desire for consumption never ends as with capitalism itself.

Rebecca Pope takes a Bakhtinian approach, viewing the female body as a site for the men to create their text; the woman's body resists this. She emphasizes the relation of the sexes to textuality in compilation and in the act of writing.

Imperialism

Other critics have looked carefully at Stoker's novel as an expression of Victorian dismay over Great Britain's powerful empire, which spanned the globe. Tensions were high as citizens imagined both collapse and revolution. Much of the populace feared intrusion from the mysterious "others" in the outlying colonies. Stoker himself felt the sting of colonization as he fought for home rule for the Irish, which had become a kind of neighborhood colony, not quite afforded the full rights of citizens. The "Irish question" in relation to Stoker's novel has interested a number of critics. Raphael Ingelbien posits Dracula as an Anglo-Irish Ascendancy figure based on comparative analysis with the

Anglo-Irish Gothic writer Elizabeth Bowen. Bowen wrote a familial memoir, *Bowen's Court*, which shows various customs seemingly native to both the Anglo-Irish and *Dracula*, suggesting that the novel was a subtle commentary on the state of the Anglo-Irish in England. Terry Eagleton suggests that Dracula is a critical characterization of the Ascendancy landlord, while Gregory Castle views the novel as an expression of Stoker's feelings of displacement as an Irishman living in London. Dracula comes to represent threats to the Anglo-Irish; he becomes simultaneously the British ruling class and the Catholics that the Anglo-Irish "ruled" in the Ascendancy. He also notes the subtle ways that Stoker critiques Catholicism throughout the novel.

Stephen D. Arata examines the text as a manifestation of concern over the "Eastern Question" facing Victorian England. Citizens and government alike worried over possible collapse and/or invasion by the "primitive" cultures coming from the East. As Dracula is transformed, Great Britain feared transition from victimizer to victim, a kind of reverse colonization epitomized by Dracula's plans for London, which include creating new members of his primitive race. In keeping with the jingoism of the time, Van Helsing reads Dracula as an infantile, unevolved brain who is nonetheless a threat to the power of scientific, reasonable England.

For readers interested in creating a biographical reading of the book, Daniel Farson's biography *The Man Who Wrote "Dracula"* offers a mix of critical information, personal remembrance (Stoker was his great-uncle), and biography. Lisa Hopkins combines criticism and biography in her work, *Bram Stoker: A Literary Life*. In addition to biographical information, readers might be interested in the plethora of academic studies devoted to the movie versions of the book. Very few stick faithfully to Stoker's text; however, the film versions give insight into the varied ways in which people have read and reinterpreted the famous story.

Certainly the future will hold additional criticism from all modes of criticism, as the story is laden with fodder for metaphoric significance, historical details, and gender/queer theory analysis. The modern attention given to *Dracula* has encouraged study of his other work, particularly in the ways in which it relates to *Dracula* itself. While Stoker himself may not have enjoyed literary celebrity, his work has enjoyed critical attention and continued in the popular consciousness for more than a hundred years with no signs of fading.

Works Cited

Arata, Stephen D. "The Occidental Tourist: *Dracula* and the Anxiety of Reverse Colonization." *Victorian Studies* 33 (Summer 1990): 621–645.

Auerbach, Nina. "A Vampire of Our Own." *Dracula: Contemporary Critical Essays.* Ed. Glennis Byron. New York: St. Martin's Press, 1999. 145–172.

Auerbach, Nina, and David J. Skal. *Dracula: Bram Stoker: A Norton Critical Edition.* New York: W.W. Norton & Company, 1997.

Bentley, Christopher. "The Monster in the Bedroom: Sexual Symbolism in Bram Stoker's *Dracula.*" *Literature and Psychology* 22 (1972): 27–34.

Bierman, Joseph S. "The Genesis and Dating of *Dracula* from Bram Stoker's Working Notes." *Notes and Queries* 24 (1977): 39–41.

Bronfen, Elizabeth. "Hysteric and Obsessional Discourse: Responding to Death in *Dracula.*" *Dracula: Contemporary Critical Essays.* Ed. Glennis Byron. New York: St. Martin's Press, 1999. 55–67.

Byers, Thomas B. "Good Men and Monsters: The Defenses of *Dracula.*" *Literature and Psychology* 31 (1981): 24–31.

Craft, Christopher. "'Kiss Me with Those Red Lips': Gender and Inversion in Bram Stoker's *Dracula.*" *Representations* 8 (1984): 107–133.

Demetrakopoulos, Stephanie. "Feminism, Sex Role Exchanges, and Other Subliminal Fantasies in Bram Stoker's *Dracula.*" *Frontiers: A Journal of Women's Studies* 2, no. 3 (Autumn 1977): 104–113.

Eagleton, Terry. *Heathcliff and the Great Hunger: Studies in Irish Culture.* London: Verso, 1995.

Farson, Daniel. *The Man Who Wrote "Dracula."* London: Michael Joseph, 1975.

Ferguson, Christine. "Nonstandard Language and the Cultural Stakes of Stoker's *Dracula.*" *ELH* 71 (2004): 229–249.

Fontana, Ernest. "Lombroso's Criminal Man and Stoker's *Dracula.*" *Victorian Newsletter* 66 (1984): 25–27.

Fry, Carrol L. "Fictional Conventions and Sexuality in *Dracula.*" *Victorian Newsletter* 42 (1972).

Glover, David. "Travels in Romania—Myths of Origins, Myths of Blood." *Dracula: Contemporary Critical Essays.* Ed. Glennis Byron. New York: St. Martin's Press, 1999. 197–217.

Griffin, Gail B. "'Your Girls That You All Love Are Mine': *Dracula* and the Victorian Male Sexual Imagination." *International Journal of Women's Studies* 3 (1980): 454–465.

Halberstam, Judith. "Technologies of Monstrosity: Bram Stoker's *Dracula*." *Dracula: Contemporary Critical Essays*. Ed. Glennis Byron. New York: St. Martin's Press, 1999. 171–196.

Hatlen, Burton. "The Return of the Repressed/Oppressed in Bram Stoker's *Dracula*." *Minnesota Review* 15 (1980): 80–97.

Hennelly, Mark M., Jr. "*Dracula*: The Gnostic Quest and Victorian Wasteland." *English Literature in Transition* 20 (1977): 13–26.

Hood, Gwenyth. "Sauron and Dracula." *Mythlore* 52 (1987).

Hopkins, Lisa. *Bram Stoker: A Literary Life*. New York: Palgrave Macmillan, 2007.

Ingelbien, Raphael. "Gothic Genealogies: *Dracula*, *Bowen's Court*, and Anglo-Irish Psychology." *ELH* 70 (2003): 1089–1105.

Johnson, Allan. "Bent and Broken Necks: Signs of Design in Stoker's *Dracula*." *Victorian Newsletter* 72 (1987): 20–39.

Kirtley, Bacil F. "*Dracula*, the Monastic Chronicles and Slavic Folklore." *Midwest Folklore* 6, no. 3 (1956).

Leatherdale, Clive. *Dracula: The Novel and the Legend: A Study of Bram Stoker's Gothic Masterpiece*. Rev. ed. East Sussex: Desert Island Books, 1993.

May, Leila S. "'Foul Things of the Night': Dread in the Victorian Body." *The Modern Language Review* 93, no. 1 (January 1998): 16–22.

Moretti, Franco. "Dracula and Capitalism." In *Dracula: Contemporary Critical Essays*, ed. Glennis Byron. New York: St. Martin's Press, 1999. 43–54.

Pope, Rebecca A. "Writing and Biting in *Dracula*." In *Dracula: Contemporary Critical Essays*, ed. Glennis Byron. New York: St. Martin's Press, 1999. 68–92.

Punter, David, "Dracula and Taboo." In *Dracula*, ed. Glennis Byron. New York: St. Martin's Press, 1999.

Raible, Christopher Gist. "Dracula: Christian Heretic." *Christian Century* 96, no. 4 (1979).

Richardson, Maurice. "The Psychoanalysis of Ghost Stories." *Twentieth Century* 166 (1959): 419–431.

Rider, John M. "The Victorian Aura of the Recorded Voice." *New Literary History* 32, no. 3 (Summer 2001): 769–786.

Riquelme, John Paul. "Toward a History of Gothic and Modernism: Dark Modernity from Bram Stoker to Samuel Beckett." *Modern Fiction Studies* 46, no. 3 (Fall 2000): 565–585.

Roth, Phyllis A. "Suddenly Sexual Women in Bram Stoker's *Dracula*." *Literature and Psychology* 27 (1977): 113–121.

Saler, Benson, and Charles A. Ziegler. "Dracula and Carmilla: Monsters and the Mind." *Philosophy and Literature* 29 (2005): 218–227.

Schaffer, Talia. "'A wilde desire took me': The Homoerotic History of *Dracula*." *ELH* 61 (1994): 381–425.

Seed, David. "The Narrative Method of *Dracula*." *Nineteenth-Century Fiction* 40, no. 1 (1985).

Senf, Carol A. *Dracula: Between Tradition and Modernism*. New York: Twayne Publishers, 1998.

_____. "*Dracula*: The Unseen Face in the Mirror." *Journal of Narrative Technique* 9 (1979).

_____, ed. *The Critical Response to Bram Stoker*. Westport, CT: Greenwood Press, 1993.

Stevenson, John Allen. "A Vampire in the Mirror: The Sexuality of Dracula." *PMLA* 103, no. 2 (March 1988): 139–149.

Twichell, James. "The Vampire Myth." *American Imago* 37 (1980).

Varma, Devendra P. "The Genesis of *Dracula*: A Re-Visit." In *The Vampire's Bedside Companion*, ed. Peter Underwood. London: Leslie's Frewin, 1975.

_____. "Dracula's Voyage: From Pontus to Hellespontus." In *Dracula: The Vampire and the Critics*, ed. Margaret L. Carter. Ann Arbor: UMI Research Press, 1988. 207–213.

Wasson, Richard. "The Politics of *Dracula*." *English Literature in Transition* 9 (1966): 24–27.

Weissman, Judith. "Women and Vampires: *Dracula* as a Victorian Novel." *Midwest Quarterly* 18 (1977): 392–405.

Willis, Martin. "'The Invisible Giant,' *Dracula*, and Disease." *Studies in the Novel* 39, no. 3 (Fall 2007): 301–325.

Dracula and Victorian Anxieties_____

Matthew J. Bolton

What determines whether any given Victorian novel still speaks to readers here on the far side of the twentieth century? Some Victorian novelists were simply such brilliant writers that the power of their language and the depth of their characterization render their work timeless. Charles Dickens and George Eliot come to mind as two such writers whose genius is evident on the level of the individual phrase and sentence. Other novelists, such as William Makepeace Thackeray or Anthony Trollope, wielded an incisive wit and satiric edge that remain undulled a century and a half on. But why have certain novels that can boast of neither genius nor wit endured? Bram Stoker's *Dracula* (1897) can offer only serviceable prose and wooden characterization, yet it has held the popular imagination for more than one hundred ten years. Its titular character, the vampire Count Dracula, has walked out of Stoker's novel and into popular consciousness, figuring in countless movies, adaptations, and advertising campaigns. In academia, meanwhile, the past two decades have witnessed a renewed interest in Stoker's novel, as critics study it through various lenses and according to various schools of thought. *Dracula* is important less for any timeless literary merit that it may possess than for the glimpse it offers a modern reader into the anxieties that preoccupied the Victorian mind. Stoker's novel holds a mirror up to Victorian culture and history, with the character of Dracula himself encoding Victorians' fears of unbridled sexuality, of the other peoples and cultures with which their empire had brought them in contact, and of what they saw as modern science's assault on the foundations of religion. That such anxieties are still a part of modern American culture should further attest to the relevance of Stoker's *Dracula* for a modern audience: the book may reveal as much about our own culture as it does that of the Victorians.

The vampire's power is fundamentally sexual in nature. Stealing at night into a sleeping victim's bedroom, materializing out of misty air or shafts of moonlight and then vanishing again, the Un-Dead seem to be linked to the unconscious. When Jonathan Harker first encounters three female vampires, for example, he cannot say for certain whether the episode actually occurred or was only a dream. He writes in his journal the next morning: "I suppose I must have fallen asleep; I hope so, but . . . all that followed was startlingly real" (39). Harker's uncertainty may come in part from his own languorous and dreamlike response to the apparitions. These women are the stuff of an erotic dream, at once strange and thrilling:

> All three had brilliant white teeth that shone like pearls against the ruby of their voluptuous lips. There was something about them that made me uneasy, some longing and at the same time some deadly fear. I felt in my heart a wicked, burning desire that they would kiss me with those red lips. (40)

Even after he has realized that these women have come not to kiss him but to bite through his throat and drain him of his lifeblood, Harker is enraptured. He recalls: "I could feel the soft shivering touch of the lips on the super-sensitive skin of my throat, and the hard dents of two sharp teeth. I closed my eyes in a languorous ecstasy and waited— waited with beating heart" (41). Count Dracula chooses this moment to rescue Harker from these lesser vampires and to spirit him back to his own bedroom. Yet Harker does not need to have been bitten by a vampire to attest to their erotic power over a mortal's desires. In the moment before the beautiful vampire sinks her teeth into him, Harker knows what she means to do to him and yet welcomes it.

The vampires that prey on Harker are undeniably real, but it is telling that the young man entertains the possibility that they are instead the stuff of dreams. If Harker can accept the possibility that he has imagined these beautiful seductresses, then he is admitting that he has had erotic fantasies in the past. This may be an obvious point, but it stands at odds with every other aspect of Harker's gentlemanly comportment. Like the other men of *Dracula*, Harker seems to be entirely devoid of sexual desire; his love for his fiancée Mina, like the love that Lucy's three suitors bear her, is a sort of reverent appreciation for purity. His feelings toward his fiancée are starkly different from the "wicked, burning desire" that the vampires engender in Harker. Yet on the morning after his encounter, Harker cannot say for sure whether the carnality that these women represent is an external reality or a private fantasy. Though sexual desire will eventually be displaced onto the figure of the corrupted and corrupting vampire, here in this early scene it is as much a part of Harker's nature as it is that of the vampire.

Stoker's novel therefore writes large the sexual repression and prudishness that have come to be associated, in the popular consciousness, with the Victorian era. While Victorian repression may sometimes be overstated or exaggerated—as in the canard that the Victorians draped their pianos and tables in order to hide the furniture's legs—it nevertheless is rooted in reality. The Victorians *were* more concerned with propriety, with proper social comportment, and with the elevation of the mind over the body than were their Georgian or Regency parents and grandparents. Yet this prudishness is itself a form of sexual hyperawareness. Sexual repression is concomitant with sexual awareness, propriety with prurience. William Gladstone, who held the office of prime minister four times, is a prime example of the Victorians' inherently conflicted attitudes toward sex.

In the early 1840s, a decade into Victoria's reign, Gladstone began what he termed his "rescue work." After leaving the Houses of Parliament at night, the prime minister would meet with prostitutes to counsel them about reforming their lives. On some level, Gladstone's work was altruistic, for he did succeed in getting some women off the streets and into reform houses (the harsh discipline of such institutions is another matter). The rescue work was consonant with the liberal Gladstone's larger agenda of social progress and reform. As prime minister, he introduced the bill that would become the sweeping Reform Act of 1867. Yet on a deeper level, Gladstone's encounters with the prostitutes were a sublimation of his own sexual desires. In his diary, he used the Greek letter lambda to indicate days on which he had scourged himself in an attempt to drive sexual fantasies out of his body (Crosby 59). Such bouts of scourging regularly followed his meetings with the prostitutes. Gladstone's diary also records his perusal of pornography. He writes of one illicit French text: "I drank the poison, sinfully. . . . I should have sheered off at the first hints of evil" (Crosby 58). The prime minister's rescue work and secret reading habits show the duality of Victorian sexual mores. A wide gulf lay between a man or woman's public persona and his or her innermost desires, and Gladstone, like so many of the Victorians whom he represented, lived a double life.

One might see the Victorian gentlemen of Stoker's novel as engaging in their own form of "rescue work." Professor Van Helsing leads Lucy's three former suitors—Dr. John Seward, Quincey Morris, and Arthur Holmwood, who eventually won her hand in marriage—to visit the tomb where she lies buried. Lucy, of course, is not dead but un-dead and has been rising by night in her vampiric form to prey on the children of London. When the four men reach the tomb, Lucy is already on the prowl, and they wait for her to return. She arrives and approaches them, and though Harker is not there to witness the scene, Dr. Seward twice uses the same adjective that Harker has used to describe the un-dead women in Castle Dracula: Lucy is "voluptuous." She still bears Lucy's form, but that form has been corrupted. Seward notes that the vampire has "Lucy's eyes in form and colour; but Lucy's eyes unclean and full of hell-fire, instead of the pure gentle orbs we knew." His response is visceral: "At that moment the remnant of my love passed into hate and loathing; had she then to be killed, I could have done it with savage delight" (226). Seward's "savage delight" has itself an erotic component to it, for he goes on confess that when Lucy called out to Arthur to join her in the tomb, "there was something diabolically sweet in her tones" (227). As for Arthur, the man who once loved the pure Lucy is now enraptured by this voluptuous thing that has usurped her place. He welcomes her embrace: "he seemed under a spell; moving his hands from his face, he opened wide his arms" (227). Only Van Helsing's raised crucifix drives Lucy away from Arthur.

Seward, Arthur, and, presumably, the laconic Quincey Morris—one of the few characters, along with the Count himself, who does not keep a diary—respond to Lucy with the same admixture of revulsion and desire that the three vampires engendered in Jonathan Harker. Like William Gladstone, they have sought out a woman of the night, witnessed the foulness of her crimes, and resisted the temptation to be complicit in those crimes. The next night they return to the tomb, where Arthur drives a stake through the vampire's heart, thereby saving Lucy's soul. Lucy's countenance attests to her having been, indeed, rescued: "There, in the coffin lay no longer the foul Thing that we had so dreaded and grown to hate . . . but Lucy as we had seen her in her life, with her face of unequalled sweetness and purity" (232).

This, therefore, is the strange dichotomy that the vampire establishes: the living woman is full of "sweetness and purity," while the undead vampire is associated with voluptuousness, carnality, and wicked desire. Stoker displaces feminine sexuality and male desire alike, locating them not in the natural realm of human relations and human biology, but in a supernatural and diabolical one. In the normal scheme of things, it seems, Lucy should be entirely sweet and entirely free of the carnal. The four men who enter the graveyard do so in order to rescue Lucy from sexuality itself. The vampire is therefore a distinctly Victorian monster in part because it represents the dangerous return of repressed sexual desire.

If the vampire is an embodiment of the repressed libido, then he renders sexual desire assailable and conquerable. Gladstone took a scourge to himself; Van Helsing and his friends can instead take a stake to Dracula. Perhaps no scene so overtly demonstrates this role as the one in which Van Helsing and the others burst into the Harkers' bedroom to find Dracula feeding his own blood to Mina. The language Seward uses to describe the scene is that of a sexual assault: "With his left hand he held both Mrs. Harker's hands, keeping them away with her arms at full tension; his right hand gripped her by the back of the neck, forcing her face down on his bosom." The count has cut himself and is forcing Mina to drink his blood so that she will become a vampire. Seward writes, "the attitude of the two had a terrible resemblance to a child forcing a kitten's nose into a saucer of milk to compel it to drink" (304). The simile is a fascinating one, for it compares Dracula's violation of Mina to the actions of a presexual child, as if Seward is willing himself to cast the scene in terms other than a rape. The scene he has witnessed is not so far off from the pornography that Gladstone and many other Victorians secretly read, yet Seward reaches for ludicrously presexual tropes with which to describe it: a child, a kitten, a saucer of milk.

Harker, meanwhile, lies senseless throughout Dracula's attack, gripped by what Van Helsing calls "a stupor such as we know the Vampire can produce" (305). This tableau of Mina framed by the senseless husband to one side and the voracious intruder to the other might be read as a metonymy of Victorian sexual repression. In *Dracula*, a man cannot be both a husband by day and a lover by night. Rather, the logic of vampirism divorces man from his sexuality, displacing it onto this unnatural nighttime intruder. Much as her husband discovered a year earlier in the castle, Mina finds the Count's attack to be at once appalling and irresistible. In her own diary, she returns to the scene that Seward had witnessed. She remembers waking to find herself gripped by a "vague terror" (309). Her bedroom was filled with a white mist, out of which the Count materializes. When he leans over Mina's throat, she confesses, "I was bewildered, and, strangely enough I did not want to hinder him. I suppose it is a part of the horrible curse that such is, when touch is on his victim" (310). Mina's response to Dracula's assault teeters on the edge of becoming an implicit justification of rape, for here the victim condones her own violation. It is important to remember that Mina's journal is in fact the work of Stoker, a nineteenth-century man, and partakes of a decidedly patriarchal attitude toward feminine sexuality, sexual availability, and desire.

Yet Mina's conflicted response to Dracula's attack speaks to something else as well. In Castle Dracula, Harker had wondered whether his encounter with the vampiric women was only a dream. Mina, having had more experience with the Un-Dead, knows Count Dracula's visit to have been real. Yet the sensations that she describes in thinking back on the encounter are distinctly dreamlike. She experiences what a clinical psychologist might diagnose as sleep-paralysis: "For an instant my heart stood still, and I would have screamed out, only that I was paralyzed" (310). This sense of terror and paralysis are common elements of a nightmare. While the Count's visitation may be real, therefore, it nevertheless partakes of a dreamlike and unreal quality. In the 1840s, when Gladstone began his rescue work, his contemporaries did not have the conceptual framework to question whether his actions were driven by subconscious sexual impulses. His critics claimed he was prurient, his allies claimed he was altruistic, but none of them would have made the more complex argument that he was motivated by both conscious and subconscious desires. By 1897, when *Dracula* was published, Sigmund Freud's writings on the subconscious had begun to change how people looked at their own and one another's layered and often contradictory impulses. *On the Interpretation of Dreams*, published in German two years after *Dracula* and translated into English in 1901, would introduce a lexicon that explored the gap between actions and their subconscious motivations: repression, displacement, and sublimation.

In a sense, *Dracula* wants to have it both ways. Sexual desire is projected onto the figure of the vampire, such that Harker, Mina, Lucy, and the novel's other heroes are rendered "pure." Yet at the same time, the dreamlike quality of the vampires' nocturnal visits allies them with the subconscious, the seat of one's primal fears and desires. Sexuality seems to hover somewhere between an internal impulse and an external threat. The series of skirmishes with Dracula might be read as a protracted process of displacement, whereby the Count comes to stand for the sex drive itself. Harker, in the end, was wrong to entertain the idea that the three succubi who appeared to him in the castle might only be fantasies conjured up by his own subconscious desires. These beautiful seductresses are, in fact, external, alien, and evil. The long chase across Eastern Europe to the gates of Castle Dracula is therefore a *reductio ad absurdum* of Gladstone's rescue work: an assault upon sexual desire itself at the seat of the *id*.

To imagine a scenario in which men vanquish abnormal sexual desire, restoring a "normal" order in which Jonathan and Mina Harker can settle down to the business of raising a family, speaks to the mood of *fin-de-siècle* Victorian England. *Dracula* was published only two years after the 1895 trial of Oscar Wilde, in which the poet and playwright was sentenced and imprisoned for engaging in a homosexual relationship. Wilde came out of prison with his health and spirit broken, and died in Paris in 1900. *Dracula* seems to share in the attitude that the court and the English public exhibited in response to Wilde: that some sexual impulses are dangerous and evil, and must be fought against. The poet was represented as a sexual predator, a corrupt man whose corruption could spread if left unchecked. Reading *Dracula* in the context of this very public trial, one may suddenly realize how programmatically heterosexual the vampiric encounters are. Harker is attacked by three women, whereas Lucy and Mina are attacked by a man. Likewise, the vampiric Lucy attempts to seduce Arthur and his male companions. The vampires are not omnivorous, and not bisexual. In rescuing Harker, Dracula hisses at the three vampiric women, "How dare you cast eyes on him when I had forbidden it? Back, I tell you all! This man belongs to me!" (41). Yet we cannot really imagine Dracula feeding on Harker himself: were the scene to be rendered with the eroticism that marks the other vampiric encounters, the effect would be scandalous for a Victorian readership still abuzz over the "crimes" of Oscar Wilde. Indeed, in a book in which the strongest relationships seem to be forged among men who gather at night for their secret rescue work of fallen women, homoeroticism would be a greater threat than vampirism.

* * *

Count Dracula may therefore be read as an embodiment of the repressed sexuality of the Victorian era. He represents "the buried life"—to appropriate the title of Matthew Arnold's famous poem—of the pure and noble characters whom he haunts. Yet this is not the sum total of Dracula's significance. Rather, the vampire is a shifting referent, standing as a marker for a whole series of Victorian cultural anxieties. Just as he speaks to the Victorians' fear of unbridled sexual desire, so too does Dracula speak to their fear of foreigners and of other races. He is a foreign foil to set off the merits of the Englishman and of his racial and cultural near-relations, the Dutch Van Helsing and the American Quincey Morris. Dracula is the consummate foreign menace, and his attempt to infiltrate and corrupt English culture would have resonated with a Victorian readership that imperialism and Darwinism had taught to draw clear lines between the Englishman and the "other."

In 1897, the sun did not set on the British Empire. British traders, administrators, and soldiers were a presence on every continent, and the Union Jack could be found flying in such disparate and far-flung locations as India, Hong Kong, Afghanistan, Egypt, and Nigeria. The term "imperialism" today has taken on a pejorative connotation; we cannot imagine any mainstream British or American politician applying the word to his or her own policy positions. In the wake of Gandhi's passive resistance to British rule of India, the word has become an accusation. For the Victorians, however, the imperial impulse was widely seen as a noble and altruistic one. How did nineteenth century Britain justify its colonial rule of foreign countries and cultures? The answer may be grounded less in economic terms than in eugenic ones, for the British Empire was essentially predicated on the idea that the English and other white European peoples were not only more culturally advanced but also more biologically evolved than their counterparts on the other continents. Samuel Wilberforce, an abolitionist member of

Parliament who died at the dawn of Victoria's reign, characterizes the British imperial mission this way:

> Their vocation [was] . . . to leave as the impress of their intercourse with inferior nations, marks of moral teaching and religious training, to have made a nation of children see what it was to be men—to have trained mankind in the habits of truth, morality and justice, instead of leaving them in the imbecility of falsehood and perpetual childhood. (Newsome 134)

To administer other countries was "the white man's burden," and many Victorians would have agreed with Wilberforce that they shared a patriarchal obligation to help rear the "childlike" races of the world. It is worth noting that Van Helsing speaks of Dracula as having a "child-brain." Yet Britain's imperial presence in so many parts of the world seems to have instilled in the Victorians a nagging fear that the relationship between the more and less advanced cultures could be reversed. Instead of the English elevating the people they have colonized, the colonized might debase the English. This anxiety concerning the weight of empire is everywhere in Victorian popular culture. Reading Arthur Conan Doyle's Sherlock Holmes stories (the first of which appeared in 1887) through the lens of colonialism, for example, one realizes how many of the mysteries that Holmes unravels have their origins not in London, but at the margins of the empire. Holmes could catalog the foreign threats that he has helped discover and eliminate: a pygmy man who kills his victims with a blowgun, a trained orangutan that climbs up a drainpipe to strangle a woman, an Indian gem that sets old friends at each other's throats. Holmes himself uses cocaine and opium, two insidious imports from the colonies, while his companion Watson bears the scars from his military service in South Africa. Holmes and Watson's adventures may unfold in London, but they are inextricably bound to the far reaches of the British Empire.

Dracula, like so many of the Holmes stories, centers on a foreign threat that has infiltrated London. Prior to moving to England, the

---

Count makes a careful study of the English language and culture. In the library at Castle Dracula, Harker finds a collection of English reference books, journals, and magazines, as well as an atlas in which he has circled the East side of London. At first, Harker is touched by the Count's interest in English life; he says that it "gladdened my heart to see" the Count reading English law. Only later will Harker realize that the Count's meticulous research is bent not on assimilation but on predation. Dracula plans his trip to London as if he were planning a military campaign. The Count's purpose in inviting Harker to Castle Dracula therefore centers not only on the purchase of Carfax, the old manor house that the Count will make his English home, but on having at his disposal a real Englishman from whom he can better learn the culture and language of his new hunting grounds. Asking Harker to correct him should he misspeak, the Count says, "I am content if I am like the rest, so that no man stops if he see me, or pause in his speaking if he hear my words, 'Ha, ha! A stranger!'" (21). Harker, as a native speaker, is to help arm Dracula to infiltrate England.

Yet while Dracula has learned the language and manners of the English, he can never truly become an Englishman. His hard-won knowledge of English life merely cloaks his essential otherness; at heart, he is still a Transylvanian. Dracula's foreignness is perhaps most obviously represented by the boxes of Transylvanian earth that he brings with him to England. This native soil—consecrated ground dug up from a cemetery—is one of the sources of the Count's strength, and he must return to lie in it by daybreak. Yet Dracula's strength is also his weakness. If he must bear his native earth with him, then he is somehow unfit to assimilate to life in England. This unfitness marks him as profoundly limited when compared to a Victorian Englishman, who can move anywhere in the world—be it India, Asia, or Africa—and thrive. Moreover, the Englishman adapts without ever compromising his essential Englishness. Dracula lacks this resiliency and adaptability, for his power is somehow bound up with his native soil in a way that of the imperial British is not.

Vampirism marks Dracula as not only culturally different from the English but biologically so. As one of the Un-Dead, he only appears to be human, and his careful cultivation of English manners cannot mask his true nature. This notion that foreignness might be rooted in biological differences rather than cultural ones may be derived from Charles Darwin's work on evolution. In *On the Origin of Species by Means of Natural Selection*, first published in 1859, the naturalist had argued that for any individual or species to survive, it must be in constant competition with others: "as more individuals are produced than can possibly survive, there must in every case be a struggle for existence, either one individual with another of the same species, or with the individuals of distinct species, or with the physical conditions of life" (76). Darwin was thinking in purely biological terms, but many of his readers were quick to apply his notion of a "struggle for existence" to social models, arguing that people and nations behave as do competing species. The mathematician and eugenicist Karl Pearson, for example, argued that imperialism itself acts out a Darwinian struggle for existence. In 1905 he wrote, "History shows me one way and one way only, in which a high state of civilization has been produced, namely the struggle of race with race, and survival of the physically and mentally fitter race" (Himmelfarb 323).

By the same token, Darwin's careful delineation of the differences between various species within a family, such as the dozens of finch species he cataloged on expedition on the *Beagle*, was sometimes misappropriated and taken as a license to draw distinctions on biological grounds between various races of people. John Beddoe, in his 1862 *The Races of Britain*, argued that a protruding jaw was a sign of primitivism and that in Britain the Irish and the Welsh should be seen as more closely related to Cro-Magnon Man and to the African than are the English. Beddoe's position, in short, was that evolution was staggered and that some ethnic groups were more evolved than others. The pseudo-science of phrenology, by which one could determine mental and moral attributes based on the shape of a person's skull, lent credence to this notion that facial characteristics spoke to developmental differences across ethnic groups and races. What gripped the imagination of the Victorian public was not so much evolution as its specter, atavism: the idea that some members of a species could regress.

The figure of Dracula seems to tap into these fears of atavism and of modern, evolved man losing ground in his struggle with some other "species"—be that the Irish, the African, or the undifferentiated masses of the urban poor. Van Helsing, Dr. Seward, and Mina all subscribe to phrenology, to one extent or another. In the world of *Dracula*, to be trained in phrenology and the Beddoe school of eugenics would be eminently valuable, for the vampire and his victims can be recognized purely on the basis of facial characteristics. After Mina has been bitten, for example, Van Helsing and the others gauge her health based on the sharpness of her teeth and the pallor of her expression. Dracula and his kind, like Darwin's finches, are physically marked as different from the species of *Homo sapiens*.

Nor is it just these people themselves whom the more civilized races should fear, but the diseases they carry. The boxes of dirt that the vampire brings to England suggest not only the foreigner who cannot adapt to his new home but also the foreigner who brings with him the dirt and disease of his native land. The figure of Dracula speaks to widespread Victorian fears that the "wrong kind" of foreigner was a threat to the public health and to public morality. Read through this lens, vampirism itself becomes a nightmarish vision of the sort of infectious disease a foreigner could bring ashore. Dracula, as loathsome as he may be, is only a carrier, an agent of infection who compromises both the physical and moral health of the English. Worse than the vampire is his vampirism, a condition that if not countered could sweep across England in epidemic proportions.

The struggle between Dracula and Van Helsing's band is therefore cast in Darwinian and imperialistic terms: an evolved race of man must overcome an atavistic and primitive one. *Dracula* may be a window into the paradoxical fear and uncertainty that ruling a far-flung empire engendered in the Victorians.

*   *   *

Reading *Dracula* in the context of Victorian notions of evolution and of the natural sciences is a complex business, however, for the figure of the vampire cuts both ways. On one hand, Dracula represents a nightmarish vision of Darwin's notion of evolution and the struggle for existence. If man can evolve, then he can also regress, and the different races of men may be locked into an evolutionary struggle that points toward either perfection or debasement. Yet on another level, the vampire is a refutation not only of Darwin but of the natural sciences *in toto*. The nature of vampirism eludes Professor Van Helsing and Doctor Seward, two eminent men of science, until they recognize that they must put down their medical books and take up the cross. Seen in this light, Count Dracula himself serves as a corrective to a general trend away from religion in the nineteenth century. He is a threat that cannot be countered through science or medicine, but only through faith.

Victorian England experienced a number of religious revivals and movements, perhaps the most influential of which was the Oxford Movement, led by John Henry Newman, Edward Bouverie Pusey, John Keble, and James Anthony Froude. The academics who spearheaded the Oxford Movement sought to reintroduce to the Church of England some of the ritual and vigor of Roman Catholicism. They argued that in the centuries since Henry VIII had split from the Roman Church, the English had lost touch with the sacramental mysteries that should lie at the center of a faith life. Their foci included apostolicism, the cult of the saints and of the Virgin Mary, and the centrality of the Eucharist to religious practice. Newman, perhaps the best known of the Oxfordians, would eventually chronicle his spiritual development in his autobiographical *Apologia Pro Vita Sua* (1864). He describes his growing interest in miracles, in the lives of the saints, and in the history of the church. The other young men who would head the movement with him were likewise drawn toward those elements of Christianity that the Church of England had long considered to smack of Papacy.

Newman says of Froude, for example, "He taught me to look with admiration towards the Church of Rome, and in the same degree to dislike the Reformation. He fixed deep in me the idea of devotion to the Blessed Virgin, and he led me gradually to believe in the Real Presence" (42). When Newman eventually converted from Anglicanism to Roman Catholicism, the act was seen by some as a great betrayal of the movement and by others as its logical end.

Many of Newman's contemporaries saw the Oxford Movement as a fundamentally reactive one: this renewed emphasis on ancient ritual and dogma was meant to counter both the advances made in scientific and industrial circles and the reforms being touted by liberals. Essayist and poet Matthew Arnold saw a movement toward English Catholicism as a misguided response to the nature of scientific inquiry. In his essay "Literature and Dogma," Arnold argued that religious people would do better to see religion as rooted in poetry rather than in fact, for poetry cannot fail one in the wake of new scientific discoveries. Poetry, in short, cannot be disproved. Yet in their own way, the members of the Oxford Movement espoused a similar position, for they saw ancient sacrament and tradition as a bulwark against the erosion of the faith. The sacraments, and particularly the sacrament of the Eucharist, ought to be the prime mode of religious expression, for these are the historical realities that connect a modern worshipper to the historical reality of Christ's incarnation on earth.

Dracula seems to affirm the Oxford vision of sacrament and ritual as central to an active faith life. At the novel's start, Harker is discomfited when a Transylvanian peasant woman implores him to wear her crucifix. He recalls, "I did not know what to do, for, as an English Churchman, I have been taught to regard such things as in some measure idolatrous" (5). Out of politeness, he accepts and wears the cross—which will ultimately help to guard him against Dracula, who cannot bear the sight of it. Van Helsing will later arm his men with crosses, which are more effective against the vampire than any firearm would be. The professor similarly makes use of the consecrated host, kneading it into a long strip with which he seals the door to the un-dead Lucy's tomb. The efficacy of the host seems to demonstrate what Newman calls "the Real Presence" of Christ in the Eucharist. The response of the vampires to the cross and the host prove that these objects are not merely symbols: they are powerful religious artifacts. *Dracula* comes down firmly on the side of the Oxfordians and of the Roman Catholics, recognizing religious objects and rituals as a source of great power. In fact, all of the characters who fight the vampire seem to undergo a gradual religious awakening, for by the novel's conclusion their various journals are studded with references to God's power and to their own belief. Dracula, a messenger of the infernal, has renewed their once-dormant belief in God.

The characters' journals themselves ought to factor into any discussion of faith and reason. In meticulously recording the events of each day, *Dracula*'s multiple narrators reveal themselves to be staunch empiricists. They believe that human experience can be summed up and categorized, that through observation and reflection they may reach logical conclusions about their experiences. At the dead center of the novel, Mina Harker and Dr. Seward, armed respectively with their typewriter and phonograph recorder, exchange accounts in order to create a more comprehensive master narrative. Mina and Harker will later collate all of the various letters, diary entries, newspaper accounts, and logs that will make up the text of Stoker's novel itself. This process of collation is a moment where the novel teeters on the edge of infinite regression and paralyzing self-reflection—the characters may seemingly do nothing new until they have recorded everything that has already happened. Yet the typist, the psychologist, and the solicitor are already moving beyond their faith in empiricism and the scientific method. Dracula—who of course keeps no account of himself—is a force that lies outside of the realm of science. To combat him, Seward and the others will have to make a leap of faith. While the martialing of reason and fact that Mina's collation represents will put the men on the vampire's trail, it is religious faith, not empirical science, that will allow them to defeat him.

* * *

Every age gets the monster it deserves. The Victorians were fascinated by *Dracula* because Stoker's monster seemed to speak to so many of their collective anxieties at once. He is a figure of excess and of negation, a stand-in for the sexual libertine, the disease-carrying foreigner, and the infidel. As such, he is a necessary corrective for a society that feared it was becoming too relativistic. Because Dracula is evil, his enemies must become good: the vampire calls on them to be more virtuous, more English, and more faithful. That Dracula has walked out of his novel and into popular culture and the collective consciousness may speak not only to the fullness of Stoker's creation but also to the fact that the Victorian anxieties he represents have never been fully resolved. Twenty-first-century American culture and politics are intimately bound up with questions of sexual propriety, immigration, and a perceived split between religion and science. It is because America is still haunted by the anxieties that Stoker's monster represents that we still find Dracula a source of fear and fascination.

Works Cited

Beddoe, John. *The Races of Britain: A Contribution to the Anthropology of Western Europe*. 1885. London: Hutchinson, 1971.

Crosby, Travis L. *The Two Mr. Gladstones: A Study in Psychology and History*. New Haven, CT: Yale University Press, 1997.

Darwin, Charles. *The Origin of Species*. Introduction by Sir Julian Huxley. New York: Penguin, 1958.

Himmelfarb, Gertrude. *Victorian Minds*. New York: Alfred A. Knopf, 1968.

Newman, John Henry. *Apologia Pro Vita Sua*. Ed. Ian Ker. New York: Penguin Classics, 1994.

Newsome, David. *The Victorian World Picture*. New Brunswick, NJ: Rutgers University Press, 1997.

Stoker, Bram. *Dracula*. New York: Signet Classics, 1993.

Modernity and Anxiety in Bram Stoker's *Dracula*

Allan Johnson

The immense popularity of Bram Stoker's *Dracula*, sustained since the novel first appeared in 1897 and reinvigorated by each additional film, stage, or literary adaptation, is perhaps not an entirely surprising phenomenon. *Dracula* is, at its very core, a deeply engaging novel that is still able to startle and concern contemporary readers even at the distance of more than a century. The impressive status that the text has earned in Anglo-American literary culture as the prime artifact of the horror genre is at least partially dependent on Stoker's masterful storytelling. Yet the sheer entertainment value of Stoker's now-infamous vampire novel is likely not the only reason that *Dracula* continues to be studied as a central work of British literary fiction and routinely subjected to intense literary criticism that seeks to examine the novel's treatment of mass culture, mental health, Freudian/Jungian subtextuality, female sexuality, reverse colonization, and modernity. That is, *Dracula* (like the Count himself) possesses deeper secrets and hidden complexities that challenge readers to enter into the dark and profoundly sinister world of the novel prepared for the unexpected.

As is common with the production of literary analysis, the style and form of academic criticism written on *Dracula* have changed dramatically in the century since the text first appeared. This essay will examine some of the most recent developments in the critical interpretation of *Dracula* (scant critical attention was paid to the novel prior to the 1970s) and begin to probe some of the directions for future study of the novel. Why has *Dracula* survived as the embodiment of our notion of the vampire while other works of vampire fiction have faded away and become forgotten? For what reasons has the novel become a significant cultural force, one that single-handedly constructed our contemporary cultural knowledge of vampire folklore? These questions are best answered through an analysis of not only *what* happens in Stoker's tale but also *why* and *how* it happens.

Dracula appeared during a transitional period in the history of British literacy. The introduction of the Education Reform Act in 1870, which had made education available to all British children, meant that, by the time Stoker's vampire novel appeared, a greater percentage of the British population were literate than ever before. We should underestimate neither the impact that this new mass readership had on the late Victorian publishing industry nor the cultural significance of the rise of "popular" genre fiction designed for Britain's newly empowered reading public. *Dracula* is, in many ways, exemplary of late Victorian styles of popular fiction, and, as critics have frequently noted, Stoker's text owes much to the popular fiction that appeared in Britain in the final decades of the nineteenth century. We might firstly recognize the influence of the gothic horror genre upon *Dracula* and, more specifically, vampire fiction such as John Polidori's "The Vampyre" (1819) and Sheridan Le Fanu's *Carmilla* (1871), both of which have been shown to be vital sources for Stoker's later work. Stoker masterfully builds gothic suspense from the very first pages of the text and, although we might anticipate the final outcome of the novel even before we begin reading (that is, the triumph of good over evil coupled with a restoration of order), Stoker teases and taunts us with unexpected surprises. Less clear are the influences of the popular styles of travel narrative and sensation fiction upon Stoker's text. The opening four chapters, which constitute the first Transylvania sequence, paint a picture of Eastern Europe as a deeply mysterious world filled with folklore and superstitions offered to the reader through the narrative voice of Jonathan Harker. Jonathan takes on the role of travel writer, and his record of his initial adventure in Transylvania serves as a vital tool in the campaign against the invading Count. *Dracula* also contains essential elements of the late Victorian sensation genre. As Francis Ford Coppola's 1992 film adaptation of the book, *Bram Stoker's Dracula*, may encourage us to remember, *Dracula* is a deeply sensual work of fiction. While rarely overtly sexual (Jonathan's encounter with the three female vampires is among the most explicit scenes in the text, and, even there, the sexual lust is embedded in the stylized drama of the scene and the murderous intentions of the vampire women), the text places much significance upon the flirtatiousness of Lucy and the virtuousness of Mina, and the dissimilar fates of these two characters may encourage us to see an attempt on Stoker's part to craft a seemingly "moral" novel in the sensational vein. We might observe, then, that *Dracula* is very much a product of the literary milieu in which it appeared.

Yet *Dracula* reaches toward the modernist style of the early twentieth century in many critical ways. It can be viewed as an early example of the "modern" novel for its style, its interest in new technology, and its depictions of newly professional women and domestic architectural space. Perhaps the most immediately striking feature of the text, and one that is suggestive of a modernist interest in the fragmentation of narrative and linear time, is its scrapbook format. Offered initially to the reader as a collection of journals, letters, and newspaper clippings from a wide range of sources, the text is only later revealed to be the file of evidence transcribed and compiled by Mina; that is, the text references its own status as a text. The preliminary note alerting readers that "these papers have been placed in sequence [and] all needless matters have been eliminated," we might later surmise, was included by the character Mina during her devoted chronicling that is shown later in the novel. Dracula, when he burns one of the two copies of Mina's manuscript, is aware how crucial the knowledge in this text could be in the campaign against him, and each of the major characters is shown to be actively aware of how important the act of documentation is. Lucy's early belief that "I must imitate Mina, and keep writing things down," is mirrored in the journal entries of each of the main characters, and they all seem keenly aware of the grave importance of documenting the strange events they encounter (Stoker 119). As Van Helsing tells Dr. Seward, "knowledge is stronger than memory"; one can see the insistence throughout the text of the fundamental value of recorded, empirical knowledge in the fight against the mysterious unknown (Stoker 130).

Like that legal style of argumentation that Mina adopts in "Mina Harker's Memorandum" immediately after the October 30th journal entry, the style of Mina's opening note makes the text seem as if it has been prepared as part of a legal case, and already we are encouraged to read this story as an entirely true account of extraordinary events. Although she began her career as a schoolteacher, Mina's recent training in stenography and typing influenced the tone of both this introductory note and "Mina Harker's Memorandum." Indeed, each of the characters in the novel has his or her own motivation or training that enables or encourages the long journal entries and letters that eventually will make up the text of the novel: Jonathan, as a budding lawyer with an interest in travel literature, is keen to record all minutiae of his travels to Transylvania; Lucy, as a friendly young woman boosted by three proposals on the same day, is eager to write long, gossipy letters to her friend; Dr. Seward, accustomed to recording long patient records on his phonograph, approaches his journal with a deeply rational and scientific attention to detail. While *Dracula* in one sense is an unconventional novel that moves away from traditional narrative styles in order to recount an episodic story through disparate textual documents, Stoker's work also confirms the significance and value of text. One can observe how the text enacts this assertion by taking the form of the very document that becomes necessary in planning the campaign against Dracula.

Perhaps more ought to be said about the actual format of these journal entries transcribed by Mina and how the technology used by these characters to record their thoughts is further suggestive of *Dracula*'s clear location in the era of early modernist literature. Jennifer Wicke's seminal article, "Vampiric Typewriting: *Dracula* and Its Media," has powerfully demonstrated the significance of the host of technological devices used in recording the individual narratives that make up the text of *Dracula*—Mina's typewriter, Dr. Seward's phonograph, the telegraph, and even the stenographic shorthand used by both Jonathan and Mina—and the implications these technologies have for the text's apparent modernity. Although Wicke acknowledges "the banal terrors of modern life" suggested in the novel by Mina's new role as a secretary, her article demonstrates the importance of mass (reproducible) media in the world of the story and the way in which the new communication technology of typewriters and phonographs prove to be the best weapon against the archaic Dracula (Wicke 468). Quincey Morris's Winchester rifle, a gun synonymous with the "Wild West" era and America's westward expansion during the second half of the nineteenth century, becomes another critical technological tool in the fight against Count Dracula. Although we may be quick to forget this as twenty-first-century readers, *Dracula* is filled with the technological inventions of the late nineteenth century, many of which would later dramatically change Western culture. *Dracula*, then, documents the rise and implementation of modern technological advancement.

Aside from this certain interest in modern technology, *Dracula* also demonstrates a clear interest in the rise of mass culture that characterized the decades surrounding the turn of the twentieth century. *Dracula* would have appeared to its first generation of readers as an extremely timely novel, and just like the Winchester rifle and typewriter, the implements of modern life such as Bradshaw's guide to train times, Kodak cameras, and common directories of people and businesses in London would have been immediately recognizable to early readers. While Dracula can transform into mist and summon bloodthirsty wolves, these powers prove to be poorly matched against the new technologies and conveniences of everyday life in England.

What purpose, then, does this clear interest in mass culture serve in the novel? Most crucially, it serves to set the very old Dracula apart from his modern pursuers: Jonathan's shorthand journal and letter to Mina are indecipherable to the Count, and although Dracula hoards train tables at his castle, it is ultimately shown to be Mina who is so accustomed to this necessity of modern life that she has a habit of memorizing train times. Much emphasis is placed on Dracula's status as a foreign invader—one who is, despite his years of study of English culture, still ultimately a stranger in a strange land once he arrives in England—and the novel foregrounds dialects and accents to demonstrate this point. Dracula's perfect German is contrasted with his deeply idiosyncratic English; the heavy Yorkshire dialect of the old man at Whitby becomes almost indecipherable to Mina and, by extension, to us as readers; Dr. Van Helsing's charming malapropisms reemphasize his status as a curious international expert. Count Dracula is aware that he will need to improve his spoken English if he intends to blend into London society, and since he cannot transform his spoken language as easily as he can transform his person, he requires a native English speaker, in the form of Jonathan, to tutor him in conversational English. The Count's primary sources of knowledge about the English language—the books and periodicals on England that he treasures—have provided him only with the general mechanics of the language, and, without the technological aid of the phonograph that later proves to be of central importance to the campaign of the Crew of Light, Dracula must keep Jonathan at the castle for as long as possible in order to practice and perfect his spoken English: "I fear that I am but a little way on the road I would travel," he tells Jonathan on his first night, "I know the grammar and the words, but yet I know not how to speak them" (Stoker 27). Jonathan is ultimately held captive and engaged in long conversations that last most of the night. It is only after Dracula has perfected his spoken English that he is finished with Jonathan and is prepared to begin his invasion of England.

There is something deeply sinister about the way in which Dracula has orchestrated, over the course of many years, his invasion of London society, and this well-planned attack is analogous—in historical context and thematic implication, at least—to the invasions of England depicted by H. Rider Haggard, Arthur Conan Doyle, and H. G. Wells. There was, in fact, a great interest in invasion stories around the turn of the twentieth century, and, as several critics have pointed out, these invasion texts are frequently indicative of a much broader social anxiety in the late Victorian period. As Stephen D. Arata has pointed out in his influential essay "*Dracula* and the Anxiety of Reverse Colonization," it is essential to remember the political context in which *Dracula* appeared. By 1897, the British Empire was entering into the early stages of the decline that would be fully realized during the first decades of the twentieth century, and already the British public was beginning to experience an anxiety about the stability of Britain's long-standing role as the single major world power. Works such as Conan Doyle's *The Sign of Four* (1890) questioned what would happen if England were to become the site of an invasion by India (the linchpin of Britain's imperial power at the time), and although Transylvania was not part of the British Empire, several significant factors about Dracula's homeland further develop this theme of reverse colonization. As Arata vitally points out, contemporary British readers would have recognized Transylvania as the site of much "political turbulence and racial strife" (122). The motif of invading conquerors is introduced into the text early when Dracula recounts to Jonathan Harker the history of Transylvania and his noble family and, as Arata has observed, the Count is shown as an emblem of a "nobleman as warrior" but also, because of his Szekely history, a "conqueror and invader" (123).

To continue to probe this reading of *Dracula* as a colonizer of England, one should consider Patrick Brantlinger's concept of the "imperial gothic," a subgenre of fiction identified by Brantlinger that engages specifically with the arrival of occult forces in England. In the imperial gothic style, characters venture to unknown parts of India, Africa, and (in the case of *Dracula*) Eastern Europe and are then followed back to London by some supernatural power. As Brantlinger notes, novels in the imperial gothic vein combine "individual regression or going native; an invasion of civilization by the forces of barbarism or demons; and the diminution of opportunities for adventure and heroism in the modern world" (230). We can recognize the instances of "individual regression" in the novel—Mina's temporary and Lucy's complete conversion to vampirism—as well as the emphasis placed on the loss of opportunities for masculine adventure—the American adventurer Quincey Morris serves to show how sheltered and protected the lives of Jonathan Harker and the Hon. Arthur Holmwood have become—but perhaps the most important aspect of the imperial gothic within the novel is the text's emphasis on social, geographical, and personal invasion. The strong academic interest in postcolonial literary criticism has made both the reverse colonization anxiety present in the novel as well as the work's position in the imperial gothic subgenre prime topics of critical conversation and debate.

Where, then, we might wonder, is critical analysis of *Dracula* headed in the future? There is growing academic interest in the representation of interior architectural space in modern British fiction, and as critics continue to demonstrate the dramatic role of architecture in literature from this period, we are encouraged to reexamine Stoker's representation of space. *Dracula* is a novel deeply concerned with houses and, more specifically, the way in which characters use architectural space to dominate (in the case of Dracula and the un-dead Lucy) or to liberate (in the case of the Crew of Light); the acquisition of property is the means by which Dracula is able to enter into London society, and much of the challenge presented to the Crew of Light is the locating of the homes that Dracula has purchased throughout metropolitan and suburban London. Although the motif of architectural space in *Dracula* is perhaps not as pronounced as the motif of mass culture or anxiety about reverse colonization, the ways in which Stoker uses domestic architecture throughout the novel to provide further comment on Dracula's invasion of London is actually indicative of a deeply modernist understanding of architectural space as a central component of identity. While a case could be made that Horace Walpole's *The Castle of Otranto* (1764) is one of the earliest literary representations of interior architectural space, Warren Hunting Smith argued in his analysis *Architecture in English Fiction* (1934) that the widespread literary representation of interior architectural space first appeared in British literature during the nineteenth century and was initially used—in the fiction of Anthony Trollope, George Eliot, and Charles Dickens, among others—primarily for "structural," "decorative," or "emotional" effects (1–2). What Stoker introduces in *Dracula*—and what becomes a key literary technique for later British modernists such as E. M. Forster, George Bernard Shaw, and Virginia Woolf—is the use of architectural space as both metaphor and symbol. We should perhaps be alerted to the critical thematic role that architectural space will later play when the novel opens with an account of the finalization of the purchase of Dracula's first London home; indeed, this interest in architectural space is sustained through to the conclusion of the text.

It is crucial that, although Dracula is portrayed as a conquering invader within the text, he is still bound by many of the physical restrictions imposed by architectural space, and the vampires in the novel seek to invade and dominate architectural spaces just as they invade and dominate their victims. Dracula's curious greeting to Jonathan at the door of his Transylvania castle provides an early suggestion of one of his primary weaknesses as a vampire: "Welcome to my house! Enter freely and of your own will. . . . Welcome to my house. Come freely. Go safely; and leave something of the happiness you bring!" (Stoker 22). Although Jonathan, as a mortal, does not require an explicit invitation to enter a home, Dracula, it is later revealed, must be invited to enter a home before he is able to move freely in and out. But here this rule is reversed: Jonathan does not require an official welcome (although he receives one), but he is then held captive in the castle and comes to realize that "the castle is a veritable prison, and I am a prisoner" (33). Not only does this strange greeting emphasize Dracula's idiosyncratic English; it also brings into the novel the motif of the permeability of thresholds and passages.

Jonathan, in his role as a journal writer, is a keen observer of architectural space and pays much attention in his long journal entries to the peculiarities of Dracula's castle. Though there is something mysterious about the castle, much of which is off-limits to Jonathan, it should be noted that Dracula's powers cannot actually alter the physical restraints of architectural space. After being left on the front doorstep by the mysterious carriage driver, whom he later suspects to be the Count in one of his several disguises, Jonathan notes that "through these frowning walls and dark window openings it was not likely that my voice could penetrate," and, even while standing outside, Jonathan already has a sense of the imposing nature of the castle and its prison-like quality (21). While he is concerned here about getting *into* the castle, this fear is later reversed and he becomes afraid of not being able to *get out* of and away from the castle. In his journal he later comments on the "odd deficiencies in the house," which are indicative of the many years that Dracula has been in residence there completely alone (26). Despite its age and apparent state of disuse, there have still been several alterations made to the castle in recent years. Jonathan finds his living quarters in the castle to be comfortable and (aside from the significant lack of a bathroom mirror) to provide him with reasonably suitable amenities. Jonathan's later recognition that the locks, which keep him out of most of the castle, are "comparatively new" provides further evidence that the castle has not fallen into a complete state of disrepair and, even more important, further emphasizes the novel's interest in the permeability of thresholds (42). Although locks can prevent Jonathan from moving through the castle, these basic restraints provide no resistance to Dracula or the three vampire women. Yet the primary difficulty in Jonathan's opening of the front door is not a lock or a supernatural enchantment but merely its weight, which can be shifted only by the powerful Dracula. Jonathan is shocked when he discovers Dracula climbing headfirst down the castle wall, suggesting that Dracula's strength and batlike prowess allow him to negotiate architectural space differently.

Now that we have examined some of the ways in which the motif of architectural space is introduced to the reader in the early portions of the novel, we can begin to dissect the connections between architectural space and Dracula's plans to infiltrate England. When Jonathan begins to describe Carfax, Dracula's estate at Purfleet, the description is not of a particularly appealing place: it is a "straggling" house, added to over many years; it retains many qualities of a medieval fortress; the grounds are heavily shaded by a large number of trees; and one of the only surrounding buildings is a mental institution (Stoker 30). This description does not paint the picture of a desirable house, but Dracula is pleased with the find and is pleased that there is a "chapel of old times" (30).

Once the narrative moves to England, this narrative interest in moving within and between architectural spaces becomes intensified. On the night of Lucy's first escape from the house in Whitby, Mina worriedly notices, "the door was shut, but not locked, as I had left it" (100). Again, because Dracula has yet to be formally invited into the house, he is not able to make his entrance and therefore requires Lucy to come outside to meet him. She, as a mortal, is able to cross the threshold with no difficulty, but, also as a mortal, she is impeded by locks, causing her to unhook the lock on her way out. The significance of the unlocked door is later emphasized when Mina, after returning with Lucy from the cliffs, locks the door and ties the key to her wrist; although Mina is still unaware of the Count's existence, Dracula is unable to get in and, now with the locked door, Lucy is unable to get out. The novel is built around images of breaking in or out of buildings, and this, like Jonathan's attempted escape from Dracula's castle, is one clear example.

While Jonathan Harker, Dr. Van Helsing, Dr. Seward, and the others might be unable to enter or leave a home because of locks or heavy doors, the vampires (Dracula and, later, the un-dead Lucy) can be similarly locked in or out of a home. The negotiation of architectural space thus becomes a central motif in the novel—and, indeed, a pivotal aspect of the novel's rising action and final, if not unexpectedly sudden, conclusion. If Dracula cannot be stopped by locks, he can be stopped by other things, and that is exactly what Dr. Van Helsing plans when he has the garlic flowers delivered from the Netherlands. By rubbing the flowers around the windows and doors of Lucy's room, he is blocking Dracula's entrance as effectively as the heavy door blocked Jonathan's exit in Translyvania. However, that proves to be only a temporary cure: the effectiveness of the flowers does not last, and Dracula is later able to approach Lucy after the garland of flowers has been removed by her hysterical mother.

The boxes of sacred earth that Dracula brings from Transylvania might be seen as another type of home—the tomb home of the Un-Dead—and after her death, the Westenra tomb becomes another home for Lucy. Although it may seem that the long scenes of the Crew of Light observing the "bloofer lady" Lucy in the middle portion of the novel are used primarily to build dramatic tension, it is important to notice how Van Helsing is testing his hypotheses and verifying the true weaknesses of the vampires. Van Helsing first proves to Dr. Seward the meaning of Lucy's un-dead condition by demonstrating to him that at night she leaves her coffin, the coffin that Van Helsing is able to open only with a saw. He then later tests Lucy's powers by filling in all of the cracks of the tomb with a paste made from communion wafers. As expected, Lucy requires at least a small crack in a structure to be able to move into it, and barred by the holy wafers Lucy is unable to enter her tomb. Lucy and other vampires, then, cannot merely pass through walls, but require at least some small opening to make their entrance. For as much power as Dracula and his minions seem to have, they are still bound by at least some of the physical restrictions imposed by architectural space. Once the Crew of Light locate Dracula's homes in Piccadilly, Mile End, and Bermondsey and (for Dracula's purposes at least) destroy the boxes of sacred earth, Dracula is forced to make a speedy retreat to Transylvania in his one remaining portable tomb. Although he first attempted to infiltrate English society by acquiring London property and perfecting his spoken English with the aid of the clerk who arranged the purchase, Dracula's plan is ultimately foiled.

Bram Stoker's *Dracula* has been the single most important influence on twentieth-century representations of vampires. Indeed, the association of vampires with Transylvania, which began with Stoker, has now become part of the customary mythology of the vampire figure in fiction. Although *Dracula* would have seemed like an extremely contemporary book to initial readers because of its connection to late Victorian popular fiction, its interest in mass media and new technology, and its association with the invasion genre of fiction that bespoke the cultural concerns surrounding the decline of the British Empire around the turn of the twentieth century, the book continues to frighten and inspire readers in the twenty-first century. Part of the appeal surrounding *Dracula* is its thematic and narrative complexity, which makes the text seem, upon first contact, a simple horror story but then allows it to open up, under closer examination, into a wider-ranging commentary on Victorian society. That Count Dracula is, in part, defeated by the tools of modernity—the technology and the keen interest in self-reflection expressed by all of the main characters—suggests that vampires can be defeated by moving into the present.

Works Cited

Arata, Stephen D. "The Occidental Tourist: *Dracula* and the Anxiety of Reverse Colonization." In *New Casebooks: Dracula*, ed. Glennis Byron. London: Macmillan, 1999. 119–144.

Brantlinger, Patrick. *Rule of Darkness*. London: Cornell University Press, 1988.

Smith, Warren Hunting. *Architecture in English Fiction*. New Haven, CT: Yale University Press, 1934.

Stoker, Bram. *Dracula*. Ed. Maurice Hindle. New York: Penguin, 2003.

Wicke, Jennifer. "Vampiric Typewriting: *Dracula* and Its Media." *English Literary History* 59, no. 2 (Summer 1992): 467–493.

CRITICAL
READINGS

Recreating the World:
The Sacred and the Profane in
Bram Stoker's *Dracula*

Beth E. McDonald

In her book *Dracula: Between Tradition and Modernism* (1998), Carol A. Senf characterizes Victorian citizens as looking "Janus-like . . . in two opposing directions" (6). While many people looked forward to the new century and to further progress, Senf writes that others looked "nostalgically to the past, a period that they *believed* [my italics] contained a clear synthesis of moral, religious, artistic, political, and social thought" (6). For many individuals, faith became a secular matter of production, consumption, and profit margins; and nature, once an example of God's rational design for the world, seemed more of an arena "red in tooth and claw" (Tennyson, "In Memoriam" 176) in which humans competed with each other for the Darwinian glory of survival of the fittest. As many late-nineteenth-century individuals came to understand how so many other species had lived and died out during the past millennia, they also had to accept their own mortality as a species; this realization called into question traditional religious promises of redemption through Christ, leaving many individuals in a condition of spiritual poverty characterized by doubt. However, the fact that men were divided over whether the alleged progress of the present time or the simpler ways of the past were best for society both morally and religiously seems to show that Victorian Britons were struggling to find some spiritual quality in their lives.

During the last decades of the nineteenth century, some Victorians sought reunion with divine mystery in study of the occult. Many turned to metaphysical organizations like the Hermetic Order of the Golden Dawn, a secret society formed by William Wynn Westcott, a Rosicrucian Freemason. Their mandate was to establish connection between the divine within man and the divine within the cosmos through the practice of magic, ritual, and the occult sciences.[1] The Society for Psychical Research, whose search for a numinous connection with the divine took place on a scientific level with the study of occult phenomena in nineteenth-century culture, also evolved during this period. Created in 1882 by a group of scholars from Cambridge University, London, and other nearby cities, the Society's purpose was to discover "whether some of the strange and unacceptable events—telepathy, clairvoyance, foreknowledge—had any basis in fact" (Sidgwick *Foreword* v). As nearly as possible a systematic and scientific method of collection, authentication, and analysis was followed; and in 1886 the information gathered by Edmund Gurney, Frank Podmore, and Frederic W. H. Myers was published in two volumes as *Phantasms of the Living*.

While Stoker would not have been aware of the numinous as such, since Rudolf Otto had not yet coined the word when Stoker was living and writing, his family history seems to indicate that he would have understood the feeling. Charlotte Stoker, Bram Stoker's Irish mother, regaled the sickly child with tales of ghosts and of the Irish banshee, whose keening cry, it was said, "presaged imminent death" (Roth 2) in the family. With this oral tradition as part of his early upbringing, Stoker would have been well versed in the qualities of non-rational experience. However, as an adult Stoker also would have been aware of the mystical side of pagan religious belief through his acquaintance with several people who practiced the art of magic.

In her biography of Stoker, Barbara Belford notes the unsubstantiated rumor that Stoker was a member of the Hermetic Order of the Golden Dawn. However, she also notes that he did have many friends who belonged to the organization and might have learned the secrets of the society from them, despite their pledge of silence on the subject. Further evidence of Stoker's awareness of the effect of an experience of the numinous might be found in his personal reaction to Henry Irving, whose reading of Thomas Hood's "The Dream of Eugene Aram" Stoker described in terms reminiscent of the hypnotic power of the Ancient Mariner, saying "so great was the magnetism of his genius, so profound was the sense of his dominancy that I sat spellbound"

(Belford 73). At the end of the reading, Stoker reportedly collapsed in apparent hysterics in the face of Irving's spellbinding power; and it is this power to hypnotize that becomes an integral part of the vampire's arsenal of supernatural weapons in Stoker's novel.

Published in 1897, *Dracula* reflects the attitudes and ideas of the late Victorian period in regard to several important issues of the day, including the importance of professional and social advancement, the significance of their own culture in the minds of nineteenth-century Britons, and the concern over what the influx of foreign influences might do to that culture and to the competition for place in society. Juxtaposed against these attitudes is the sense that in *Dracula* faith has taken second place to the professional advancement of many of the characters. As the men and women of the novel are confronted by the numinousness of the vampire, the search for salvation becomes more important; however, they approach their spiritual quest more as a community, or even a committee, than as individuals. Perpetuating the sacredness of their own cultural world view, when that view is threatened, they seek to fortify its crumbling foundations through the reestablishment of its secular sacredness, rather than through an actual reunion with the divine on a higher level of spiritual awakening that might be signified by a change in their world view.

Transforming the epistolary style of earlier, realistic novels, such as *Pamela* (1740–42) and *Clarissa* (1747–48) by Samuel Richardson, Stoker's work transcribes a Gothic nightmare whose multiple versions might raise doubt as to the reliability of any of the versions, despite his use of realism. However, when Jonathan Harker finally realizes what the women of castle Dracula and Dracula himself represent, he feels the weight of the truth of the events that have transpired. Later, also, when Mina Harker compiles all of the characters' individual stories into one, acceptance of the situation as real must follow. Once the various events are put in perspective, the fears of the individuals become the fears of society. If society is to be protected, the individuals must form a community and use their combined powers to destroy Dracula and his women. Their more secular search and destroy mission against the vampires becomes a spiritual journey that requires them to call on their faith, imagining themselves to be crusaders upholding the sacredness of British society.

Instead of forming a relationship with God and remaking the world in a more cosmic context on an individual level, as the Ancient Mariner has done, the group in *Dracula* works in a more communal, almost corporate, fashion, forming a small committee of dedicated men (and one woman) banded together for the good of the larger British community. Although Dracula is, like the Mariner, a figure of the numinous condemned to wander eternally, unlike the Mariner he is not allowed to tell his story and can take no active part in the healing of society. In Stoker's novel, the human characters are in power, despite Dracula's divine status, because they control the narrative. While the Mariner is constrained to serve the divine by becoming a vehicle for reconnection with it, the humans in *Dracula* make a decision to serve themselves and their larger society as protectors of the already established cultural system. For them, Dracula is not a vehicle of revelation or transformation, but a threat to the conservative, established order of British Victorian society that must be destroyed. Although the group calls on God in times of danger, by denying the sacred, though negative, aspects of the vampire, they deny the divine a place in their secularized world; and while the Mariner answers the question of the human place in the world by positing the unity of all things under God, the humans who destroy Dracula answer the same question by choosing to believe in the righteousness of their own established secular power, which they perceive as sacred.

In *Haunted Presence: The Numinous in Gothic Fiction*, S. L. Varnado utilizes Rudolf Otto's philosophy of the non-rational to argue that "the *mysterium tremendum et fascinans*, with its associated categories of the sacred and the profane" (1), is at the heart of Gothic literature. Applying Otto's theory of the negative numinous, in his chapter "The Daemonic in *Dracula*," Varnado argues that Bram Stoker's novel "dramatizes the cosmic struggle between the opposing forces of darkness and light, of the sacred and profane . . . , sweeping racial, geographical, even ontological counters in its wake" (97–98). In accordance with his interpretation of the opposition of good and evil in Otto's definition of the negative numinous, Varnado reads the sacred in *Dracula* as "benign" (108) and the profane as evil. While his analysis has much merit, due to the perceived evil of the vampire characters in the text, he does not explain what universal principles are behind the cosmic conflict in the novel. However, employing religious historian Mircea Eliade's critical studies of the sacred and profane helps illuminate the mythic patterns in the text and demonstrates why it is important that Dracula be destroyed.

Also drawing on Otto's investigation of the non-rational, Eliade defines the numinous as threshold or journey experience, a "boundary situation . . . man discovers in becoming conscious of his place in the universe" (*Images and Symbols* 34), and describes the polarities of sacred and profane as "two existential situations assumed by man" (17) in relation to the cosmos. Impelled by dread, Eliade argues, the subject of an encounter with the numinous feels a sense of "profound nothingness" (*Sacred and Profane* 10) and acknowledges the non-reality of his earthly existence as a feeling of profaneness that is in opposition to the sense of absolute reality that surrounds the sacred. This feeling of powerlessness causes many individuals to seek ways to resacralize the world. Eliade defines two ways in which the religious person might recreate the world as a sacred cosmos: spatially, by projecting four horizons from a central point or forming a symbolic vertical axis through a central point to above and below earth; and temporally, by ritual repetition in imitation of the gods creating the world from the body of a primordial being most often characterized as a serpent or dragon. In Eliade's study of world religions, this being defines metaphorically the chaos which existed at the beginning of time when the world was formed, and which exists again each time the world loses its sacredness. For the proponents of the primitive religions Eliade studied, this primordial chaos often is experienced as a condition that must be vanquished so that order may be instituted in or restored to a society. For Eliade, a feeling of the numinous and a resultant yearning to be close to the divine are evoked thematically through the opposition of the sacred and profane, divine order and primordial chaos. In *Dracula* this theme is carried out on several levels as the conflict between vampire and living human becomes a reenactment of a mythic ritual in order to preserve the sacredness of the British world.

My examination of the novel mainly deals with the various representations of sacred and profane space and time within the text. However, inherent in the numinous experience is a wish to believe in God and the possibility of reunion with the sacred, leading the characters to engage in mythic rituals in order to establish their relationship with the divine. As the characters in the text confront the numinousness of Dracula, they must also confront their own apathetic faith in God; therefore, this analysis leads eventually into a discussion of faith and belief and why it is important to the late Victorian culture that the vampire be destroyed.

"Transylvania Is Not England": Sacred and Profane Space

According to Eliade, all "space is not homogeneous" (*Sacred and Profane* 20) but is perceived as either sacred or profane, order or chaos. Manifestation of the sacred reveals a fixed point or center where a person experiences absolute reality directly; all spaces outside this center are profane, "without structure or consistency, amorphous" (20). To transform profane into sacred space, individuals recreate the habitations of their immediate world, from their countries and cities to their houses and even their bodies, by visualizing a sacred center; however, this point then becomes a threshold point where the profane may also reveal itself. In *Dracula*, sacred and profane spaces, in opposition and intruding upon one another, are represented by England and Transylvania and the individual habitations and characters associated with them, so that both sacred and profane seem fluid and change qualities depending upon the influence of Dracula.

Sacred and profane spaces are represented initially by the polarity of West and East, England and Transylvania. Jonathan Harker's first diary entry records the impression that he is "leaving the West and entering the East" (Stoker 1)[2] as he travels to Transylvania. Although England is considered the "polar opposite of Transylvania" (Varnado 105) and the "rational center of the novel" (105), Victorian Britain may represent more than rationality in its opposition to Transylvania. If, as Eliade writes, every primitive religious individual considers his or her own world consecrated space with the world outside it unconsecrated, and if, as he also states, colonization is a method of consecration of profane space, then one might see Britain's exploration and colonization of other more primitive countries as a consecration of profane space by a country that considers itself in possession of a stronger sense of the sacred.

In his speech at the second reading of the Australian Colonies Bill before the House of Commons on February 18, 1850, Charles Adderley spoke of colonization as the "destiny" (32) of the English people. The former motives of war and commerce, which once had been behind the English proclivity toward imperialism, had been replaced by "a motive higher than either" (32). From this motive, which Adderley articulated as "the desire of spreading throughout the habitable globe all the characteristics of Englishmen—their energy, their civilization, their religion and their freedom" (32), it is not difficult to infer that, through the belief of most Englishmen in the superiority of their culture and in their right and duty to expand their world, the country of England itself acquires a higher dimension of meaning and can be interpreted as the sacred center of the British Empire.

Representing the East, Transylvania also incorporates both sacred and profane space. For people belonging to many of the early religious systems analyzed by Eliade, a belief existed that at the limits of any sacred microcosm lies profane space, a "dangerous region of the demons, the ghosts, the dead and of foreigners—in a word, chaos or death or night" (*Images and Symbols* 38), which threatens the sacred cosmos with destruction, regression, and chaos. In *Horror and the Holy: Wisdom-Teachings of the Monster Tale*, Kirk J. Schneider does examine the sacred aspects of several horror tales in spatial terms, as either "*constrictive* [or] *expansive*" (7). However, although arguing that *Dracula* is hyperconstrictive due to Harker's feelings of fear and the representations of imprisonment in the text, he fails to account for the representations of chaos that are an important cause of Harker's fear.

In *Dracula*, the chaos of profane space is represented in several ways; however, writing in *Our Ladies of Darkness: Feminine Daemonology in Male Gothic Fiction*, Joseph Andriano argues that the "circle is . . . the most pervasive archetypal symbol in *Dracula*" (113) with the sacred circles formed by the heroes of the novel in opposition to the unholy circles of the vampires represented by the "whirlpools, vortices, and circles within circles" (114). As Harker begins his journey, he describes Transylvania in terms of watery chaos, as the "centre of some sort of imaginative whirlpool" (Stoker 2) of superstition; and later Dracula characterizes it as "the whirlpool of European races" (28). In Emily Gerard's *The Land Beyond the Forest*, which Stoker read while researching Transylvania, her discussion of Romanian superstition includes a reference to the whirlpool as a place to be avoided because it is considered the residence of a water spirit, "the cruel water-man who lies in wait for human victims" (200).[3]

Further representations of the circle also show up repeatedly during Harker's confusing journey from Borgo Pass to Dracula's castle. A "living ring of terror" (Stoker 13) surrounds him as the wolves gather about the coach and menace him while the driver is off searching for the blue flames he and Harker have seen flickering in the darkness. Later in the novel, the chaos of the vampire is juxtaposed against the order of the sacred as Professor Van Helsing and his band of men work to save Mina. When Mina has been partially turned to a vampire by Dracula and wears the circular imprint of the Sacred Wafer on her forehead as a sign of her profaneness, Professor Van Helsing places a "Holy circle" (369) of the blessed wafers about Mina to protect her from the female vampires. Furthermore, at the climax of the novel, it is a "ring of men" (376), Jonathan Harker, Quincey Morris, Arthur Holmwood, and Dr. John Seward, who do their sacred duty by ridding the world of Dracula.

In addition to the circular images, the chaos of storm and wildness is also important in engendering Harker's fear. He records in his diary that on crossing the mountains through the Borgo Pass it "seemed as though the mountain range had separated two atmospheres, and that now we had got into the thunderous one" (Stoker 9). In *The Essential Dracula*, Leonard Wolf annotates this passage, noting that Stoker is informing the reader "that Harker is passing from the civilized to the primordial" (14). This is Harker's threshold experience at the edge of the numinous, as he crosses over from the order of his familiar world to the chaos and danger of the unknown land beyond the forest.

For Otto, the power of the numinous lies in the subject's realization of the possibility of death and his fear of the mystery of existence beyond that death; and as Dracula will later remind Harker, "Transylvania is not England" (Stoker 21). As a wildly primitive and largely unknown part of the world, Transylvania is a netherworld of superstition and death, a place which Harker will later characterize as a "cursed land where the devil and his children still walk with earthly feet!" (53). In Transylvania, Harker will be confronted with the destructiveness of profane space in the form of the living dead and their habitations. Language fails him as he journeys into a world where the Babel of "queer words" (6) spoken by the various nationalities disconcerts him. The odd behavior of the peasants protecting themselves from the evil eye and their insistent offerings of various superstitious and religious objects of the Catholic faith also leave the Protestant Harker uneasy, hesitant and wondering, open to the eventual experience of the numinous in the form of the vampire. Having ventured into the chaotic zone of Transylvania, he must recognize that beneath his rational, empirical façade he stands powerless in relation to Dracula.

Harker's journey has embodied the chaos of the East as opposed to the order of the West. However, Stoker also develops the Transylvanian landscape as a model of sacred and profane space within itself. According to Eliade, the cosmos may be recreated by projection of an imaginary axis that extends vertically above and below the horizon point. The central point of this *axis mundi* is considered the communication point between heaven, earth and the underworld; and Eliade suggests that an extremely common representation of the abode of the gods is "a Mountain . . . situated at the Centre of the World" (*Images and Symbols* 42). In Harker's description of Transylvania, one can see the representation of an *axis mundi*. The road which he and his fellow passengers travel winds in and out of "the green swelling hills of the Mittel Land" (Stoker 7) which rise toward the Carpathian Mountains. This middle land takes on the aspect of earthly paradise as Harker describes its "forests and woods" and "a bewildering mass of fruit blossom—apple, plum, pear, cherry" (6), all carpeting the green grass with their petals. Suddenly, one of his companions, crossing himself in reverence, directs Harker's eye to a mountain peak looming above them. He refers to this mountain as "'Isten szek!' [or] 'God's seat!'" (7).

In these passages, it is clear that the peasants operate in this earthly middle ground in touch with a God whose abode is the peak of this lofty mountain and with the underworld in the form of Dracula's castle, and Dracula himself, to whom they show a particular aversion. Although Dracula's castle is not technically under ground as one might expect a representation of the underworld to be, and although the coach and its passenger must ascend to reach it, the castle signifies the underworld because the burial crypts far below the earth are Dracula's resting place. It is, however, in its representation as a threshold or horizon that Transylvania itself becomes important as a site of the numinous.

From the middle land of earthly existence Harker must cross the threshold into the hell of Dracula's castle and face the probability of physical death without hope for a spiritual afterlife.

Chaos at the Center: Ruins and Madhouses

According to Eliade, many religious people recreate the *imago mundi* by settling a country or establishing a city and also construct their homes by imitating the patterns of the cosmos; therefore, "cosmic symbolism [can be] found in the very structure of habitation" (*Sacred and Profane* 53). As the sacred can be represented in a house, the profane may be, also; and Dracula's castle "stands as a symbol of the *mysterium tremendum*" (Varnado 101). However, the castle itself produces only feelings of uneasiness in Harker, not the level of fear or dread that the *mysterium tremendum* is capable of evoking. Although the uneasiness Harker feels when confronted with the mystery of Transylvania and its people does grow stronger once he is in the castle and has met Dracula, it only becomes the full blown dread of the *mysterium tremendum* once he is assured of the horrible existence and the mysterious power of the vampire.

If Transylvania represents profane space, Dracula's castle represents the vortex of chaos. The castle is a maze of corridors, rooms, and locked doors, which for Harker come to illustrate his lack of knowledge and, therefore, his powerlessness in the presence of Dracula. As the guest of Dracula, Harker lives a "strange night existence" (Stoker 25) in which his imagination runs wild, producing even more anxiety. Within this realm of chaos, Harker attempts and fails to find some kind of order and safety. Although he feels safe upon first entering the one forbidden room that he finds unlocked in the castle, his feeling, based upon what he imagines about the former occupants of the room, is illusory. Then, after he has experienced the horror of the female vampires, he looks upon his own room in the castle as a refuge from danger; however, at the center of chaos, true sanctuary does not exist. At the mercy of these "devils of the Pit" (53), Harker lives in fear of death, wondering how he can escape from the danger.

Up to this point, Harker's experience in Dracula's castle has been one of an uneasy sense of danger; however, once he has met the vampire women, he suffers the horror that characterizes Otto's definition of the numinous in its negative aspect. This feeling causes him to fall to his knees in prayer, insisting that, if he dies at the hands of the vampire women, he will be spiritually ready. At this point, he apprehends the sacred in its positive character. As it rises, the sun strikes the highest point of the gate to Dracula's castle which Harker can see from his window; and it seems to him "as if the dove of the ark had lighted there" (46), pointing the way to safety. Like Noah in his ark, Harker is delivered from his "sea of wonders" (18) to a new birth, a second creation of the world from watery chaos. After the cataclysmic events of the previous days, Harker's fear dissipates, and he realizes that he must take action to save himself. He must risk death by imitating Dracula, climbing out over the precipice of the castle to escape. Although, like many men, he dreads the unknown "Hereafter" (46), Harker's dilemma is more urgent than most. Fear of being turned into one of the Un-Dead makes the choice of possible death a necessity for Harker. In the end, it seems, he prefers the unknown and hope for a spiritual life to the decidedly purgatorial existence of vampirism, as he risks his mortal life climbing down the wall and escaping the female vampires

In the primitive systems of religion studied by Eliade, profane space is commonly represented as having no fixed point of reference; and this amorphous and neutral space will erupt in the heart of seemingly sacred space when Dracula lands at Whitby, England, bringing with him a chaos that will threaten an already shaky English order. The sun will set with a vengeance on the British Empire when he arrives. As Dracula arrives in England aboard the *Demeter*, however, Stoker reminds the reader of Dracula's connection to Coleridge's wandering Mariner. The wind dies and the stormy seas are replaced by a dead calm; and Mina remarks, quoting Coleridge's Mariner, that the only ship visible, a foreign ship, seems "as idle as a painted ship upon a painted ocean" (Stoker 76; Gardner line 113). This is the dead calm before the true storm of Dracula's presence is felt in England.

If discovery or projection of a sacred center is equivalent to the creation of the world, as Eliade posits, then Dracula's invasion of England becomes a de-creation of the sacred, extending chaos to the religious institutions and habitations of the British population. Just as houses are considered as forms of the *imago mundi*, holy sites and sanctuaries are considered even more so because they are sanctified religious structures and, as such, are supposed to be "proof against all earthly corruption" (Eliade *Sacred and Profane* 59); however, in the potentially profane world of England, holy sites and sanctuaries are no proof against Dracula. Since, as Eliade argues, no place exists exclusively as sacred or profane, Dracula has always had his own privileged places, sanctuaries as it were, to which he can retreat. For centuries, his *sanctum sanctorum* has been his Transylvanian castle and the tomb deep beneath it in the old chapel; however, when he decides to travel to England, he must make use of more portable sanctuaries. Harker records his understanding that the vampire can "only rest in sacred earth" (Stoker 297), information which he has learned from Professor Van Helsing's reference to the belief that the graves of Dracula's heroic ancestors have sanctified the soil for Dracula's sanctuaries. Although Wolf notes that he finds no evidence in either folklore or history to support Professor Van Helsing's observation, the precedent does exist in Eliade's research of primitive religions. Eliade argues that many primitive people felt a sacred connection to the earth because they believed their original ancestors came from it; and Dracula also partakes in a more profane way in what Eliade describes as the "religious experience of autochthony" (*Sacred and Profane* 140), which is "the feeling . . . of *belonging to a place*" (140), of having a connection with the native soil of one's own land. Dracula's autochthonic connection with the earth of his native land is represented by the fifty boxes of "friendly soil" (Stoker 31) which he has shipped to England to serve as sanctuaries for him.

However, in Britain, Whitby Abbey, the estate of Carfax, the insane asylum, and Hampstead Heath also represent types of sanctuary, which have been rendered profane and, therefore, provide other privileged places for Dracula and for Lucy once she becomes a vampire. In his chapter "Sacred and Desecrated Space: The Cathedral and the Ruin in the Gothic Novel," in *The Cartographers of Hell: Essays on the Gothic Novel and the Social History of England*, Alok Bhalla argues that the foundation of the "religion and religious institutions" (72) represented in Gothic novels lies in the "economic, political and cultural conditions of a given society" (72). Although he concedes to Eliade's finding that the cathedral is sacred space and, quoting Eliade's *Sacred and Profane*, agrees his assertion that the sacredness of the cathedral allows the worshipper to "make a 'religious valorization of the world'" (Bhalla 74; Eliade 23), he makes a more pessimistic argument that the cathedral produces only the realization of human inability to restore the sacred relationship of primordial times. He describes the Gothic ruin as an amorphous place which holds no promise of a "return to a divine origin" (74) and characterizes the Gothic ruin as "a region of moral and spiritual desolation, a desecrated space tainted with sin and corruption" (79). As such, these places represent a world devoid of "spiritual meaning or purpose" (80), which for the characters in *Dracula* may be indicative of the time in which they live. However, Bhalla has missed an extremely important point. For both Eliade and Otto, spiritual value is not irretrievable; the feelings of unworthiness felt by the person who has encountered the sacred, in either its negative or positive guise, cause the person to recognize his longing to reclaim the sacred and to seek out ways to do so. The Gothic ruin only indicates that mankind has failed in his responsibility to maintain and renew the sacredness of his world; it does not represent the sacred as irredeemable. In *Dracula*, the ruins in England are a sign that humanity must change or be caught up in the chaos of a profane life, which is perceived by many religious people to be a living death with no promise of spiritual release.

Whitby Abbey, once a religious sanctuary, has been in ruins since its sacking by the Danes in 867 (Wolf 84) and is purportedly now only fit to house ghosts.[4] Even the parish church standing between Whitby Abbey and the town of Whitby itself is surrounded by a ruined graveyard. According to Mr. Swales, the gravestones are "simply tumblin' down with the weight o' the lies wrote on them"; and "nigh half of them" (65) have no body in them at all since the men were lost at sea. The old man tells Mina Murray that not only the graves but also the memories of the dead themselves are not held sacred by the living. One grave in particular belongs to a suicide; and it is here that Dracula takes shelter when he arrives in Whitby. This grave is a privileged place for him, since, according to the research of both Montague Summers and Leonard Wolf, in vampire folklore a person who committed suicide was considered susceptible to becoming a vampire. However, the suicide's grave is also a logical hiding place for Dracula because the disrepair of the graves and the lies that have been written on them suggest the absence of true sanctity in British society.

In Whitby, there exists the same polarity of West and East that Harker had noticed on his travels to Transylvania. The suicide's grave and the death seat above it are on the East cliff, while the town and the hotel where Mina and Lucy are staying are on the West cliff. Once Dracula has brought Lucy under his influence, he can invade the town and her rooms at the Crescent and eventually move even further west to her home at Hillingham, near London. When the novel's action moves on to Purfleet, outside London, the intrusion of profane into sacred space becomes even more apparent. Since in primitive religious belief structures may take the cosmos as a "paradigmatic model" (Eliade *Sacred and Profane* 45), Carfax may be considered an *imago mundi*. The estate purchased by Dracula represents the world in two ways, as a structure of habitation and as a representation of intersection. Harker's description of the estate to Dracula refers to the derivation of the name Carfax from "*Quatre Face*, as the house is four-sided agreeing with the cardinal points of the compass" (Stoker 23). Moreover, in Eliade's study, an intersection is considered a sacred representation of the world. As the human universe stretches out from the sacred center "toward the four cardinal points, the village comes into existence around an intersection" (*Sacred and Profane* 45). Carfax can be perceived as an *imago mundi* because it is situated at a crossroads in Purfleet. Although Harker only describes the house as being on a side road, the structure aligns with the four compass points by virtue of its name. In *The Essential Dracula*, Wolf employs *The Oxford Dictionary of Etymology* definition of Carfax as "a place where four roads meet, especially as a proper name" (31); he also makes an interesting point that Carfax is a perfect choice for Dracula's English lair because suicides were traditionally buried at crossroads.

Regardless of its sacred orientation, this estate is now a model of chaos, abandoned and in ruins. Harker tells Dracula that Carfax is comprised of an ancient keep and church (Stoker 23) and several additions made haphazardly over the generations. The high wall surrounding the property has long been in disrepair and the iron parts of the gate are exceedingly rusted. These descriptions of Carfax not only suggest a lack of order, but also a lack of the responsibility that the English society should have taken for the sacredness of its habitations. The fact that Dracula will now inhabit this place shows that the profane has invaded the symbolic center of the Victorian world; yet this center is empty and in ruins because the British people have neglected the sanctity of their own space.

At this place of intersection, however, Carfax is not the only sight of profane activity. Here is another residence, an insane asylum owned by Dr. John Seward. Although by the late nineteenth century the stereotypical madhouse had evolved into a hospital atmosphere with a more humane approach to the care and cure of patients, the insane asylum in *Dracula* should still be considered more a center of chaos than of order. According to Andrew T. Scull's *Museums of Madness: The Social Organization of Insanity in Nineteenth-Century England*, both strait waistcoats and chaining were methods used in the early eighteen hundreds to restrain patients. Dr. Seward's reference to the use of the strait waistcoat and to the chaining of the inmate Renfield in order to restrain him indicate that Seward is still making use of earlier methods and mechanics for keeping the asylum's patients in a condition more like prisoners' than sick people's.

As a privately owned "lunatic asylum" (Stoker 23), Seward's establishment also may be associated with the profane side of existence in the economically oriented British culture. Private asylums arose as business ventures in the eighteenth and nineteenth centuries and had to make a profit in order to survive; therefore, the doctors in charge not only became the "arbiters of mental normalcy" (McCandless 341) but also had a monetary stake in diagnosing someone as insane. Furthermore, the opposition of sacred and profane space is seen in the isolation of the asylum from the so-called normal community. By locating the asylums outside the city, the foreignness or "'otherness' of the insane was emphasised by their geographical separation from 'normalcy'" (Mellett 46); and in *Dracula*, Harker assures the Count that the asylum cannot be seen from the grounds of Carfax Abbey. This isolation will give Dracula access to the lunatic Renfield and, later, to Mina (Murray) Harker when she is left in the asylum by her husband and the other men, ostensibly to protect her as they all go in search of Dracula.[5] Like Harker in Dracula's castle, Mina is isolated from the outside world and from the additional knowledge that the men are gathering on the danger Dracula poses to them all. Her isolation and ignorance of this knowledge indicates a lack of control in chaotic space; Mina has been placed in a vulnerable and profane position in relation to Dracula's great power. The asylum offers her no sanctuary, no safety; and while the men are out searching for his hiding places, there is no one to stop Dracula from making Mina one of his vampire women.

Another place of chaos within the sacredness of Britain is Hampstead Heath. In *Literary England*, David E. Scherman and Richard Wilcox refer to Hampstead Heath as "an expanse of wasteland" within the confines of the London suburbs. According to data in Henry Mayhew's *London Labour and the London Poor*, prostitution was prevalent there (Mayhew 266).[6] For Lucy, once she is a vampire, the graveyard near Hampstead Heath becomes a place of sanctuary. From there the demon Lucy, her vampire body now representative of the chaos brought to England by Dracula, roams the lonely domain of Hampstead Heath preying on children.

Good Women and Great Men, Demons and Lunatics

Eliade maintains that when primitive individuals perceive the world as a creation of the gods, they apprehend themselves as a part of that creation and discover within themselves "the same sanctity . . . [apparent] in the cosmos" (*Sacred and Profane* 165). This discovery, he argues, causes them to assimilate the cosmic patterns of the world into individual life and reproduce the cosmos on a human scale. Therefore, for Eliade's primitive individual, the human body can be considered as either sacred or profane; and "passing beyond the human condition finds figural expression in the destruction of . . . the personal cosmos" (177). In *Dracula*, the characters represent the opposition of sacred and profane space on a personal level. However, as a group, a large part of what they come to represent is the sacred order of the cosmos, at least the British cosmos.

Good Women

The main female characters in the novel, Lucy Westenra and Mina Murray, represent the sacredness of such institutions as society and family; yet both women have the potential to become profane. As a representative of British womanhood, Lucy rather typifies the fears of many British men in regard to the Victorian New Woman.[7] She is a woman who wants to marry three men; and this sexually rebellious attitude places her squarely on the side of the profane, making her susceptible to Dracula. Lucy's surname Westenra also allies her with both the sacred and the profane. Most interpretations, according to Wolf, call attention to the displaced "r" to give the reading "Western" to Lucy's last name, identifying her name "symbolically as 'Light of the West' (Wolf 71). He also notes that her name has been interpreted as a derivative of 'Lucifer' and mentions Mark M. Hennelly's suggestion in his article "*Dracula*: The Gnostic Quest and Victorian Wasteland," that her name stands for "'the principle of right light'" (71). However, there is a further interpretation to be explored. According to Christopher Frayling's *Vampires: Lord Byron to Count Dracula*, Stoker had E. A. Wallis Budge's *The Mummy: Chapters in Egyptian Funereal Archeology* (1893 edition) in his library at the time of his writing of *Dracula*, and Frayling lists this book as "relevant to the writing" (346) of the text. In light of the information in this book, one might interpret Lucy's last name as divided into the syllables West-en-Ra, 'en-Ra' most often translated in the Budge book as 'of the Sun.' Her name might then be interpreted as 'Light of the Western Sun,' which would associate it with sunset, thereby identifying her even more strongly with the vampire who can only rise from the grave at that time.

Unlike Lucy, Mina Harker is considered "practical and ambitious" (Varnado 105) and dreams of helping her husband with his work. This description may align Mina with the rational; however, she demonstrates even more strongly that she is allied with both the sacred and profane. Mina is characterized as wife, mother, and sister in relation to the men in the story, all sacred familial relationships. In addition, she is described in religious terms. Professor Van Helsing's description of her as "one of God's women" (Stoker 188) resembles the standard description of a nun's relationship to God; and, after she has exchanged blood with Dracula, she is described as a "martyr" (290) when she vows to die before she would hurt any of the others. However, Mina also is allied with Eve when she gives Professor Van Helsing a shorthand copy of her diary to read, excusing her wish to astonish and puzzle him by laying the blame on "some of the taste of the original apple that remains still in our [women's] mouths" (183). In identifying herself with Eve, she has characterized herself as transgressor and so is a suitable victim for Dracula, as Lucy was for different reasons.

After the exchange of blood, however, Mina recognizes herself as "unclean" (Stoker 296) and profane; but she has no power to recreate herself again as sacred. Soon she begins to feel a strange sense of freedom and becomes more affectionate with Harker than usual. Although Lucy and Mina may represent the rational and the sacredness of English society, Dracula's penetration of them both with his fangs may be interpreted as a penetration of chaos: into heart of the personal cosmos and, through them, into the center of the sacred British cosmos. It will be up to Mina's husband and the others to resacralize the bodies of both Mina and Lucy and the world of England with the death of Dracula.

Great Men

If one looks at the relationships between the men, one can see the beginnings of the group structure that will be brought against Dracula. Dr. Seward, Morris, and Holmwood have formed strong ties of friendship through sharing adventures in the Marquesas, South America, and Korea; Seward, Holmwood, and Professor Van Helsing, in their turn, share the same kind of connection, and more so, because Dr. Seward saved the life of Professor Van Helsing by sucking the poison from his wound after Holmwood accidentally injured him. As comrades in danger, these men have already formed a community within the larger social structure, participating in a relationship which honors the sacredness of life, friendship, and duty, among other things; and these are the men who become the foundation of the forces of the sacred to which later will be added Jonathan and Mina (Murray) Harker.

Arthur Holmwood's name also aligns him with the sacred in two important ways. First, the surname Holmwood establishes his connection with the sacred. Holmwood is another name for the holm-oak, a bush often defined as the holly because of a resemblance in the foliage; and the holly is a sacred plant signifying "death and regeneration" (Walker

406). In relation to the meanings of holly, in his study *The Golden Bough*, Sir James Frazer found the mistletoe plant to be connected with divinity as it was considered supernatural, growing on oak trees as it does without benefit of roots in soil. Then, the name *Arthur* brings up the obvious connection with King Arthur, a fifth-century British hero of both historical and mythic proportions, whose leadership consolidated the tribes of Britain to repel its enemy, the Saxons. Furthermore, the connection between Arthur Holmwood and King Arthur takes on a tripartite pattern if one takes into account the association of Irish hero Finn MacCumhal and King Arthur.

Finn was the leader of a band of men called the Fianna, who, according to historical and folklore research, were most often characterized in early texts as social outcasts who survived by "hunting and warring" (Nagy 18). As outlaws, these men functioned "outside or on the margins of the tribal territory or community" (18). However, through time and the telling of the tale, as so often happens, the character of Finn and his band was transformed; they came to be perceived as the champions and protectors of Ireland. Many experts in Celtic literature find a bond between King Arthur and Finn, considered in their respective folklores to be heroic, cultural figures and leaders of bands of men who protect their respective lands from enemies again; and Finn is often described in later tales as the "'Irish Arthur'" (MacKillop 63).

A particular tale of Finn may be relevant here. In *Gods and Fighting Men: the Story of the Tuatha De Danaan and of the Fianna of Ireland*, Lady Augusta Gregory retells the tale "The Hospitality of Cuanna's House" which Stoker quite possibly was familiar with from the stories his mother told during his Irish childhood. While hunting with his band one day, Finn MacCumhal and his friends see a giant carrying a pig on his back. A heavy mist rises suddenly, hiding the road and the giant; and when it clears, they discover a house with two wells near it. On the edge of one well is an iron vessel; on the other is a copper vessel. The occupants of the house welcome them; and soon Finn becomes thirsty. Caoilte, one of Finn's band, is sent by the owner of the house to bring water from either well. He brings water in the copper vessel. This water tastes like honey while Finn is drinking it, but it turns to gall in his stomach, causing "fierce windy pains and signs of death" (264). Caoilte is sent out again and this time brings water in the iron vessel. When Finn drinks this water, it tastes of "bitterness" (264); but afterward, he feels better. The old man explains that the two wells represent "Lying and Truth; for it is sweet to people to be telling a lie, but it is bitter in the end" (266). By the same token, though the truth may taste bitter when first heard, in the end it is sweet. It may be this idea that Stoker is trying to impart when he has Professor Van Helsing tell Arthur that they all "will have to pass through the bitter water to reach the sweet" (Stoker 170), especially since he reiterates this sentiment two more times in the course of the novel (202 and 213).

For Holmwood, as for all of them, the truth of Lucy's existence as a vampire may be bitter in the beginning, but later, after the men have returned her to a more blessed state in death, memory of her can be sweet again. In light of the connection between these legendary heroes, Arthur and Finn, it seems probable that Stoker combined them in the character of Holmwood, both by naming him after King Arthur and by incorporating the story of Finn in the repeated references to bitter and sweet water. As the only aristocrat in the group, Arthur Holmwood represents something of the divine himself in his connection to the heroic nobility of the legendary king Arthur. He also represents the more chaotic polarity through Finn the Irish outlaw hero. In addition, it is foretold in the tales of both noble and outlaw that they will be resurrected when their respective countries are in desperate need of them; and, in his act of staking Lucy, Arthur Holmwood becomes the sacred agent of death and resurrection for her.

The group's connection with the sacred is apparent in other characters as well. As a newly made solicitor, Harker is now a member of the middle class, serious about his new duties. In the rational world these attributes are admirable; but in the non-rational world they will avail him little. Once Harker crosses over into Transylvania, his journey becomes a rite of passage, and he becomes the initiate. When subjected to the mysterious actions and words of the peasants, he is ignorant of their true meaning and so is only uneasy; but as he gathers knowledge of Dracula and the three women, the horror of both his own and society's fate nearly paralyzes him. After his escape from the castle and the female vampires, he suffers from brain fever, his hair turns white overnight, and he is reported to be raving "the secrets of God" (Stoker 103). To some extent, although he seeks to deny his knowledge, once he survives his ordeal in Transylvania, he is a wise old man figure because he has immediate experience of the vampire, which Professor Van Helsing, for all his knowledge, does not have; and his foreign journal, in turn, becomes for the others a narrative of initiation into the numinous.

However, despite the fact that he has no direct experience of the vampire, Professor Van Helsing's role in the group seems the most important. As the oldest of all the men, Professor Van Helsing represents a kind of father figure to the younger men. His experiences of the world are far greater than those of the other men; and he has his Catholic faith and his knowledge of medicine and of folklore as weapons to combat Dracula. As a metaphysician and the leader of the band of men who will destroy Dracula, Professor Van Helsing represents the sacred in the role of warrior priest, as a St. George, leading the fight against the evil dragon—chaos. Dr. Seward, Holmwood, and Morris join Professor Van Helsing, as they had in earlier years, eventually drawing Jonathan and Mina Harker into their ranks, to become a force in service of the sacred.

Demons

If Professor Van Helsing is the good father figure, leading his band of children in a sacred ritual, Dracula is the evil father who has some of the same characteristics as Professor Van Helsing but who has turned them to the service of evil. As a representation of the negatively numinous, Dracula embodies both sacred and profane space. Dracula embodies some of the aura of the sacred hero; he is, as he tells Harker, the "heart's blood" (Stoker 29) of his people. It is widely believed that Stoker at least partially patterned Dracula after Vlad Tepes, a ruler of Wallachia in the 1400s, who, according to historic documents, used impalement as a form of punishment, and sometimes as a source of entertainment. If accounts of Tepes are true, one might rather interpret the connection of Dracula to him as a signification of the profane; but, despite these reports, Tepes was not and is not considered a monster in his own country. To this day, he is considered a hero for driving the Turks from the borders. According to research done for their book *Dracula, Prince of Many Faces: His Life and Times*, Radu R. Florescu and Raymond T. McNally, history professors and Dracula experts with several books on the subject to their credit, found that through Romanian folklore Vlad Tepes became a national hero on the order of America's George Washington. The Romanian oral tradition characterizes him as "a law-upholding statesman who is implacable in punishing thieves, liars, idlers, or people who otherwise cheated the state" (216). As a "rational despot" (216) he attempted to "centralize his government by killing unpatriotic anarchical boyars" (216), and his exploits were believed by the people to be socially and morally right. It is this interpretation of history that connects Tepes and Dracula as heroes and allows Dracula to represent sacred space.

Dracula also has at his control what appear to be divine powers—to control the animals and the weather, to turn to motes of dust or bats, and to read minds. Although these powers would seem to ally him with the sacred, they represent Eliade's description of profane space in several ways. Dracula reacts with horror both to religious objects and to the natural, folk remedies of garlic, mountain ash or rowan and wild rose given to Harker by his fellow coach passengers. These represent a more superstitious approach toward danger and are meant to protect the intended victim or dispatch the vampire. Emily Gerard writes that Romanian superstition calls for the mouth of a suspected vampire to be filled with garlic, in addition to the cutting off of the head as a precaution against vampirism (185). As an agent against plague and various supernatural evils, in Romania garlic is used both to detect the vampire and to prevent attack. On both St. Andrew's and St. George's Eves windows and doors are anointed with garlic to keep vampires away. In addition, Gerard also found that it was "usual to lay the thorny branch of a wild-rose bush across the body to prevent it leaving the coffin" (186). Montague Summers also records that in Saxon superstition in Transylvania on St. George's Day it was customary to place branches of the wild rose bush on the gates of the yard to keep out witches (309). Moreover, the mountain ash or rowan, a member of the rose family, was customarily planted in churchyards and at door of houses and barns to protect people and animals from evil spirits (Melton).

Dracula's abilities to shape-change, become invisible, and read thoughts also demonstrate his profane nature because they are not ultimate powers. His shape-changing and invisibility are limited to night time and noon; and his ability to read thoughts is contingent upon his first having a blood link with the person through an act of vampirism. Furthermore, as the living dead, Dracula represents a man whose *personal cosmos* has been destroyed, who has passed "beyond the human condition" (Eliade, *Sacred and Profane* 177). He is and is not human at the same time—both a man and a "monster" (Stoker 51), a hero of the wars against the Turks and a "criminal, and of criminal type" (342), according, as Mina Harker says, to Nordau and Lombroso, nineteenth-century physician and criminologist, respectively, whose theories argued that criminal behavior was degenerative and a reversion to the primitive.[8] Dracula, although he was once a living, breathing human and a hero, is now a daemonic corpse; still of human form, he now is characterized by Harker as having a "marked physiognomy" (Stoker 17). As Harker and his fellow vampire hunters come to know Dracula more fully, they find in him a physical, rather than spiritual, immortality, prodigious strength, and uncanny powers of metamorphosis and control of animals and people. These aberrations link him to the primitive and, therefore, to the criminal type.

These are not the only qualities of Dracula that make him profane, however. He is foreign; and, according to the analysis done by Carol A. Senf and Stephen D. Arata, as a foreigner, Dracula may represent the British fears of colonization by other countries and/or cultures.[9] Moreover, in many of the more primitive religions that Eliade researched, colonization is considered a form of creation of the world and, as such, is always considered a consecration (*Sacred and Profane* 32); therefore, as the creator of a "new order of beings" (Stoker 302), Dracula will, in effect, colonize and consecrate England to the profane. Dracula penetrates to the sacred center of the British Empire and brings chaos into an already partially desacralized world characterized by industrialism and profit making, but because Dracula is a vampire, his destructive power also means desacralization of the human body. Although the vampire cannot procreate in a normal human fashion, he creates by destroying, taking over an already existing body and turning it into the living dead and an already existing universe and returning it to primordial chaos. His creations all have the same attributes and desires; and all are parasites living off the blood of a human host, just as Dracula does. In light of the parasite-host relationship between vampires and humans, the forces of the sacred fear Dracula's ability to create more beings like himself because his way will lead to a profane, parasitic existence for all of them. It is this fear that produces the sense of extreme powerlessness and dread in the human subjects as they realize death as a vampire will result only in an amorphous and perverse version of mortal life.

The images of chaos are even stronger when applied directly to the body of the vampire. In England, in her memorandum to Professor Van Helsing and the others, Lucy Westenra tells of the visit of Dracula that precipitates her mother's death through descriptions of chaos resembling those Harker had used earlier to portray Transylvania. Dracula arrives as cloud of "little specks" (Stoker 143) which seem to blow in through the window broken by the wolf; then, these specks are further described as "wheeling and circling round like the pillar of dust that travelers describe when there is a simoom in the desert" (143). A simoom is a dust storm—hot, dry, heavy with sand, and dangerous to travelers as it sweeps across the deserts of Africa and Arabia during the spring and summer months. Of Arabic derivation, from the word *samm*, which means *to poison*, the word is particularly apt to describe the entrance of Dracula, especially in light of the earlier revelation to Mina by Sister Agatha about Harker's almost premonitory ravings of "wolves and poison and blood" in the throes of the "violent brain fever" (99) induced by his stay at Castle Dracula. The pillar of dust that Lucy describes also has implications of the danger Dracula poses. In *The Land Beyond the Forest*, Gerard makes reference to the whirlwind as denoting "that the devil is dancing with a witch, and whoever approaches too near to the dangerous circle may be carried off bodily to hell" (197). This description of the whirlwind has dangerous implications for Lucy. Struck with fear, she cannot avoid the phenomenon that is Dracula. Like the whirlwind in Gerard's example of Romanian superstition, the destructive and chaotic space that is Dracula will eventually carry Lucy off to the underworld of vampirism.

Figures of chaos prevalent in the description of Transylvania as profane space extend to the characterization of the vampire women as well. At the castle, the second time Harker is confronted by the vampire women they are described first as dispersed matter, "quaint little specks floating in the rays of moonlight" (Stoker 44). Then, taking more solid shape, they seem to organize "in clusters in a nebulous sort of way" (44). Later, near the end of the novel, Professor Van Helsing and Mina see the vampire women form out of the "whirling mist and snow" (368) of the Transylvanian landscape. In *Our Ladies of Darkness: Feminine Daemonology in Male Gothic Fiction*, Joseph Andriano discusses the ability of the female vampires or lamiae of *Dracula* to shape-change from solid form to the chaos of dust and swirling snow and vice versa. In an analysis of the numinous qualities of the vampire, the ability to shape change shows its divine, as well as profane, character. The numinous object is dangerous in and of itself, as an objective reality, because of its perceived power. However, its transformation at will into a chaos of whirling, floating obscurity—amorphous, undetectable, and dangerous—only adds to the mystery and creates the sense of shuddering horror which Otto feels characterizes the negatively numinous. In addition, these descriptions of whirling, wheeling, circling substance taking form or dispersing also indicate that the fate of those who are transformed into vampires will be dissolution into the primitive state of chaos.

Renfield, the Lunatic

Perhaps the most complicated character in the novel, Renfield, the lunatic, evokes both the sacred and the profane in various ways. In his desire for immortality, Renfield seems to suffer from a form of religious mania in which, as Dr. Seward puts it, "he will soon think that he himself is God" (Stoker 100). In Book II of *Degeneration*, Max Nordau argues that mysticism is a form of "religious delirium" (45) and a "principal characteristic of degeneration" (45). Mysticism is, he writes,

> A state of mind in which the subject imagines that he perceives or divines unknown and inexplicable relations amongst phenomena, discerns in things hints at mysteries, and regards them as symbols, by which a darker power seeks to unveil or, at least, to indicate all sorts of marvels which he endeavors to guess, though generally in vain [Nordau 45].

Renfield's preoccupation with blood as the symbol of life and with the coming of the "Master" (Stoker 100), who will bestow upon him immortal life, seems to echo Nordau's definition of mysticism as a degenerative mania.

Within the text, however, the evidence for diagnosis of Renfield as a religious maniac comes because he does not distinguish between Dr. Seward and the attendant, treating them both with a somewhat arrogant indifference and disregard. Because Renfield does not differentiate between the rank of doctor and attendant, Dr. Seward feels the lack of proper respect for his station and draws the analogy that the "real God taketh heed lest a sparrow fall; but the God created from human vanity sees no difference between an eagle and a sparrow" (110). However, Renfield's own analogy of the bride and bridesmaids shows that he recognizes the difference in importance of people. He tells Seward that "the bride-maidens rejoice the eyes that wait the coming of the bride; but when the bride draweth nigh, then the maidens shine not to the eyes that are filled" (111). In *The Essential Dracula*, Wolf notes that the spiders are comparable to the bridesmaids overshadowed by the appearance of the bride. If Dracula is to be the bride, Renfield is cast in the role of groom, according to Wolf; and "Dracula's murderous visit to Renfield takes on the meaning of a macabre consummation of a monstrous wedding night" (133). Certainly, the bride-maiden-spider analogy works; however, I believe that the bride-maidens are also Dr. Seward and the attendant, both of whom Renfield feels are unimportant now that Dracula has arrived.

Eliade describes the profane individual as one for whom "the universe does not properly constitute a cosmos—that is, a living and articulated unity; it is simply the sum of the material reserves and physical energies of the planet" (*Sacred and Profane* 93–4); and this description seems to have implications in the novel. As Dracula feeds on the blood of living humans, Renfield feeds on insects, spiders, and birds, totting up their numbers in his little book as if the sum of them will give him a greater and longer life. He even goes so far as to stab Dr. Seward in the wrist with a dinner-knife and then lap up his blood from the floor. However, Eliade also proposes that most primitive humans had an obsession with recovering the world as it was in the beginning. This obsession is characterized by a thirst for sacredness; and in light of this, Renfield's mental problem could also be interpreted as allying him in some respects with the sacred.

In *Will Therapy and Truth and Reality*, psychoanalyst Otto Rank argues that, while "the more normal, healthy, and happy" (250) person willfully accepts the empirical world as reality, the neurotic suffers "not from a painful reality but from painful truth" (251) because, spiritually, the neurotic sees "through the deception of the world of sense, the falsity of reality" (251). In Rank's understanding of the psyche, the individual cannot survive without illusions, "not only outer illusions such as art, religion, philosophy, science and love afford, but inner illusions which first condition the outer" (250). If the average person has adapted the individual will to accept the truth which society sets forth as reality, the neurotic person's focus on self-consciousness is a denial of that will and a refusal to accept what society deems reality. The moment an individual begins see through the false reality created by society, the willfully created reality is destroyed; and the person's relationship to the world of the senses changes. In refusing to accept a willfully created reality, the neurotic shares a deeper sense of the world with Eliade's religious individual, who sees the earthly world as illusory and the mystical world of the gods as the true reality. If one considers Renfield's insanity as a denial of his own will in response to the more powerful will of the numinous object Dracula, then one might also read his mental state as a spiritually true perception of the world. His preoccupation with blood then might be examined as an attempt to reproduce the sacred reality of the world.

According to Eliade's exploration of early religions, "ritual cannibalism . . . is the consequence of a tragic religious conception" (*Sacred and Profane* 106), in which sustenance is "not given in nature," but is "the product of a slaying" (103), and in which blood sacrifice helps religious individuals re-actualize their relationship with the cosmos. In *Voyage of the Beagle* (1839), Charles Darwin, nineteenth-century proponent of the survival of the fittest evolution theory, comments on the primitive land of New Zealand being "the centre of the land of cannibalism, murder, and all atrocious crimes!" (313). This description reminds one of Jonathan Harker's description of Transylvania. In *Dracula*, cannibalism takes place each time the vampire feeds, whether it is

Lucy or the other female vampires feeding on the children, or Dracula himself feasting on the sailors, Lucy, or Mina. Participation in this kind of cannibalism seems to be entered into for the most obvious of motives—the sustenance gained allows the vampires to survive. Even one of the humans, Dr. Seward, has partaken of blood when he sucked the wound of Professor Van Helsing to save his life.

However, the most insistent ritual of cannibalism is demonstrated in Renfield's zoöphagous behavior. His connection with the world, his sense of being, depends upon blood; and he even goes so far as to try to convince Dr. Seward that his redemption hangs upon his getting a cat or even a kitten. According to Sir James Frazer's studies of early cultures in *The Golden Bough*, many primitive individuals believed that ingesting the flesh of animal or human gave them the attributes of that entity. If the entity happened to be divine, the individual believed he or she would acquire some part of those divine powers as a result of the act. For Renfield, "the blood is the life" (Stoker 234); and he is counting increments of life with every fly, spider and bird, hoping through this blood sacrifice to gain immortality. Wolf notes that the expression *for the blood is the life* is part of a proscriptive Old Testament passage (Leviticus 17: 11–13) that forbids the eating of the blood in order for the Israelites to distinguish their religion from those who practiced human sacrifice (181). It is not in that sense, however, that we should view Renfield's cannibalism as profane. Renfield's cannibalism is in search of salvation—a state of grace with the cosmos, represented by the divine aspects of Dracula. However, the potentiality for evil inherent in Dracula stains Renfield's attempt at salvation, because his salvation will be only physical if he receives the immortality the vampire is prepared to give.

"Truly There Is No Such Thing as Finality": Sacred and Profane Time

Eliade's study proposes that, in the perception of various worldviews, time, "like space, is neither homogeneous nor continuous" (*Sa-*

cred and Profane 68) and, as such, encompasses the sacred and profane as existential situations for humans. Sacred time is posited as *"primordial, mythical time made present"* (68) through periodic repetition of sacred rituals and myths, and is, therefore, eternally recoverable, and effectively non-temporal, outside human time. Profane time, on the other hand, is believed to be "continuous and irreversible" (*Images and Symbols* 57) and of finite "temporal duration" (*Sacred and Profane* 68). While Eliade considers the non-religious person to be aware of his or her existence only within the profane time of a life circumscribed by birth and death, he believes religious individuals perceive themselves as living within both sacred and profane time, aware of their existence in finite time but returning periodically to sacred through reenactments of sacred rituals. For Eliade's religious individual, the eternal present of the mythical event makes possible the profane duration of time; and the year is the temporal dimension of the cosmos, circular in nature with a beginning and end, yet infinitely renewable each year with the cosmic rhythms of seasons, days, and nights.

"In This Matter Dates Are Everything"

As Mina Harker attempts to put together the entries of all the participants into a comprehensive narrative in *Dracula*, she records in her own journal her feeling that "in this matter dates are everything" (Stoker 224); therefore, chronological order must guide her transcription of events. In the novel, the sacred calendar is of first importance. The action begins on May first and ends November sixth. May first is an important date on the sacred calendar. A celebration of regeneration of the land, it is also a day honoring Saint Walpurga. According to canonical history, St. Walpurga, an 8th century English nun and abbess at Heidenheim, Germany (Cooper 299), became confused in legend with the pagan fertility goddess Waldbourg. Through this mix-up, Walpurgis Night became associated with the activity of witches and even vampires. Although the date of celebration in honor of St. Walpurga was changed to February to discourage her celebration being confused with the pagan one, Walpurgis Night remains the primary festival night of witchcraft.

This night also is associated with Johann Wolfgang von Goethe's *Faust*, in which the aged scholar makes a deal with Mephistopheles in order to gain all knowledge and experience. In part one of the play, Goethe uses the Walpurgis Night celebrations of the witches to illuminate the chaos that characterizes Mephistopheles and his dwelling place in the underworld; and in part two, as Faust searches for Helen of Troy, Goethe sets the action against a Walpurgis Night festival from classical Greece. Stoker's *Dracula*, influenced as it must have been by his close association with actor Henry Irving, who played Mephistopheles innumerable times, originally opened with a chapter, later published under the title "Dracula's Guest," that takes place on Walpurgis Night.

This night is significant to a discussion of *Dracula*, since it is a night, as Sir James Frazer maintains in *The Golden Bough*, when witches and all evil spirits are said to have great power. It is also the time of Beltine (Beltane) in Ireland, the beginning of summer and renewal. November, particularly the first week, is important as Hallowtide, the season of All Saints; and November first is All Saints' Day, the Christianized version of Samhain, which in Irish legend is the "beginning of the dark season . . . , especially associated with the dead and the underworld" (Ó hÓgáin 403). Samhain celebration was held on October 31, All Hallows' or All Saints' Eve, and was considered a propitiatory gesture in response to the "threatening and warlike . . . powers of destruction" (Sjoestedt 69) which characterized the intrusion of the spirits into the earthly world.

The idea behind the pagan celebration of these days seems to be "that crucial joints between the seasons opened cracks in the fabric of space-time, allowing contact between the ghostworld and the mortal one" (Walker 372). In pre-Christian Celtic belief, a retaliatory relationship existed between the mortal and immortal worlds, which not only allowed the spirits to threaten mankind at this time but also allowed humans to enter their world and "to attack in their turn those mysterious dwellings which for one night lay open and accessible" (Sjoestedt 72). According to research by folklorist Dáithí Ó hÓgáin, in Irish folklore and myth "many of the supernatural adventures of heroes . . . are said to have taken place at this time" (403). Whether one uses pagan feast days or their Christianized counterparts as a time frame in which to map the events in the novel, it is clear that the plot of *Dracula* takes place within a cyclic, sacred calendar of summer and winter, birth and death, with the possibility of a cosmic rebirth for the forces of the sacred and their society when Dracula is killed. Harker ventures into Transylvania as the fabric of time and space is rent in May and helps Dracula to take up residence in the world of men. Once loosed upon the world, Dracula cannot be driven back across that border between the two worlds until the next tear in the fabric is effected during Hallowtide or Samhain.

The cyclic nature of days and nights also is important in a discussion of sacred and profane time. While the human characters live their day from sunrise to sunset, Dracula's daily span is inverted. His earthly life has been profaned by his vampirism and is now a perversion of human life. Many humans perceive death to be a return to the womb of the earth (Eliade *Sacred and Profane* 140); however, Dracula is profane so he can not rest peacefully. Although he is seen a few times during daylight, he is generally constrained to rising at sunset and returning to his bed at sunrise. In Transylvania Dracula manages to invert Harker's time schedule. He keeps Harker talking all night, manipulating him into conforming to his own more profane time schedule; and soon Harker's lack of sleep wears on him, increasing his uneasiness. Harker records how his diary seems like the tales of the "'Arabian Nights' [where] everything has to break off at cockcrow—or like the ghost of Hamlet's father" (30). Like Shahrazad, Harker is given a reprieve from a sure sentence of death each morning; like Hamlet, Harker cannot know if his experience is real or not. Once he is in Transylvania, he is plunged into the abyss that separates sacred and profane time, where primitive evil haunts the night and daylight is the only sanctuary.

For Eliade, the temporality of the human condition is defined as a "'historical situation'" (*Images and Symbols* 58). As a representative of the rational West, Harker lives in historical time and tries to place his destination Transylvania in an historical context. To this end, he searches for information on the area in that icon of historical artifacts, the British Museum, but can find no map pinpointing the exact location of Dracula's home. However, he does gain some information on the history of the area and on the traditions and superstitions of the inhabitants. Time, though, becomes much more urgent and more personal as Harker begins his journey. As he travels to Transylvania, he seems to move back in time, to travel outside of time. However, here the clock time of Great Britain is irrelevant; the cycles of seasons and of sunrises and sunsets dictate the actions of the people. Transylvania is a place of late trains and early coaches, as the driver of the public conveyance hurries through Borgo Pass, hoping to miss meeting Dracula's coach. Once Harker has exchanged the public coach for Dracula's private one, his journey is confusing as time seems to repeat itself. The coach seems to cover the same ground repeatedly; and the driver seems to stop repeatedly, going off into the darkness where they have seen blue flames flickering.

When Dracula and Harker finally arrive at the castle, Harker notices that time and the elements have taken a great toll on the carved stones of the edifice. However, time within Castle Dracula seems to stand still. The furniture and bed hangings, though clearly ancient, are in excellent condition; and Harker records that similar ones he saw in England's Hampton Court were in a much more dilapidated condition. Later, as Harker tells Dracula that Carfax has existed in one form or another since "medieval times" (23), the audience is given its first clue about Dracula's great age. He replies to Harker that he is "of an old family," (23) and used to old houses. A house, he maintains, "cannot be made habitable in a day; and, after all, how few days go to make up a century" (23). In the case of the vampire's immortality, the number of days it takes to make a century are not many in relation to the endless nights spent in the service of survival.

The next night, as Harker questions Dracula about the history of Transylvania, the conversation leaves Harker feeling as though Dracula had experienced it all personally. Dracula explains this away by calling it pride of house and name which a boyar feels. His is a history both sacred and profane, including, as it does, tales of how the Szekelys and Dracula himself were born out of blood-drenched colonizations by Icelandic tribes and by the Huns and of the heroism of rulers who continually drove back the Turks and shook loose the oppressive grasp of Hungarian rule. Dracula's history has lost its significance, however. His legendary and historical associations, and his heroism, though once great, are far in the past.

By May 15th, Harker's fear has increased greatly; he knows himself to be a prisoner and has seen the Count's lizard-like descent from a window of the castle. Harker's empirical mind calls for facts and exploration and he finds himself in a room he romantically imagines was the part of the castle occupied in much earlier times. Here he juxtaposes against the history of the long dead occupants of the room the fact that he is sitting at their writing table, using shorthand, a method of transcription which "is nineteenth century up-to-date with a vengeance" (Stoker 36). Yet the incongruity of his actions in this old place makes him aware of living in both sacred and profane time as he writes "unless my senses deceive me, the old centuries had, and have, powers of their own which mere 'modernity' cannot kill" (36). On first entering this room in Dracula's castle, Harker had felt a sense of the history of the place and a closeness to the inhabitants of the castle because of the history he imagined for the woman who once might have used the writing desk in the room; however, this sense of the past soon turns profane as he encounters the vampire women. The historical time, which he perceives in his imagination, does not exist; it is not recoverable.

Later, Harker awakens in his own bed; and the next day's journal entry recaps his experience with the vampire ladies, an experience that he cannot identify as dream or reality. However, evidence supports his belief that the experience was reality when he discovers his watch is not wound as he is "rigorously accustomed" (Stoker 40) to doing before bed. A few days later, the urgency of time is brought home to Harker with a finality that is horrifying. Dracula requests that he write three letters post-dated for June 12, 19, and 29, each indicating his progress toward home. At this request, Harker records "I know now the span of my life" (41). Harker is to be left at the mercy of the vampire women when Dracula leaves for England.

"Time Is on My Side"

At this point the novel's action moves on to England. Dracula lands at Whitby where Mina Murray and Lucy Westenra are on holiday. He has done his homework, having discovered much more about England than Harker did about Transylvania, from English magazines, newspapers, and books on all subjects "relating to England and English life and customs and manners" (Stoker 19). Dracula's history and the profaneness of the time that delineates his existence can now include England.

Here the ruins of Whitby Abbey and later Carfax represent profane time, historical and irrecoverable, both places dating from far in the past. However, it is here that the span of a lifetime is brought to the forefront again. In Whitby, Mr. Swales, the old man whom Mina and Lucy meet at the seat where a suicide is buried, sensing his death is imminent, talks to Mina of how long he has lived. Indicating that "a hundred years is too much for any man to expect" (74) to live, he tells Mina that he smells death on the wind and that if the "Angel of Death" (74) were to come that very night, he would be ready to go. Mr. Swales is allied with the forces of the sacred in his belief in the immortality of spirit; however, the death he has sensed on the wind from the sea is Dracula.

Unlike the mortal Swales, Dracula has lived centuries beyond the life-span that Swales feels is beyond human expectation, and because of his extended existence, he is a representative of profane time. Eliade claims that the profane individual has a "*pessimistic vision of existence*" (*Sacred and Profane* 107) because the end of linear time is death. For this person, Eliade posits, repetition has no religious meaning. When repetition is no longer "a vehicle for reintegrating a primordial situation, and hence for recovering the mysterious presence of the gods, that is, *when it is desacralized*, cyclic time becomes terrifying" (107). In its terrifying aspect, cyclic time is perceived as "a circle forever turning on itself, repeating itself to infinity" (107), as the references to the whirlpool and the nebulous shapes of the vampire in the novel demonstrate. Dracula's life goes on year upon long year as he is resurrected only bodily within historical time frames. As a figure of the negatively numinous type, Dracula seems outside of time in a way, because he lives forever. However, he is caught in history and cannot recover sacred time. For Dracula, there is no renewal because there is no death. Therefore, time means nothing to Dracula; true death is not for him. As he tells Professor Van Helsing and the others, time is on his side, and his revenge upon them can be meted out eternally.

Eliade claims that for a non-religious person time constitutes the deepest existential dimension linking life from beginning to end, but a religious individual refuses to live solely in the historical present. For him or her, the cosmos is a model for other kinds of doing and creation; and repair of the cosmos through ritual is a religious act, an "*imitatio dei*" (*Sacred and Profane* 88) in which the object repaired becomes a "mythical archetype" (88). With each original act associated with the creation of the cosmos, according to Eliade, religious individuals believe they have the opportunity to transfigure their existence and renew their connection to the sacred and their place in the cosmos. By virtue of this eternal return to sources of the sacred, human existence appears to be saved from nothingness and death. The important point here is that modern secular individuals live within a sense of empirical, linear time that is considered by many religious men to be profane. However, traditional, more religious people claim to live within a sense of sacred time that is cyclical, recurring periodically to reconstitute the cosmos.

Sacred time is demonstrated near the beginning of the novel, when on his journey Harker sees the people worshipping at the shrine by the side of the road. They cross themselves in a "self-surrender of devotion" (Stoker 8), seemingly detached from the earthly world around them. Harker seems to be a profane man because he lives in profane time and space as represented by Victorian Britain's seeming concentration on profit and promotion; but later, after Harker learns the truth about Dracula's castle, he attempts to connect to sacred time as he surrenders to a need for spiritual intervention. Having seen the vampire women for the second time and realized that Dracula means to leave him to them, he throws himself on his knees in prayer; and the next morning, rising for what he feels is his last day, he again sinks to his knees resolved to be spiritually ready if death, in the form of the vampire women, should come for him.

Once the action of the novel moves to England, the idea of spiritual surrender is suggested by Mr. Swales who indicates his readiness to face Death by raising up "his arms devoutly" (Stoker 74), his lips moving as if in prayer. Also, as Lucy Westenra is dispatched to the spiritual world, Professor Van Helsing reads the prayer for the dead over her; and later, once Mina Harker is turning into a vampire, she asks for this same prayer to be read, as if her funeral were taking place at that moment. Sacred time is also manifested in the novel when Professor Van Helsing states of Mina that "good women tell all their lives, and by day and by hour and by minute, such things that angels can read" (184). The humans in the text, however, fear profane time. Time presses upon Harker who focuses on the "minutes and seconds so [preciously] laden with Mina's life and happiness" (292) that are passing so quickly while he and the other men discuss what to do about Dracula. Bitten by the vampire for the third time, Mina is in eternal danger because her soul is at risk.

Eliade claims that "in the experience of sacred time" (*Sacred and Profane* 65), a religious person can apprehend the cosmos "as it was *in principio*, that is, at the mythical moment of Creation" (65). In rituals, as in the myths that generate them, the individual attempts to make contact with what is perceived as the absolute reality of the sacred and, in so doing, the individual hopes to transcend the profane condition of a historically oriented existence, reuniting with cyclical time and returning to an originating moment in the renewal of the cosmos out of chaos. The historical reality of the human characters in *Dracula* is superseded over time and through knowledge of what Dracula represents by a sacred reality; and the human characters become a force for the sacred, recreating their world with the death of the vampires. However, as a force of the sacred, they perceive their duty to God as a duty to protect British social values.

"A Duty to Do": Reenacting the Ritual

In *Dracula: Between Tradition and Modernism*, Carol A. Senf describes Harker's diary as a chronicle of "underlying prejudice against practically everything foreign" and sees in it a growing sense that what Harker finds "exotic" at the beginning of the journey soon becomes "suspect and ultimately evil, as Harker changes from tourist to patriot" (36). According to her reading, Dracula is a foreigner whose invasion is feared by the men of England "during a period in which England was intent on preserving her colonial holdings and may even suggest the fear of reverse colonization" (37); and Harker's patriotic reaction against helping him to colonize England, when echoed by the others, becomes a communal pledge to "destroy all that threatens their beliefs" (37). However, Harker's reaction to Dracula's monstrosity is patriotic only in so far as he wishes to preserve his England. While patriotism is a sacred duty on a nationalistic level, if one looks at the composition of the band of men who destroy Dracula, patriotism is too narrow a concept for what these men are doing. Although England is the sacred center of Harker's world, one must not forget that Morris is an American, a frontiersman in the tradition of Jim Bowie. Since, during the Victorian period, England and America were two of the most important countries in the Western world, linked through a common language and an industrialized economy, they might both be considered sacred in the eyes of their citizens, and the pledge which Harker and the others make to destroy Dracula is a pledge to save not just England, but also the world, from chaos.

As representatives of cosmic sacredness, Professor Van Helsing and the others have become aware of the non-rational or numinous, and through that awareness they have come to recognize the more profane side of themselves and to understand their obligation to society. In the novel, the Victorian sense of duty takes on both profane and sacred natures, acquiring a sacred dimension of meaning when duty to business becomes the higher duty to "rid the world of such a monster" (Stoker 51) as Dracula. In Transylvania, both Dracula and Harker tend only to business. For Harker "duty [is] imperative" (5); as a newly made solicitor sent to Transylvania to complete the sale of property in England to Count Dracula, Harker's responsibility is the business of his firm. However, duty takes on a sacred character in England, when Professor Van Helsing must convince the others of their responsibility to return the un-dead Lucy to the proper condition of bodily death and spiritual life and to rid the world of Dracula. It is at this point that the second method Eliade posits for transforming the profane world into a sacred one becomes important in the novel, as the forces of the sacred set out to destroy the transformed Lucy.

Eliade argues that most primitive religions believed that the gods had to slay and dismember the marine monster or primordial being to create the world from it; and to recreate the human world as sacred space, the individual must imitate this ritual. Many primitive, religious societies believed in imitating the gods even when the act "verged on madness, depravity, or crime" (*Sacred and Profane* 104). In *Dracula*, although the desecration of graves and bodies, and even the crime of house-breaking which the men must commit in order to fulfill their purpose, may seem like "unhallowed work" (Stoker 200) to them, yet it is holy work in defense of the sacredness of human life and English society. For Professor Van Helsing, he and the other men are like medieval Crusaders, who should look upon themselves as instruments of God's will. The crusade of the forces of the sacred is likened to Christ's bearing of his cross for world sanctification. However, Eliade argues that, although of a sacred nature, Christianity is also a religion "sanctified by the incarnation of the Son of God" (*Sacred and Profane* 72) and, therefore, "historically conditioned" (111). As such, Christianity may be seen to demonstrate a new dimension of the presence of God in the world, which Eliade terms salvation history; and the sacred and profane meet at this point. In *Dracula*, the forces of the sacred must imagine themselves to be crusaders for the holy cause of their own historically based religion in order to validate their actions in resanctifying the world within their more modern value system; and they call upon God to defend a social view of the cosmos predicated on duty and profit. However, regardless of the fact that they must imagine themselves as soldiers of God acting out of a sense of solemn and sacred duty, they are still repeating an age old pattern of recreation of the world in order to beat back chaos from the borders of their world.

To reconsecrate their world, the men must first kill and dismember Lucy Westenra. Professor Van Helsing tells Holmwood that he has "a duty to do, a duty to others, a duty to you, a duty to the dead" (Stoker 206–207); and that obligation is to stake her through the heart, cut off her head, and fill her mouth with garlic. At the tomb of Lucy, as Professor Van Helsing reads the prayer for the dead over her undead body, he counsels Holmwood to "strike in God's name" (216), in order that Lucy's soul might be redeemed from Dracula's power and that she might find the peace he has promised. After Lucy's true death is accomplished, the men will take on another sacred duty: saving Mina Harker from the same terrible fate. However, when Dracula's existence in England is threatened, as his sanctuaries are found out and his boxes of earth are purified with blessed wafer, he retreats to the safety of his own country; but the forces of the sacred are not to be stopped. They follow Dracula back to the origin of chaos in Transylvania.

Devils, Dragons, and Dragon-slayers in the "Heart of the Enemy's Country"

Since whatever space the religious person inhabits is considered a sacred cosmos, according to Eliade's study, attack from outside the cosmos threatens to desacralize it, to turn it to chaos. Attacks are, therefore, in his estimation, equivalent to "ruin, disintegration, and death" (*Images and Symbols* 39); and, in many world views, enemies are considered to be "demons, and especially . . . the archdemon, the primordial dragon conquered by the gods at the beginning of time" (*Sacred and Profane* 47). In *Dracula*, the foreign chaos of Dracula has invaded England, attacking the human characters and turning their cosmos to chaos, and the only way to restore the sanctity of their world is to destroy the vampire. To this end, the forces of the sacred become dragon-slayers, risking all to penetrate to the "heart of the enemy's country" (Stoker 354) and kill the primordial dragon, Dracula.

Devils and Dragons

In *Vampires in the Carpathians: Magical Acts, Rites, and Beliefs in Subcarpathian Rus'*, Pëtr Bogatyrëv, Russian folklorist and ethnographer, argues that "belief in sorcerers, vampires, and forest spirits is reinforced by the fact that the Church also teaches about the existence of the Evil Spirit, the Devil" (137), causing people to meld their notions of folk spirits with their concept of evil. Eliade maintains that "the conception of the enemy as a demonic being, a veritable incarnation of the powers of evil" (*Images and Symbols* 38) is an idea which has survived through time; and Otto connects the feeling of horror inherent in an experience of the negative numinousness of demons to the fury of Lucifer and his status as a fallen angel. "The devilish" (*Idea of the Holy* 106), he maintains, has some part of the divine in it, yet is opposed to it by having a "potentiality of evil" (106) in its divine wrath. If one looks at Dracula's history, as he tells it to Jonathan Harker, one can see that he is connected to the devil through the history of his blood ties with the Szekelys who are said to have come from Scythian witches mated with devils and with the blood of the Berserkers brought into his land by the marauding Ugric tribes of Iceland (Stoker 28).

However, Dracula is represented as both a dragon and devil in other ways. He is affiliated with both, first when Harker has reached the eastern side of Borgo Pass and records their passage into the "thunderous" (Stoker 9) zone. This affiliation becomes clear if one looks at Emily Gerard's work in reference to local superstitions about weather. In her recording of local Romanian superstitions, she finds a connection between thunderstorms and the legend of the "*scholomance*, or school, supposed to exist somewhere in the heart of the mountains and where the secrets of nature, the language of animals, and all magic spells are taught by the devil in person" (198). According to legend, at the end of the course of study, one of the ten students would be required to remain with the devil as an assistant to help him "in 'making the weather'— that is, preparing the thunderbolts" (198). Gerard also records how the peasants believe that "a small lake immeasurably deep, and lying high in the mountains to the south of Hermanstadt, is supposed to be the caldron where is brewed the thunder, under whose water the dragon lies sleeping," (198) in fair weather. To wake the dragon is to invite the storm. In the novel, Professor Van Helsing relates some of the history of Dracula to the others, including his connection with the Scholomance and the dealings which Dracula's family had with "the Evil One" (Stoker 241) who taught the dark arts there.

Moreover, the last leg of Harker's journey to castle Dracula begins from the hotel in Bistritz on May fourth, "the eve of St. George's Day" (Stoker 4), a day on which, as Montague Summers writes, "the power of vampires, witches and every evil thing" (*Vampire in Europe* 312) is strongest, a day celebrated in honor of St. George, heroic "soldier-martyr" (Baring-Gould 93) and legendary dragon-slayer. The Eastern legends of St. George, both Christian and Muslim, refer mostly to his suffering for religion; however, reminiscent of the myth of Perseus and Andromeda, the Western myth incorporates a fight with a dragon whose depredations were destroying the town of Silene in Libya. Tribute was first paid in animals, then in human lives as the supply of animals was depleted. Finally, the king's daughter was chosen as tribute, taken to the lake, and offered up to the beast. As George passed by the lake, he saw her weeping. Discovering what had caused her fear and sadness, he vowed to save her. As the dragon rose from the water, George made the sign of the cross, recommended himself to God, and went to fight the beast. His prowess with the sword so mesmerized the dragon that George was able to tie the princess's girdle about its neck and lead it into town. Through this miraculous feat, George converted and baptized thousands of men, women, and children; then he cut off the head of the dragon (Baring-Gould *Curious Myths of the Middle Ages*).

In *The Essential Dracula*, Wolf notes that in the legend of this saint "the dragon represents Satan" (8), as it does in *Dracula*, since in the Romanian tongue "*Dracul* . . . means both 'dragon' and 'devil'" (8). Some of the names bandied about by the peasants on the coach with Harker are "'Ordog'-Satan" and "'vrolok' and 'vlkoslak'" (Stoker 6), which Wolf, referencing Montague Summers' research, annotates as having the same meaning as "*vârcolac*" (Wolf 10). Summers describes the *vârcolac* as "a third type of vampire . . . thought to be an extraordinary creature which eats the sun and moon and thus causes eclipses" (306). In addition, in her article "The Vampire in Roumania," Agnes Murgoci connects Eastern European belief in the vârcolaci with the moral that "God orders the vârcolaci to eat the moon, so that men may repent and turn from evil" (25).

Wolf also draws attention to folklore's connection of buried treasure with dragons; the source of this connection, he feels, can be found in the ancient practice of burying heroes in caves or barrows along with treasures for the afterlife and the fact that snakes find burial caves and barrows suitable habitations. Though, in *Dracula*, the sites of buried treasure are easily located because of the blue flames, the treasure is not so easily obtained because of the powers of evil that roam the land on St. George's eve. However, it is clear that Dracula has the ability to find the valuables cached underground. Upon his arrival at the castle, Harker first notices treasure of immense value as he assesses the furniture, curtains, bed hangings, and table service. Later, when Harker climbs into Dracula's room looking for a key to help him escape, he finds a hoard of jewels and gold from many countries and periods. As the dragon guarding the treasure, Dracula also has an advantage in finding and appropriating it for his own purposes.

Moreover, from Dracula, Harker learns not only of the monetary treasures, but also of the soil being "enriched by the blood of men, patriots or invaders" (Stoker 22). In the early history of the region, Dracula's ancestors led the fight for freedom; but now those heroic times are over and "blood is too precious a thing in these days of dishonourable peace" (30). For Dracula, the days of honor are over, and blood is precious to him now only as it can continue his own life. He has lost his cosmic connection and become profane. Only his battle fury is left, turned into a struggle for survival instead of dedicated to a larger more sacred cause for society. Again, later, in England, the characters representing the sacred learn that blood is precious through Renfield's preoccupation with the food chain and his repeated assertion that "the blood is the life" (141). Then, as Lucy Westenra suffers from the bite of the vampire, it is the blood of brave men that she needs. To save her, Holmwood "would give the last drop of blood" (121) in his body; and Professor Van Helsing, Morris, and Dr. Seward eventually are called upon to sacrifice their blood for her, also; however, it is Dracula who gets all of this blood in the end when he finally makes Lucy Westenra a vampire. Moreover, Morris gives his life's blood in the destruction of Dracula, sacrificing himself to regenerate society and save

Mina Harker's from a vampire's existence. The dragon Dracula guards the treasure of monetary riches which English society values so much for the power which it provides; but the forces of the sacred find that they also must value the treasure of more spiritual forces. A victory over the primordial dragon is a victory over chaos, a victory over the material profane life ruled by the value of riches by the forces of the spirit.

Dragon-slayers

According to Eliade, "struggles, conflicts, and wars for the most part have a ritual cause and function," where repetition of the conflict is in "imitation of an archetypal model" (*The Myth of Eternal Return* 29) for creating the cosmos through violent means. Sacrifice is made in order to sanctify the world anew as an *imago mundi*; and a ritual death is required for the resacralization of society. The forces of Western sacredness imitate the gods when they kill and dismember the profane Lucy Westenra in a bloody ritual, impaling her in her coffin with a sharpened stake, then cutting off her head and filling her mouth with garlic. The female vampires at the castle all are dispatched in the same way, as a primordial dragon should be; however, Dracula is destroyed differently. Harker cuts Dracula's throat with his Kukri knife while simultaneously Morris penetrates Dracula's heart with his Bowie knife. Although there has been a lot of literary speculation over the decades as to whether Dracula truly died at the hands of Jonathan Harker and Quincey Morris, one must believe he did. While the classic tools for dispatching the vampire were not used in Dracula's case, the Kukri knife that Harker uses on Dracula is a ferocious instrument of death, much like a machete in its size and form, with a curved double-edged blade, known for its ability to shear through small tree trunks with ease. With some degree of force behind it, the Kukri knife would shear the head from the body in one stroke. Moreover, the Bowie knife that Morris carries is almost as formidable a weapon as the Kukri. With a length of fifteen inches from end to end and a double-edged blade, it would be a suitable weapon with which to stake the vampire.

However, regardless of how the vampire is dispatched, it would seem that the effect is the same; the cosmos is again restored to sacredness. Eliade writes that "the true sin is forgetting" (*Sacred and Profane* 101) what happened in the beginning of time; and the story of Mina's courage which at the end the men vow to tell young Quincey Harker when he is old enough to understand is a sign that they will not forget, but will pass that knowledge on to him, making him capable of recovering sacred time for future generations.

"In Dread . . . Is Some Need of Belief": Faith and the Numinous

Eliade argues that "death is often only the result of . . . indifference to immortality" (*Images and Symbols* 56), indifference to the sacred. In *Dracula*, the vampire is a threat to the other characters on both a physical and spiritual level because they are indifferent to his sacred qualities. He represents what humanity can become if its faith in God and sacred duty to the cosmos are not taken seriously and periodically maintained. However, since the foundations of religious faith had been called into doubt over the decades of the nineteenth century, many people of the late Victorian period could not confidently turn to traditional religious beliefs for relief from their spiritual crisis. This is true of the characters in *Dracula*, who create their own brand of sacredness based on social, economic, and political values and draw on the occult only to reestablish that world in the face of the vampire's threat to their society and to themselves. Eliade's study of early religions argues that "it is the experience of death that renders intelligible the notion of *spirit* and of *spiritual beings*" (*Occultism, Witchcraft, and Cultural Fashions* 34); and for many religious individuals, he maintains, death is not the end of life, only the beginning of another mode of existence. Drifting into the unknown darkness, the person seeks to conquer death by transforming it into a rite of passage, the beginning of a new spiritual existence. In initiatory contexts, death signifies passing beyond the profane, unsanctified condition to an experience of the sacred and the responsibility of being human. Numinous dread is felt in anticipation of death and is, therefore, an initiation into the human condition. Through death, it is supposed, a person changes from body to spirit; and, likewise, in the experience of possible death "man becomes aware of his own mortality" (35), the reality of his physical presence in the universe. In confronting the numinous, a person is confronting himself or herself; the profane side of the person's personality with all its worldly desires comes under scrutiny in its conflict with a spiritual yearning for eternal life. The value of the numinous experience is sacred truth, a higher understanding of the human relationship with the gods and of an innate yearning for faith in an afterlife.

The humans in *Dracula* struggle with the mystery of vampirism and the ontological truth it reveals; and it is faith that in the end gets them through their ordeal, regardless of the fact that what they are protecting is a historically structured sacredness. The dread that the forces of the sacred feel at the numinous experience of the vampires reaffirms their need for faith in a spiritual existence. As they all strive to understand the meaning behind the mystery of Dracula, the "mystery of life and death" (Stoker 192), Professor Van Helsing tells Mina that despite the facts of the case which she has transcribed from Harker's journals, she "will need all [her] faith" (218) to deal with the situation before them. Then, on the way back to Transylvania in pursuit of Dracula, his former journal showing the way for the others, Harker writes "it is in trial and trouble that our faith is tested—that we must keep on trusting; and that God will aid us up to the end" (289). They put their fates in God's hands, as "drifting reefwards . . . faith is our [their] only anchor" (310) in the chaos of a sea of troubles. Their modern belief in science and the industrialized world must give way to a reliance on older traditions. Professor Van Helsing tells the other men that when they catch up to Dracula they must trust "to superstition . . . at the first; it was man's faith in the early, and it have its roots in faith still" (328). Belief in their own God gives them the courage they require to face the negative numinousness of Dracula; trust in the traditions and superstitions of earlier times, when there was no doubt of a divine presence in the world, gives them the tools and the power to recreate their world in imitation of the gods.

Eliade argues that to experience sacred space and time is to reveal a longing to reactualize the primordial situation of creating the world. In his analysis of early religions, Eliade found that many people believed that sacred space and time was renewed each year with the rebirth of the land; and when each new year began, chaos had to be overcome once more. So, too, would this be true on a larger scale at the end of a century or a millennium. Humanity's terror of each new century or new millennium may be perceived as a terror of chaos and the possibility of death without renewal. The longing to live in the presence of the gods then may be expressed as an unquenchable thirst for being, a need to exist as a spiritual entity as well as a physical one. This thirst for being may be manifested as the individual's will to take responsibility for the sacredness of his or her own society, as Professor Van Helsing and the others do when they seek out Dracula, risking possible nonexistence and dissolution into chaos and death to imitate the gods and return their profane world to sacred space. As numinous fiction, *Dracula* is a story of salvation, of initiation into the sacred, despite the fact that their sacredness has a secular slant. In their confrontation with the negatively numinous vampire, the humans evaluate their own evil potential and their longing for reaffirmation of a spiritual future because the chaos of the unknown, the chaos of living death, is too frightening.

From *The Vampire as Numinous Experience: Spiritual Journeys with the Undead in British and American Literature* (Jefferson, N.C.: McFarland & Company, Inc.): 86-128. Copyright © McFarland & Company, Inc. Reprinted by permission of McFarland & Company, Inc.

Notes

1. Known members of The Hermetic Order of the Golden Dawn include William Butler Yeats, Algernon Blackwood, and Aleister Crowley, among others.

2. This and all future references to *Dracula* are from the World's Classics paperback edition published by Oxford University Press in 1983.

3. In *Vampires: Lord Byron to Count Dracula*, Christopher Frayling reproduces sections of Stoker's research notes from Emily Gerard's book. Stoker's working and research notes for *Dracula* are housed at the Rosenbach Museum in Philadelphia.

4. Leonard Wolf, in *The Essential Dracula* (an annotated version of *Dracula*, New York: Plume/Penguin, 1975), and Raymond McNally and Radu Florescu, in their *The Essential Dracula* (annotated version of *Dracula*, New York: Mayflower Books, 1979) all note that the "white lady" of Whitby Abbey is thought to be the ghost of St. Hilda, the first abbess of Whitby monastery in the seventh century. Brewer's *Book of Myth and Legend* (J. C. Cooper, ed.) defines the "white lady" as a "kind of spectre, the appearance of which generally forebodes death in the house" (301).

5. In the early eighteenth century, Daniel Defoe alleged "that men often disposed of unwanted wives" (McCandless 339) in private asylums. Elaine Showalter's *The Female Malady: Women, Madness, and English Culture, 1830–1980* (New York: Random House, 1985) contains an interesting study of the treatment of women diagnosed as insane during the nineteenth century.

6. Highwaymen also found this spot particularly attractive for their activities, and the Spaniard's Inn, on the edge of Hampstead Heath, where Professor Van Helsing and the others dine, was the setting for Alfred Noyes' poem "The Highwayman."

7. For more information on the *New Woman* and the role of sexual freedom in *Dracula*, see: C. F. Bentley's "The Monster in the Bedroom: Sexual Symbolism in Bram Stoker's *Dracula*" (*Literature and Psychology* 22 [1972]: 27–34); Phyllis A. Roth's "Suddenly Sexual Women in Bram Stoker's *Dracula*" (*Literature and Psychology* 27 [1977]: 113–21); and John Allen Stevenson's "A Vampire in the Mirror: the Sexuality of *Dracula*" (*PMLA* 103 [March 1988]: 139–49).

8. Hungarian physician and disciple of Cesare Lombroso, Max Nordau (1849–1923), in his most famous work, *Degeneration*, published in 1892, argued that culture had deteriorated and retrogressed, and that criminals, prostitutes, the insane, and artists were degenerate types. Lombroso (1836–1909), known by many as "the father of modern criminology" (Wolf 403), argued a theory that the congenital criminal is an aberrant mental type showing regression to primitive behavior.

9. Discussions of the fear of reverse colonization in *Dracula* can be found in chapter five of Carol A. Senf's *Dracula: Between Tradition and Modernism* (New York: Twayne/Prentice-Hall, 1998) and in Stephen D. Arata's article "The Occidental Tourist: *Dracula* and the Anxiety of Reverse Colonization." (*Victorian Studies* 3, no. 4 Summer 1990: 621–45).

The New Naturalism:
Primal Screams in Abraham Stoker's *Dracula*_____

Carrol L. Fry and Carla Edwards

The behavioral sciences have long been a fertile seed ground for literary-critical approaches. In 1910 Ernest Jones wrote "Hamlet and Oedipus," an article published in *Journal of the American Psychological Association* that applied Sigmund Freud's writings to literary analysis, reasoning that if characters in works of literature come alive as real people, they can be psychoanalyzed. Generations of critics have continued exploring literature through Freudian concepts. Carl Jung's ideas have also attracted a great deal of attention among literary critics. Maude Bodkin's *Archetypal Patterns in Poetry*, published in 1934, is an early approach, to be followed by many others. Today, variations on both approaches are legion.

Sociobiology and the parallel field of psychobiology (for brevity's sake, we use the term sociobiology here to describe both), newer developments in behavioral studies, also offer the potential to become a powerful hermeneutic methodology in the study of literature and film. Closely related to Jung's description of the collective unconscious, sociobiology suggests that a "whisper within" leads us to programmed responses that transcend reason and the conscious mind. Sociobiology differs from Jung's findings in presupposing that the whisper emanates not from symbolic intuition but from millions of years of adaptive behavior and inhabits the most basic level—the human gene. Like Freudian and Jungian concepts, sociobiology offers a promising approach to literary analysis. In the absence of a better name, we will call it primal-traits criticism.

Sociobiology focuses on visceral-level responses rather than cerebral; thus, an application of concepts from this field to literature seems most fruitful for works with powerful primal and mythic appeals. Many works could be fruitfully analyzed with a primal-traits methodology, from ancient epics to the latest slasher movie. But the tale of terror, a type of literature long recognized to evoke strong response at the unconscious level, offers an excellent example for analysis through primal-traits criticism. Therefore, we will apply this approach to a signature work of the horror genre: Abraham Stoker's novel *Dracula*. The novel obviously exerts a powerful pull on the popular imagination. *Dracula* has not been out of print since its publication and has inspired a plethora of vampire novels and films. This appeal, and indeed that of many others of the horror genre, rests on fictional conventions that have long endured for a very good reason. They whisper messages to readers at the most primordial level: instinctual responses. Stoker's novel seems founded on four narratives: fear of the predator, territoriality, male bonding and cooperation, and protection of the female. These narratives in the novel, especially the last three, interact in creating its power over succeeding generations of readers by evoking a response, sociobiologists might say, emanating from our genetic heritage.

With his *Origin of Species*, published in 1859, Charles Darwin created a revolution in the way humanity thinks of itself. The great religions of the west, Judaism and Christianity as well as Islam, posit the assumption that God gave humanity a special place in the creation, "dominion over the fish of the sea, and over the fowl of the air, and over every living thing that moveth upon the earth" (Genesis 1:28). Darwin, on the other hand, describes humanity as one of millions of species engaged in what he called the great "Struggle for Life," the battle to adapt to an environment that is the true arbiter of survival. Individual members of the species that have some trait privileged by the environment are fittest to survive. They breed to pass on this adaptive trait and cause the species to change physically through natural selection (see *Origin of Species*, iii, 55).

Darwin's findings caused spiritual indigestion of various sorts, suggesting, as they do, not only that humankind evolved from "a hairy quadruped, furnished with a tail and pointed ears, probably arboreal in its habits, and an inhabitant of the Old World" (*Descent of Man*, xxi,

633), but that it evolved from this earlier form through the iron laws of evolution: adaptation to changes in the environment through natural selection and survival of the fittest. Christianity remained in denial through the nineteenth century, and conservative Christian sects cling doggedly to the "Genesis" version of creation even today.

Sociobiologists' interests lie in the study of animal behavior with application to human behavior, and ultimately, in fact, to the study of human nature itself. Chapter Nine of Carl Degler's *In Search of Human Nature* offers an excellent review of the literature of sociobiology. However, E. O. Wilson's *Sociobiology: The New Synthesis* created much of the controversy surrounding this field in 1975 and has remained the standard text.

In this work, Wilson applies the successful studies of animal and insect populations to human behavior. He responded to criticism of his findings with *On Human Nature*, published three years later. In both books, he begins with the Darwinian assumption that species evolve through adaptation to the environment by individuals, who, as the fittest, survive and pass on their genetic heritage. But Wilson expands the discussion from the purely physical adaptation described by Darwin to adaptive social behavior. This key issue inspired the controversy over his works. The environment, he posits, rewards not only species' physical characteristics but also those group behaviors most beneficial to survival. Cultural practices and behavior, in other words, may become survival traits if they are adaptive. Then, over millennia, these behaviors become part of the species' heritage at the instinctual level. Wilson's initial assumption about this approach stated in *On Human Nature* seems especially interesting for the study of the arts and for a primal-traits critical methodology:

> If the brain evolved by natural selection, even the capacities to select particular esthetic judgments and religious beliefs must have arisen by the same mechanistic process. They are either direct adaptations to past environments in which the ancestral human populations evolved or at most

constructions thrown up secondarily by deeper, less visible activities that were once adaptive in this stricter, biological sense. (2)

Wilson posits that not only our beliefs and the actions based on these beliefs but our responses to real or fictional situations emanate from what David Barash calls "the whispers within," subtle voices from tens of thousands of years of human evolution and located in genetic matter. Of human behavior, Wilson writes, "Before the curtain is drawn and the play unfolds, the stage has already been partly set and much of the script written" (130).

This sociobiological approach is fascinatingly similar to Jung's concepts and parallels them in many respects. Calvin Hall and Vernon Nordby describe Jung's collective unconscious in terms similar to the findings of Wilson and others on instinct: "What is learned through experience by previous generations can be inherited by future generations, and does not need to be learned by them anew. Habits become instincts" (40). Jung, however, followed Jean-Baptiste Lamarck's views on evolution: that is, species may learn from experience and build this experience into their genetic heritage in a relatively short period of time. Darwin denied Lamarck's view in favor of natural selection and survival of the fittest, a process that demanded far longer for the evolution of a species. Sociobiology and psychobiology assume Darwin's approach. But Wilson and Jung agree on a basic principle: capacities for response are built into our nature at the most primordial level—the "germ plasma" to Jung and the human gene to Wilson.

The two approaches immediately differ in terms of application, however. Jung developed his theory of archetypes, symbols that represent the collective experience of the species as related to myth. Sociobiologists focus on patterns of animal and human behavior: aggression, territoriality, kin relationships and sexual rituals, for instance—all qualities that gave some adaptive advantage for the species.

One fundamentally Darwinian assumption underlies sociobiologists' thinking. They find that the drive to procreate the species subtly directs nearly all other patterns of behavior. In *Origin of Species*, Darwin wrote, "In looking at Nature, it is most necessary to keep the foregoing considerations always in mind—never to forget that every single organic being may be said to be striving to the utmost to increase in numbers" (iii, 59). The "tangled bank" passage in *Origin*, in which the author describes a mass of plants, with each individual trying to choke out others so that it and its progeny can survive, states the case for the procreational drive quite clearly (iii, 65). Wilson puts the matter only a little differently: "The brain exists because it promotes the survival and multiplication of the genes that direct its assembly. The human mind is a device for survival and reproduction, and reason is just one of its various techniques" (*On Human Nature*, 2). Robin Baker puts the matter in another way:

> our sexual behavior has been programmed and shaped by evolutionary forces that acted on our ancestors to make them who they were—and that still act on us today. The main thrust of these forces is, however, directed at our *bodies*, not our *consciousness*, though our bodies use our brains to manipulate us into behaving in a way dictated by this programming. (xiv)

In other words, sex isn't just important: it is everything, because the whispers within tell us to make ourselves immortal through procreation. The pleasure and mystique of human sexuality, say sociobiologists, is an evolutionary adaptation to inspire propagation: all else is ritual.

Sociobiologists also speak of the epigenetic traits of behavior, those traits that lead to both the physical and mental development of the individual. In *Consilience*, Wilson writes,

> What we inherit are neurobiological traits that cause us to see the world in a particular way and to learn certain behaviors in preference to other behaviors. The genetically inherited traits are not memes, not units of culture, but rather the propensity to invent and transmit kinds of these elements of memory in preference to others. (163)

A primal-traits critical methodology would argue that "prepared learning" leads readers to respond to certain stories when we finally encounter them, even though the response may not have pre-existed the encounter.

The continuing popularity of *Dracula* bespeaks the potency of the novel's hold on the popular imagination. Stage productions toured England and the United States soon after the book was published, attracting large audiences everywhere. *Nosferatu*, the first film adaptation, appeared in 1921, early in the history of cinema. Because F. W. Murnau, the German director, had failed to get permission to use Stoker's story, the film was soon withdrawn from circulation. But Tod Browning's Universal Studio's adaptation in 1930, starring Bela Lugosi, opened a floodgate of Dracula films that has extended to the new millennium. The primordial power of the story seems beyond question.

Surely fear of the predator who would consume us is one of the most primal of responses. Texts that portray the predator-prey relationship stir the sublime shiver of vicarious fear, and Dracula is precisely such a predator. Wilson mentions serpent aversion as a type of prepared learning. Not all people, he asserts, fear snakes, but they can learn such fear more easily than affection or indifference for them. Assuming humanity's common ancestors were, as Darwin postulated, "arboreal in their habits," such a predisposition to a predator that hunted our "hairy quadruped" forebears in the trees seems a likely inheritance. Predator stories abound in the literature of all nations, from the Big Bad Wolf to the werewolf to the popular slasher films, in which a different type of predator (interestingly enough, often somehow dehumanized by mask or disguise) stalks teenagers. But the vampire tale has the greatest currency in the twentieth century of any such story line. The vampire is, after all, as the Count says of the wolves outside his castle, one of the "children of the night," a being well suited to trigger visceral fear of predators that hunted our primordial ancestors in the dark.

Stoker establishes the vampire's role as a hunter-predator early in the film. In one of the most oft-quoted scenes in the novel (especially in

Freudian analyses), Jonathan Harker strays outside his room in Dracula's castle, against the Count's advice, and he awakes to find himself the prey of the Count's wives. Dracula enters the room "as lapped in a storm of fury" to save him, waving the wives away. When they complain, he tosses them a bag, from which there emanates "a gasp and a low wail, as from a half smothered child" (38). Clearly, the Count has been a-hunting and shares his prey with the wives. But they too are predators. Freudian analyses of the novel stress the sexual suggestiveness of the wives, whose "wanton" and "voluptuous" beauty reeks of sexuality, as they bend over a supine Harker and place their lips on his neck, while he waits "in a languorous ecstasy . . . with beating heart" (38). But the "kisses" that they anticipate are his blood. Harker has strayed into the dark, and predators have found him.

The predator/prey plot thickens when Dracula stalks Lucy Westenra successfully. He lures her outside her home to drink her blood, and manages to gain entry later to prey on her again, ultimately causing her to become a vampire. Then she too is a hunter and preys upon children in London as "the bloofer lady." The hunt then shifts to Mina Harker, who falls victim to the predator when he gains access to her through Renfield. The vampires' drinking of their victims' blood must resonate at the primal and instinctual level as the action of a hunting predator because, as Renfield so correctly quotes from the Bible (Deuteronomy 12:23), "the blood is the life!" (141).

A more sophisticated level of conflict arises when a band of sturdy heroes defends its territory against this predator, who is an "other," an outsider and an invader. Wilson defines territory as "one of the variants of aggressive behavior" and states that a "territory" is "an area occupied more or less exclusively either directly by overt defense or indirectly through advertisement" (*On Human Nature*, 107). In *The Territorial Imperative*, Robert Ardrey establishes territoriality as one of the most common instinctual responses across species boundaries. Ardrey writes,

We act as we do for reasons of our evolutionary past, not our cultural present, and our behavior is as much a mark of our species as is the shape of a human thigh bone or the configuration of nerves in a corner of the human brain. If we defend the title to our land or the sovereignty of our country, we do it for reasons no different, no less innate, no less ineradicable, than do lower animals. The dog barking at you from behind his master's fence acts for a motive indistinguishable from that of his master when the fence was built. (5)

Social animals, a designation that certainly includes humankind, establish individual as well as group territory. College roommates sometimes draw a line down the middle of their dormitory room floor, and the fences of suburbia probably have the same purpose as the natural or constructed barriers that separate nations.

Darwin articulates a few basic principles developed by modern sociobiologists when he discusses the evolution of a moral faculty in Book One of *Descent of Man*. In Book Three, he notes that the willingness to help others does not "extend to all individuals of the species, but only to those of the same community. As they [helping behaviors] are highly beneficial to the species, they have in all probability been acquired through natural selection" (xxi, 634). Darwin goes on to state that humanity "is impelled by the same general wish to aid his fellows; but has few or no special instincts" (xxi, 635). However, he seems to have understood that the social instincts, as he called them, lead to certain types of behavior.

Sociobiologists take Darwin's line of thought further, assuming that in the first hunter-gatherer societies, men operated cooperatively to kill game, led by a dominant male. Barash puts the case well: "Efficient hunting often requires group coordination, obedience to authority and a high degree of conformity, especially if the prey is large and dangerous. During this stage of our evolution, those who fitted in and were good 'team players' almost certainly left more descendants than those who stubbornly insisted on individual action" (186–87). Evolutionary descendants of the primitive hunting party are everywhere visible to-day in varieties ranging from African tribes whose conflicts result in massive genocide to Sunday afternoon NFL confrontations in which spectators listen to the same whisper within as they urge their tribe of highly paid warriors on to greater effort against the invading other. Those who study aggression agree that, as Wilson says, we are "strongly predisposed to respond with unreasoning hatred to external threats"—specifically to our territory. Wilson goes on,

> we tend to fear deeply the actions of strangers and to solve problems of conflict with aggression. These learning rules are most likely to have evolved during the past hundreds of thousands of years of human evolution and, thus, to have conferred a biological advantage on those who conformed to them with the greatest fidelity. (*On Human Nature*, 119)

An assumption follows that imaginative portrayals of territorial conflict and defense of territory by a brave band of men would strike a sympathetic chord in the unconscious of reader or viewer.

The issue of territory arises early in *Dracula*. Jonathan Harker leaves his own territory and enters Dracula's, despite the warning of the peasants he meets, when he comes to the Borgo Pass, a rather clearly defined territorial line in the novel. We have passed from the mundane world of humanity to the realm of the king of the Vampires, clearly an other, a being different from those on whom he will prey. Harker crosses yet another territorial line at Dracula's castle when the Count tells him, "Welcome to my house! Enter freely and of your own will!" Dracula must make his guest cross the final territorial boundary voluntarily. Stoker no doubt adapts this act of will on the part of the guest from the tradition that evil must be invited into the house, as portrayed in Coleridge's "Christabel," when Christabel must practically carry the evil Geraldine, apparently fainting, across the threshold of her home. Like Geraldine, Dracula must be invited into the house of his victims, with Renfield serving as his go-between later in the novel, inviting him into the asylum where he can prey on Mina Harker.

But on a much larger scale, Dracula assumes the role of territorial invader when he arrives in England, having prepared himself by studying the culture, history, language and arts of this new territory in order to infiltrate it and populate it with his own kind. Interestingly enough, he must take a part of his own territory with him, the caskets of Transylvanian earth, and these caskets become an important focus in the plot, as the Crew of Light strive valiantly to find and destroy them. Van Helsing's lectures to his *posse comitatus* on vampires, focusing on their supernatural abilities and limitations, underscore Dracula's otherness as a territorial invader, a being well suited to set off bells of primal alarm in the unconscious of the reader. And early in the novel, when Jonathan Harker finds Dracula in his coffin, his journal entry stresses the potential of such an other as invader and also as predator: "This was the being I was helping to transfer to London, where perhaps for centuries to come, he might, amongst its teeming millions satiate his lust for blood, and create a new and ever widening circle of semi-demons . . ." (51). Later, when Dracula has begun his work in London, Van Helsing speculates about the effect of the invasion: "He [Dracula] is experimenting, and doing it well; and if it had not been that we have crossed his path, he would be yet—he may be yet if we fail—the father or furtherer of a new order of beings . . ." (302). Thus, the issue is species extinction. As Van Helsing tells his crew, "But to fail here is not mere life or death. It is that we become as him; that we henceforward become foul things of the night like him . . ." (237). Thus, the plot of the novel makes the reader respond to a basic principle articulated by Darwin and modern sociobiologists: humanity's instinctive loyalty to its own group within its own territory.

When Van Helsing learns the nature of Lucy Westenra's condition, he forms a band of sturdy men to do battle with this hated other in what seems clearly a defense of territory by the equivalent of the primitive hunting pack. When they go on the offensive with their strike on Dracula's hiding place, Van Helsing warns the group, "My friends, we are going into a terrible danger . . ." (249). The group persists after Dracula flees London, pursuing him to Transylvania, where they do battle with his Gypsy minions. They must invade his territory to destroy him because they recognize that he will return. Van Helsing lectures his fellows: "he [Dracula] is not one to retire and stay afar. . . . His glimpse that he have had [sic] whet his appetite only and enkeen his desire" (320–21). Dracula can simply outlive them and then return.

All of the passages describing the exploits are redolent of male bonding with the group led by an alpha male, Van Helsing, the "leader of the pack," emblematic of primitive hunters. They work as hunter-warriors to find and exterminate the other, the territorial invader. The group strategy that they employ, the same approach no doubt used by Neolithic hunters of wooly mammoths, proves more successful, and adaptive, than Dracula's solitary approach to survival. The conflict between a human hunter group and a territorial invader who threatens our species must generate powerful reader appeal from the instinctive level. After all, as Van Helsing describes his and his friends' work, they fight "for the good of mankind, and for the honour and glory of God" (321).

In *Dracula*, however, more than territory is at stake from a primal-traits critical perspective: a female must be saved. Barash takes note of Samuel Butler's comment that "a chicken is but an egg's way of making more eggs," and gives it a hard-line sociobiologist's perspective with, "A more modern view might be that a chicken is a device invented by chicken genes to enhance the likelihood of more chicken genes being projected into the future. People are . . . temporary, skin-encapsulated egos, serving as complex tools by means of which their potentially immortal genes replicate themselves" (21). Evolutionary biologist Robin Baker's research found that even male spermatozoa compete with the spermatozoa of other males within the female's reproductive tract, and he postulates, "a good part of the sexual behavior of a male—even one who has never consciously doubted his partner's fidelity—is driven by the [instinctive] need to either prevent the woman from exposing his sperm to competition or, failing that, to give his sperm the best chance of winning that competition" (xv).

Although, thus far at least, both sexes participate in the human replication process, in male-dominated hunting societies, where warfare over territory is endemic, protection of the females as the source of the gene pool and future of the group would be of paramount importance, albeit an unconscious response from the most pressing of inward admonitions. A primal-traits approach would note that in the myth of Troy, after the Greeks slaughtered the Trojan warriors when the city fell, the rape of the Trojan women was the next order of business. And in *The Odyssey*, Odysseus mentions that his first exploit after leaving Troy was to sack the city of the Cicones, massacre their men, and take their women. He goes on,

> I depeopl'd it [the city],
> Slue all the men, and did their wives remit,
> With much spoil taken, which we did divide
> That none might need his part.
> (*Chapman's Homer*, I, 152)

A primal-traits critical perspective would suggest that the whisper within prompted the warrior hearers or readers of these folk epics to inwardly nod with approval at the spread of the Achaeans' genes to another population.

In *Dracula*, Stoker gives us two women, Lucy Westenra and Mina Harker, ravaged by a territorial invader. Several passages from the novel seem especially important from a primal-traits perspective regarding protection of the female. Before Van Helsing takes his band off to do battle, he tells Lucy why she must stay behind: "You are too precious to us to have such risk. . . . We are men and are able to bear; but you are our star and our hope . . ." (242). The future bearer of children and custodian of the gene pool cannot be placed in harm's way. While

Mina does help find Dracula later in the novel, when the male hunting party goes out to confront him at Carfax Abbey, she stays discreetly at home at this point (where, ironically, Dracula comes to visit); and her husband writes in his journal, "I am so glad that she consented to hold back and let us men do the work" (247). Later, when she awakes at night to find Quincey Morris protecting her and Jonathan, she cries, "Oh, thank God for good brave men!" (311).

Then when Van Helsing and his posse confront Dracula in his London lair, he snarls at them, "Your girls that you all love are mine already; and through them you and others shall yet be mine . . ." (306). The invader thus boasts that his progeny will dominate the human species. And when he possesses Mina Harker, he gloats that she, "their best beloved one," is now "flesh of my flesh; blood of my blood; kin of my kin" (288). The allusion to Adam's description of Eve as "bone of my bones, and flesh of my flesh" (Genesis, xi: 23) suggests that the territorial invader and other has truly made the woman his own, as indeed comes near to being the case. But from a primal-traits perspective, the reader might respond to the inward murmur of fear for the community's genetic future. The sexual suggestiveness of the passage indicates that Dracula has not only seduced the community's women but infected them with vampirism. Lucy becomes a vampire and other, not of the human species, and Mina seems well on the way to the same fate.

Van Helsing follows the same approach when he invades Dracula's territory. A first order of business when he and Mina Harker arrive at Dracula's castle is to take care of the vampire's wives, who, like him, are other to Van Helsing and his friends. The phallic stake in the heart which he gives each of them is surely as sexually suggestive as Dracula's bite on the neck. Each territorial invader, first Dracula and then Van Helsing, has done what the Greeks did at Troy: take the community's genetic heritage for himself. The novel's appeal at the level of instinct or the unconscious to a species steeped in territorial conflict and defense of the community's genetic heritage has unique power.

In B. F. Skinner's *Walden Two*, Frazier articulates the author's philosophy of social determinism: "in the long run, *man is determined by the state* . . . men are made good or bad and wise or foolish by the environment in which they grow" (257). Skinner suggests that humans are lumps of clay waiting to take the form given them by the potter's wheel of social experience. Sociobiologists give quite a different spin to determinism. The more extreme view in the field holds that the clay has not only already been moulded by evolution but the wiring for behavior has been installed.

Neither position takes into consideration the changing meaning of the word "environment." In a technologically developed country, the social behavior of primitive peoples is no longer adaptive. When an aircraft can shoot down an enemy plane from 100 miles away with a missile, physical strength seems beside the point: the hand that rocks the cradle can pull the trigger. And when the word *environment* means a fiercely competitive world marketplace where success depends not on skills in the hunt for animals but on technological innovation, the nation that calls on the brain power of both sexes and all races is more likely to adapt and survive than one that prevents fullest utilization of human resources. One suspects that the evolution of culture will progress much more rapidly in the next century, with the whisper from without—the demands of a society in the throes of rapid change— quieting and eventually altering the nonadaptive whispers from within. Perhaps the Genome survey will finally tell of us our nature and even let us change it more rapidly. But until then, we can only look on the comedy and tragedy of humanity as we too often respond to the instinctual promptings that are not adaptive, exploited at the least damaging level by fiction and film and at the truly dangerous level by political and religious demagogues, and say, with the Bard, "Lord, what fools these mortals be!"

From *Midwest Quarterly* 47, no. 1 (Autumn 2005): 40-54. Copyright © 2005 by Midwest Quarterly. Reprinted by permission of Carla Edwards.

Bibliography

Ardrey, Robert. *The Territorial Imperative: A Personal Inquiry into the Animal Origins of Property and Nations*. New York: Dell, 1966.

Baker, Robin. *The Science of Sex: Sperm Wars*. New York: Basic Books, 1996.

Barash, David. *The Whisperings Within*. New York: Harper and Row, 1979.

Hall, Calvin S., and Vernon J. Nordby. *A Primer of Jungian Psychology*. New York: Taplinger, 1973.

Nicoll, Alardyce, ed. *Chapman's Homer*. 2 vols. Princeton: Princeton University Press, 1967.

Darwin, Charles. *Origin of Species by Means of Natural Selection*. 6th Edition. New York, 1890.

_____. *Descent of Man and Selection in Relation to Sex*. New York: Collier, 1900.

Degler, Carl N. *In Search of Human Nature: The Decline and Revival of Darwinism in American Thought*. New York: Oxford University Press, 1991.

Skinner, B. F. *Walden Two*. New York: Macmillan, 1978.

Stoker, Abraham. *Dracula*. New York and Oxford: Oxford University Press, 1983.

Wilson, Edward O. *Consilience*. New York: Vintage, 1999.

_____. *On Human Nature*. Cambridge: Harvard University Press, 1978.

Dracula's Earnestness:
Stoker's Debt to Wilde_____

Samuel Lyndon Gladden

Bram Stoker's relationship with—and to—his fellow Irishman and author, Oscar Wilde, has attracted the examination of a number of scholars, most of whom point to the men's connections and commonalities: in their nationality and education; in their professions and their struggles to be taken seriously as truly British writers; in the subject matter of their works; and in their relationships with Florence Balcombe, a woman who early on encouraged Wilde's amour, only later to become Stoker's wife. Of these studies, a few seminal biographies of both writers best summarize recent findings and conclusions about the Stoker-Wilde relationship. In *Oscar Wilde*, Richard Ellmann notes that although in their married lives the Stokers and Wildes did remain on socializing terms, the close relationship between Florence and Oscar became rather strained after Florence's acceptance of Bram's proposal of marriage, and particularly after Florence's failure to deliver the news personally to her former suitor.[1] Such a sentiment is echoed by a number of Wilde's biographers and is suggested, at least to some degree, by Wilde's letter to Florence in September of 1878 acknowledging her engagement but bemoaning her failure to convey the news herself, and requesting the return of a small gold cross engraved with the name "Wilde," which he had presented her during their courting days.[2]

Whatever rift might have opened between Oscar and Florence, however, soon closed, and when in 1885 Oscar and his wife Constance took up residence in the midst of the glamorous Chelsea artistic set at 16 Tite Street, just around the corner from the Stokers, the couples became frequent guests in each other's homes.[3] Alas, *The Complete Letters of Oscar Wilde* includes only one communication to Stoker, but Wilde wrote to Florence off and on throughout his life, even closing a letter postmarked on 22 February 1893, "with kind regards to Bram . . ." (Wilde, *Complete Letters* 552). Clearly, Wilde's relationship with both

Stokers, separately and together, includes a long and friendly history, making even more surprising Stoker's apparent eagerness not only to erase Wilde from accounts of his personal and professional lives but also to demonize him in *Dracula*.

Belford notes that in *Dracula*, which appeared just eight days after Wilde's release from Reading Gaol and flight from England, Stoker uses the word "wild" and its derivatives thirty-four times,[4] and she asks whether these allusions might have operated as "coded messages to [Stoker's] exiled friend" (Belford, *Bram Stoker* 218). I find the suggestion of friendliness underlying Belford's speculation highly problematic, particularly given the arguments of the scholars whose work I describe below, all of whom develop a forceful case for finding in *Dracula* Stoker's careful and calculated extrication of himself from Wilde—Stoker's passing of the harshest of judgments on the friend he once seconded for the Philosophical Society at Trinity College (Ellmann 103), the very man who, in his prison-house letter to Lord Alfred Douglas, recognized that he "stood in symbolic relations to the art and culture of [his] age"[5] and with whom any association would, clearly, have been read in a similarly and, I believe Stoker feared, an *uncontrollably* symbolic fashion.

Ten years after *Dracula*'s publication, Stoker's 1907 volume *Henry Irving: Personal Recollections* "[omitted] Wilde's name from a list of one thousand notables entertained at the Lyceum," the theater Stoker managed, where Irving performed many of his most acclaimed roles (Belford, *Bram Stoker* 308). Such self-censoring seems much more consonant with the traditional critical reception of the Stoker-Wilde connection. Yet still, Belford notes—albeit speculatively—that legend has Stoker meeting Wilde in exile and providing cash support for his ruined friend:

A story still circulates that Stoker brought money to Wilde when he was destitute in Paris. It is pleasant to imagine Stoker arriving at the Hotel d'Alsace and Wilde's surprise and pleasure at seeing him. They would go first to the Café de la Régence for Courvoissier, and Wilde would order a box of gold-tipped cigarettes. They would dine at the Cafe de Paris and talk of Trinity, of Florence and her beauty. That one evening they would be Dubliners. (246)

Regrettably, the evidence for Stoker's continued good will toward his disgraced friend and colleague remains sketchy at best, leaving Belford merely to imagine, to invent, gestures of affection, moments of reconciliation—a position difficult to hold in the face of the much stronger evidence of the Stoker-Wilde rift I find carefully coded throughout *Dracula*'s pages.

A handful of studies of *Dracula* have pointed to the novel's scrutiny of Wilde and the so-called "degeneracy" he had come to symbolize by 1895, the year Stoker prepared his *magnum opus* for publication.[6] Judith Halberstam set the stage for many of these readings by situating *Dracula* amidst emerging discourses of monstrosity, finding in the novel typically Gothic concerns with race, class, and gender, and pinpointing Stoker's exposures and repudiations of degeneracy, Jewishness, and non-capitalist models of economy. Christopher Craft and Talia Schaffer read *Dracula* as a demonization of Wilde, finding in the vampire a stand-in for the looks, the actions, and the desires—in short, for the sensibilities—of a new sort of figure emerging at that particular fin de siècle: the male homosexual.[7] In his essay on *The Importance of Being Earnest*, Craft considers the symbolic and imaginative connections of Wilde to vampires and vampirism, concluding that Wilde comes to figure as a diagnostic "type," a name and an image that stand for unspeakable desires.[8] Such a positioning of Wilde as vampire also informs Craft's essay "'Kiss Me with Those Red Lips': Gender and Inversion in Bram Stoker's *Dracula*," which posits that the novel "does not dismiss homoerotic desire and threat" but instead "simply continues to diffuse and displace it,"[9] chiefly by heterosexualizing homosexual investments: "[Stoker's] sexualized women are men too," Craft insists, and throughout the novel, "blood substitutes for semen" (453, 454).

Schaffer argues even more specifically that "*Dracula* reproduces Wilde in all his apparent monstrosity and evil, in order to work through this painful popular image of the homosexual" (398). Schaffer reads the novel as tracing "Stoker's imaginative identification with Wilde" (398), and she argues that the vampire "represents not so much Oscar Wilde as the complex of fears, desires, secrecies, repressions, and punishments that Wilde's name evoked in 1895"; similarly, Schaffer finds in Jonathan Harker, the vampire's antithesis, the symbolic manifestation of Stoker, a figuring that situates Stoker as what we might think of as an anti-Wilde, a complicated self-modeling embedding both acknowledgment and disidentification (398). *Dracula*, Schaffer argues, "functions as both accusation and elegy," for "Stoker used the Wildean figure of Dracula to define homosexuality as simultaneously monstrous, dirty, threatening, alluring, buried, corrupting, contagious, and indestructible" (399). Schaffer points to Stoker's peppering of *Dracula* with the word "wild," arguing forcefully that this key adjective functions, both aurally and symbolically, as a reference to Wilde himself, so that, for example, the "wild desire" that overtakes Harker as he opens Dracula's coffin[10] implies a desire of the "Wilde" sort, a homosexual desire played out on Stoker's pages as one man's anxiety about an intimate proximity to and knowledge of the body of another (399): as Harker feels his way around the Count's blood-engorged body (his tumescent phallus, according to such readings), carefully exploring Dracula's pockets for the keys to the castle, he searches also for control, for release, for phallic mastery. Throughout, Schaffer argues that just as Harker represents Stoker—and, by extension, all upstanding, respectable late-nineteenth-century men—"Dracula is a kind of basin in which images of Wilde-as-monster float" (399).

And so in the novel *Dracula* we find things wild, just as in the character Dracula, these critics insist, we find Wilde himself. What these studies have failed to note, however, is Stoker's recurrent use of the term "earnest" and its derivatives, which suggests to me a specific and significant debt to Wilde's greatest dramatic achievement, *The Impor-*

tance of Being Earnest, the very play whose success was punctuated by Wilde's arrest for acts of gross indecency, the play whose run ended shortly after Wilde's sentencing and communication to Reading Gaol for two years' hard labor. It is unquestionable, given Stoker's position as one of the most important theatrical managers in London, that he would have known Wilde's preeminent stage piece quite well; equally certain is that Stoker would have appreciated the irony of *Earnest*'s plot in the coming-undone of Wilde's life, for Wilde's play lays bare earnestness as an act, a sham, that conceals its very opposite, just as Wilde's trials strip him of his carefully cultivated veneer of respectability, exposing even that as a "shallow mask of manners" veiling the darker side of Wilde's private life.[11] References to earnestness resound throughout *Dracula*, and an account of the types and uses of that term may contribute to work begun by Ellmann, Belford, Halberstam, Craft, and Schaffer in making sense of Stoker's complicated relationship with Wilde, as well as of *Dracula*'s complicated relationship to homosexuality.

Eve Kosofsky Sedgwick insists that "there is no evidence of Wilde's [credence in contemporary theories] of gender inversion—. . . the trope of the woman's soul trapped in a man's body, in the famous 1869 phrase of Karl Heinrich Ulrichs,"[12] the man Hubert Kennedy calls the first theorist of homosexuality, perhaps best known for coining the term "Uranism" to describe homosexual desire. Ulrichs diagnosed sufferers of such a condition as "Uranistes," an identity one may hear echoed playfully in the name "Ernest" and, more generally, in the duplicitous earnestness Wilde's piece lampoons, a coded reference solidified several years earlier in J. G. F. Nicholson's *Love in Earnest*, a collection of poems celebrating same-sex love, which circulated widely among "gay" literary circles and which Wilde would almost certainly have known, whether specifically or merely by reputation.[13] That Wilde would nonetheless have rejected Ulrichs's conclusions about the origin and etiology of Uranism, however, remains unquestioned. Wilde famously rejected all essentialist models of identity, remarking in *The Picture of Dorian Gray* that "being natural is simply a pose, and the most irritating pose I know";[14] nonetheless, Wilde would certainly have been cognizant, as were others in his social/sexual circle, of such late-Victorian *lingua franca* for these secret desires and activities.[15] By 1899, four years after Wilde's "fall" and the widespread recognition of the real presence of same-sex relationships throughout the Empire (and indeed throughout the world), the sexologist's terminology had become sufficiently well known for the category of "Uranian" to be included in Magnus Hirschfeld's diagnostic questionnaire for prospective "patients," thus indicating the transfer of terminological knowledge and mastery from physicians to patients, both actual and prospective (Sedgwick 66).

I believe that Stoker appropriated the word "earnest" from its double context—as the principal term in the title of Wilde's last great triumph, and as a near-homophone for a circulating name for unspeakable love—and launched that double context into his novel by way of his uses throughout *Dracula* of "earnest" and its derivatives. Whether or not Stoker knew of the earnest/Ernest/Uraniste connection strikes me as ultimately less important than the fact that "earnest"-ness offered one more avenue through which Stoker found a means for incorporating—and excoriating—Wilde throughout *Dracula*; in my reading, Wilde's construction of earnestness as a slippery, duplicitous term resonates throughout Stoker's register, as well.

Aside from Stoker's direct invocations of "earnest" and its derivatives, *Dracula* includes several other allusions to Wilde's play as well as to Wilde's personal yet very public position in the dark days of his scandal and fall. Lucy's posing to Mina of the question "'. . . why are men so noble when we women are so little worthy of them?'" (Stoker 199) directly echoes Gwendolen's observation to Cecily that it is ". . . absurd to talk of the equality of the sexes. Where questions of self-sacrifice are concerned, men are infinitely beyond us" (Wilde, *Earnest* Act 3). When, on his first morning in Castle Dracula, Jonathan recognizes familiar titles in the Count's library, he notes that these include "the Army and Navy Lists" (Stoker 167), and upon finding these Jonathan feels a sense of comfort—feels, indeed, "great delight" (166)—just as at the conclusion of *Earnest* Jack finds solace by coming to know his true identity and, thus, finding his salvation, in the record of his father's name ". . . in the Army Lists of the period," which he characterizes as "delightful records [that] should have been my constant study" (Act 3). Elsewhere in Stoker's novel, Dr. Seward observes Renfield "sitting out in the middle of the floor on his stool" (371). Seward understands the lunatic's "pose" to be "generally indicative of some mental energy on his part" (371) and, thus, of the danger Renfield's scheming may forewarn. In the same way, one might argue, the posings of Jack and Algernon throughout Wilde's play threaten to topple Victorian earnestness and prudery just as, more generally, the revelation of Wilde's "posing as a Somdomite [*sic*]," as the Marquis of Queensberry so notoriously misspelled his accusation, threatened to topple all of Victorian society from its tottering perch. In these several ways, *Dracula* addresses *Earnest* and earnestness; yet by invoking Wilde's key comic term, Stoker encodes an even more trenchant critique of Wilde and of the effaced earnestness the playwright celebrated—a precipitous, precarious earnestness that ultimately crushed Wilde beneath its fall.

By my count, *Dracula* contains twenty uses of the term "earnest" and its derivatives—more than half as many as the novel's uses of forms of the word "wild," which Belford and Schaffer both point to as indicative of the novel's investment in examining Stoker's friend, colleague, and rival Wilde (Belford, *Bram Stoker* 217).[16] Following Wilde, Stoker constructs "earnest" as a polyvocal sign, an instrument for articulating simultaneously more than one aspect, more than one quality—and even, in some cases, suggesting its removal from qualities generally included with traditional definitions of the term. One of Stoker's uses of the term reminds us of the syntactical ambiguity of "earnest," for what we generally think of as an adjective may also function as a noun: in an entry from his journal, Jonathan Harker indicates that he paid a moving-man "his day's wages . . . for the privilege of asking him a few questions on a private matter," and that he offered the man "an earnest" for his trouble (Stoker 366). Already doubled in its use-value, the now-noun form of Wilde's pet adjectival term takes on another meaning, as well: an earnest may denote "money, or a sum of money, paid as an installment, esp. for the purpose of securing a bargain or contract."[17] "Earnest," then, operates as a means for exchange, an offering made in anticipation of receiving something the earnest-giver desires; at the same time, it stands for nothing in and of itself, an empty place-holder that merely *suggests*—promises, with only itself as its guarantee—that what is expected will follow. Indeed, the whole of the charade of *The Importance of Being Earnest* works in exactly this doubly nominative way.

More generally, Stoker draws on the term "earnest" to remark in individuals the visible qualities that term connotes, to engage in what I call somatic inscription: Lucy Westenra writes of Quincey P. Morris that "he looked so earnest . . . that I shall never again think that a man must be playful always, and never earnest, because he is merry at times" (199). Existing alongside its opposite, mirth, earnestness appears here as a physically legible indicator of man's *other* disposition, the serious aspect of his Janus-like nature. Wilde's use of earnestness as a somatic inscriptor informs some of the most comic observations in *Earnest*, as well, such as when Algernon, upon discovering the secret of Jack's real identity—that he isn't really Ernest at all—remarks that, "You look as if your name was Ernest. You are the most earnest looking person I ever saw in my life. It is perfectly absurd your saying that your name isn't Ernest" (Act 1). For both Wilde and Stoker, earnestness takes form as a readable sign, a mark of somatic inscription that tells the tale of the body's trustworthiness, respect, and honor; yet such a proposition ultimately fails, certainly throughout *The Importance of Being Earnest*, and to a less obvious degree throughout *Dracula* as well, for those who are first "read" in such a way—Mina, for example—later come under suspicion, and those who are initially seen as untrustworthy—Renfield—nevertheless model earnestness so convincingly that those around them find their diagnostic schema at a loss to measure that elusive quality.

"Earnestness" figures throughout *Dracula* in both its adjective and adverb forms to denote the seriousness and importance of the gestures, work, and attitudes of a variety of characters, both major and minor. Jonathan Harker notes that in his carriage ride to Castle Dracula, "one by one several of the passengers offered me gifts, which they pressed upon me with an earnestness which would take no denial" (Stoker 158); these gifts, a crucifix among them, Jonathan initially regards as trinkets, as worthless nothings, but as he finds himself in increasingly vulnerable situations, Jonathan takes these up as modes of protection, believing sincerely in the same silly objects presented to him so earnestly as he made his way to certain doom. Similarly, Seward records the shock of the vampire-hunters at Van Helsing's revelation of the unholy use intended for a sacred relic: "'The Host. I brought it from Amsterdam. I have an Indulgence,'" Van Helsing announces, and Seward records that this "was an answer that appalled the most sceptical of us, and we felt individually that in the presence of such earnest purpose as the Professor's, a purpose which could thus use the to him most sacred of things, it was impossible to distrust" (323).

In her journal, Mina notes Arthur Godalming's appreciation of her care in making an exact record of all the vampire-hunters have endured; according to her account, Godalming praises her by observing that "'I don't quite see the drift of it; but you people are all so good and kind, and have been working so earnestly and so energetically, that all I can do is to accept your ideas blindfold and try to help you'" (339). Later in the same entry, Mina characterizes Godalming's sorrow over Lucy's death as "so earnest," and she remarks on Godalming himself as "in earnest" (340). And even in moments of contention, as when Dr. Seward expresses distrust of Renfield, he admits nevertheless that "he certainly did seem earnest. . . . I only hope we have done what is best. These things, in conjunction with the wild work we have in hand, help to unnerve a man" (354). Obviously, the use of the word "wild" in conjunction with that which "unnerve[s] a man" directly invokes Wilde and the scandal he had come to signify; but more covertly, the passage refers again to Wilde by way of its use of the term "earnest," here as in Wilde's play a marker of dual personality, a descriptor of one who seems dedicated to that in which he believes, yet who proves unreliable for the uses of others, one committed (to himself) yet untrustworthy (to others)—an echo of the type of "bunburyist" both Jack and Algernon exemplify throughout Wilde's work.

Like Renfield, Mina, too, operates as a figure who stands between the vampire and its hunters, an earnest yet potentially untrustworthy bridge between good and evil. Even when admitting her own frailty, her potential to work against the forces of good, Mina asks her husband "in earnest" to promise to reveal nothing to her of the vampire-hunters' plans (417). Sincere in her declaration of untrustworthiness, Mina appears here as Renfield redux, and as Wilde's own duplicitous brand of earnestness reembodied. And when Van Helsing suggests that the vampire-hunters may fare better without Mina's full confidence of their plans, Seward records in his diary that he "answered earnestly, for I did not want him to weaken in this matter," saying that "'I agree with you with all my heart'" (360). The very excessiveness of Seward's statement, not to mention its carefully *performed* earnestness, begs the question of whether earnestness here is sincere or forced, natural or posed. Later in the novel, Seward seems less divided about his attitude toward earnestness, when his command to the hypnotized Mina that she speak is followed by his protestation that "'it is proof . . . Madame Mina . . . if proof be needed, of how I love and honour you, when a word for your good, spoken more earnest than ever, can seem so strange because it is to order her whom I am proud to obey!'" (434). In this case, earnestness works to set right an unintentionally toppled order, to remind Mina that although Seward commands her, it is because he loves her so deeply, because he directs her in earnest only and ultimately to enable Mina to restore command over herself—and because Mina already has command over his affections.

Twice in *Dracula*, Stoker repeats exactly phrases that contain the word "earnest," establishing, although to a much lesser degree, the very sort of verbal ec(h)onomy that structures the operatic nature of Wilde's play.[18] Jonathan records an encounter with Van Helsing in which the Dutchman informs him of Mina's pure nature by remarking that "'we shook hands, and he was so earnest and so kind that it made me quite choky'" (305). In a parallel scene, Mina records her private conversation with Lord Godalming, in which he expresses his extreme grief over Lucy's condition, his knowledge that she is near death; Mina notes that "he was so earnest, and his sorrow so fresh, that I felt it would comfort him," and she promises that if ever she needs "a man's help," as did Lucy, she will not hesitate to call on him (340). In both moments, an earnest expression finds confirmation in both the actions and the written record of the one to whom it is addressed—Van Helsing's to Jonathan, and Godalming's to Mina.

The second paired set of uses of "earnest" includes a unique descriptor, "deadly," which reminds us of the difference between Stoker's earnestness and Wilde's, for where in *The Importance of Being Earnest* the titular quality is invoked as a comic ruse, a pose, in *Dracula*, earnestness stands alongside sincerity and commitment as an eternal quality rather than a fleeting, baseless attitude. One of Mina's letters to Lucy suggests that language itself signals earnestness in Stoker's sense, that the seriousness of language reinforces the sincerity of earnestness—a sharp contrast to Wilde's style, in which comic language helps to unmoor earnestness from any attitude in particular: Mina writes that Jonathan addresses her as "'Wilhelmina,'" and upon hearing him articulate her full, formal name, she realizes that "I knew then that he was in deadly earnest, for he has never called me by that name since he asked me to marry him" (237). Later in the novel, as Seward records his observations of Van Helsing trying desperately to save Lucy's life, he writes that "I never in all my experience saw the Professor work in such deadly earnest. I knew—as he knew—that it was a stand-up fight with death, and in a pause told him so" (272). In both cases, "deadly earnestness" reinforces the true nature of earnestness it-self, reinvesting the noun with the denotation of which Wilde's play had robbed it, righting "earnestness" here with "deadly," Stoker's very serious—deadly earnest—syntactical truss.

Double uses of the word "earnest" are not limited to near-echoes, however. In fact, one repetitive use of the term underscores the earnest-ness of "earnest" itself, the need for that quality to be doubled before it may be taken as true: when Van Helsing suggests the vampire-hunters enter Lucy's tomb, Seward responds first by asking, "'Professor, are you in earnest; or is it some monstrous joke?'" and then by concluding, without waiting for any response, any verbal or physical sign, "'Pardon me, I see that you are in earnest'" (319). In *Dracula*, earnestness may be proven, but always and only on decidedly flimsy grounds: earnest-ness has recourse only to itself in verifying its presence, as Seward's repetition of the term suggests. Following *Earnest*, then, *Dracula* con-structs Wilde's descriptor as an empty signifier, a mere placeholder that searches elsewhere for its true meaning; like Jack and Algy drawing on the false personae of Ernest and Bunbury, earnestness looks to its (sim-ilarly empty) doubling for confirmation, validation, and control.

Clearly, Stoker's use of "earnest" enters into a dialogue with Wilde's, and some of Stoker's language actually acknowledges, à la Wilde, that earnestness may exist separately from—apart from, rather than as a part of—other terms of respectability. Renfield insists to Seward that "'I am sane and earnest now'" (353), a formulation that distinguishes, rather than joins, clarity of mind and purity of intention. And while Mina couples earnestness with a term of respectability by remarking that "'I know that all that brave earnest men can do for a poor weak woman, whose soul is perhaps lost . . . you will do'" (420), elsewhere she writes that ". . . it did me good to see the way these brave men worked. How can women help loving men when they are so earnest, and so true, and so brave!" (442), an exclamation that again separates ear-nestness from other markers of masculinity and respectability, suggest-ing that, as in Wilde's play, earnestness may be a quality we expect of men, but its true meaning, its ultimate resonance, remains ever-shifting, making the earnestness of earnest men knowable only by the other qualities that surround it, ultimately revealing earnestness to remain wholly separate from those qualities with which we assume its association. In both *Dracula* and *Earnest*, we find that earnestness in and of itself can never be known, for just as Lady Bracknell remarks of the Court Guides—"I have known strange errors in that publication" (Wilde, *Earnest* Act 3)—earnestness remains a slippery signifier, meaning both itself and its other, both the thing socially valued and the thing eschewed.

Finally, near *Dracula*'s end, Stoker's final use of the term "earnest" accompanies the release of Mina from the vampire's curse, signified by the vanishing of the communion-wafer scar from her forehead: "The sun was now right down upon the mountain top," Mina writes,

> and the red gleams fell upon my face, so that it was bathed in rosy light. With one impulse the men sank on their knees and a deep and earnest "Amen" broke from all as their eyes followed [the mortally injured Quincey's] pointing of his finger. The dying man spoke:—
>
> "Now God be thanked that all has not been in vain! See! the snow is not more stainless than her forehead! The curse has passed away!"
>
> And, to our bitter grief, with a smile and in silence, he died, a gallant gentleman. (Stoker 459)

Here ends the main portion of Stoker's narrative, followed only by Jonathan's note describing the happy lives of the novel's main players some seven years hence. Stoker's final invocation of the word "earnest" in *Dracula* thus accompanies the removal of the vampire's scourge and the erasure of the threat that monster posed to the good, sincere people with whom he came in contact, those whose reputations he literally and figuratively stained—just as Wilde's long history with Stoker threatened to stain Stoker, as well. With the eradication of the vampire, the stain lifts, and, simultaneously, earnestness disappears from Stoker's narrative. It is this disappearance, I argue, that echoes the disappearance of Wilde's "stain" on Stoker's reputation, manifested in Stoker's exposure and excoriation of Wilde, his disidentification with his friend and fellow Irishman, throughout *Dracula*'s pages. *Dracula*'s earnestness reveals Stoker's complicated debt to Wilde, and in concluding the novel that demonizes his one-time friend, Stoker settles that debt once and for all, atoning for the connection that marked him and extinguishing forever any further associations with the fellow Irish writer Stoker saw as his other, the double by whom Stoker clearly feared he might well have been vamped.

From *English Language Notes* 42, no. 4 (June 2005): 62-75. Copyright © 2005 by *English Language Notes*. Reprinted by permission of *English Language Notes*.

Notes

My sincere thanks go to my research assistant, Alissa Burger, who helped in the final preparation of this article for publication, as well as to the Department of English Language and Literature and the College of Humanities and Fine Arts at the University of Northern Iowa, under whose shared auspices Alissa was assigned to work for me during the spring term of 2004.

1. Richard Ellmann, *Oscar Wilde* (New York: Knopf, 1988) 103.

2. Oscar Wilde, *The Complete Letters of Oscar Wilde*, ed. Merlin Holland and Rupert Hart-Davis (New York: Henry Holt, 2000) 71–73.

3. Barbara Belford, *Oscar Wilde: A Certain Genius* (New York: Random House, 2000) 131.

4. Barbara Belford, *Bram Stoker: A Biography of the Author of Dracula* (New York: Knopf, 1996) 217.

5. Oscar Wilde, *De Profundis*, 2nd ed. (New York: G. P. Putnam's Sons, 1909) 36.

6. Stoker began preliminary research for *Dracula* in 1890, but it was not until 1895 that he began to write the novel in earnest—concluding it, Talia Schaffer argues, "one month after Wilde went to jail" ("'A Wilde Desire Took Me': The Homoerotic History of *Dracula*," *ELH* 61.2 [Summer 1994]: 398). Schaffer reviews at greater length than I the connections and divisions that suture the Stoker-Wilde relationship; see especially her pages 381–97. Nina Auerbach also makes much of the significance of the Stoker-Wilde relationship to the genesis of *Dracula*, writing that "I suspect that Dracula's primary progenitor is not [the best-known vampires in nineteenth-century literature] Lord Ruthven, Varney, or Carmilla, but Oscar Wilde in the dock" (*Our Vampires, Ourselves* [Chicago: U of Chicago P, 1995] 83).

7. I use the term "homosexual" loosely here, fully realizing the problematic status

of such nomenclature around the time of Wilde's trials, when such an identity—though technically "named" some decades earlier—first became visible to the public-at-large. While Wilde would not have used the term "homosexual" to describe himself or his activities, the linking of homosexuality to Wilde—and to Wilde's double life, which I treat here under the trope of earnestness—has been considered at great length by a number of critics, perhaps most trenchantly by Ed Cohen in *Talk on the Wilde Side: Toward a Genealogy of a Discourse on Male Sexualities* (New York: Routledge, 1993) and by Alan Sinfield in *The Wilde Century: Effeminacy, Oscar Wilde, and the Queer Moment* (New York: Columbia UP, 1994).

8. Christopher Craft, "'Alias Bunbury': Desire and Termination in *The Importance of Being Earnest*," *Representations* 31 (Summer 1990): 19.

9. Christopher Craft, "'Kiss Me with Those Red Lips': Gender and Inversion in Bram Stoker's *Dracula*," *Representations* 8 (Fall 1984): 107–33. Rpt. in *Dracula*, ed. Nina Auerbach and David J. Skal, Norton Critical Editions (New York: W. W. Norton, 1997) 447.

10. Bram Stoker, *Dracula* in *Three Vampire Tales*, ed. Anne Williams, New Riverside Editions, series ed. Alan Richardson (Boston: Houghton Mifflin, 2003) 192–93.

11. Oscar Wilde, *The Importance of Being Earnest* (New York: Dover, 1990) Act 2.

12. Eve Kosofsky Sedgwick, "Tales of the Avunculate: Queer Tutelage in *The Importance of Being Earnest*," *Tendencies*, Series Q, series ed. Michele Ania Barale, Jonathan Goldberg, Michael Moon, Eve Kosofsky Sedgwick (Durham: Duke UP, 1993) 56.

13. See J. G. F. Nicholson's *Love in Earnest* (London: Elliot Stock, 1892), *passim*. Nicholson's use of the term "earnest" as a euphemism for desire, and particularly for same-sex desire, presents the most contemporary turn on an etymological tradition. The *OED* cites two now-obsolete forms of the word, "earnful," which describes a person who is "anxious, full of longing desire; sorrowful," and "earning," which describes "longing desire; poignant grief or compassion."

14. Oscar Wilde, *The Picture of Dorian Gray*, ed. Donald L. Lawler, Norton Critical Editions (New York: Norton, 1988) 10.

15. See Sedgwick 65–67 on emerging late-Victorian notions of Germanness as code for what we might now think of as "gay language," or homosexual parlance.

16. See also Schaffer, *passim*. In the absence of a Stoker concordance, such a count is difficult to authorize, but I draw here from the work of my students in English 034, Critical Writing about Literature, particularly Lorena Knight, Ned Kelley, and Jonathan Fasselius, whose careful reading helped me reach this tally.

17. "Earnest," *Oxford English Dictionary*, Compact ed.

18. By "verbal ec(h)onomy," I refer to the system of exchange, the economy, of language, in which words or phrases are echoed—repeated, more or less exactly—in ways that reverse the play's positions of power. In this way, economy becomes real exchange, one person trading the position of power with another by way of a verbal deployment that repeats the language of the first speaker, taking for the second the power now forfeited by the first. I write at much greater length about this concept in my Introduction to an edition of *The Importance of Being Earnest*, which I am currently preparing for Broadview Press.

Dracula:
Righting Old Wrongs and Displacing New Fears_____

Jimmie E. Cain, Jr.

In 1897, the year of *Dracula*'s publication, Karl Marx's daughter, Eleanor Marx Aveling, and her husband Edward brought out a collection of Marx's letters and articles featured in the *New York Tribune* during the Crimean War. The Avelings' stated purpose for publishing at this particular time was a renewed interest in the "ever-recurring Eastern Question." Although the Eastern Question had "entered upon another phase" with the growth of "Social Democracy" in the Balkans,

> One thing [. . .] remained constant and persistent: the Russian Government's policy of aggrandizement. The methods may vary—the policy remains the same. To-day the Russian Government [. . .] is, as it was in the "fifties," the greatest enemy of all advance, the greatest stronghold of reaction [viii–ix].

Two years earlier, in 1895, Russia and England were once again at loggerheads over Turkey. The cause, in this instance, was Turkish atrocities among the Armenians, a people residing on the border of the Ottoman and Russian empires. Salisbury, then Prime Minister, suggested in 1896 that the European great powers finally resolve the Eastern Question by partitioning the Ottoman Empire amongst themselves. Russia, however, bitterly opposed the plan, for it stymied her ambition to control the Black Sea and Dardanelles. Although Salisbury threatened to send the fleet back to the Black Sea to thwart any possible Russian incursions, nothing more than a diplomatic flap between Russia and England ensued. By 1897 the Turks had ceased their attacks on the Armenians, and war was averted. Nevertheless, the crisis revealed that the "old rivalries and antagonisms" between England and Russia lived on (M. S. Anderson 256–259).

At the very time, then, when Bram Stoker was finishing the novel *Dracula*, anti-Russian sentiments were again running high in England. It is important to place the novel in this context, for as Daniel Pick suggests, *Dracula* "must be read in relation to a whole set of late nineteenth- and early twentieth-century concerns, images and problems" (83). Of special concern in *Dracula* is what Rhys Garnett generally terms "a fear of the emergence of a superior and necessarily antagonistic rival" (30). That rival, I argue, is Russia and her Slavic client states in the Balkans, who posed political, social, military, economic, and racial threats to Victorian middle class stability. For the most part, the middle-class fears articulated in *Dracula* had their source in the social and political changes evolving in England subsequent to the Crimean War of 1854–1856. The novel, therefore, serves both to allay these anxieties and to assuage the national embarrassment over the abysmally flawed conduct and frustrating outcome of the Crimean War by re-enacting the conflict in a manner wholly favorable to England.

So far this study has shown that Stoker matured in a culture hostile toward Russia and her Slavic kin. In 1854 at age seven, the invalided Stoker heard and saw jingoistic accounts of Russian savagery and bestiality in his parents' daily conversations and readings from the popular press. Later as a young adult he listened to first-hand reports of the fighting in the Crimea from his father-in-law. In his early years as acting manager of the Lyceum Theatre, Stoker learned of the political and foreign policy aims of the war from Gladstone during their many meals at the Beefsteak Room. From his work with George Stoker on *With the Unspeakables*, Stoker participated in the crafting of a derogatory polemic aimed at Russians and other Slavic peoples, notably the Bulgarians. These attitudes were reinforced through his association with Arminius Vambery, Stepniak, and, to some degree, Rudyard Kipling. Therefore, by 1890 when he began work on *Dracula*, Stoker had lived for thirty-six years in an environment rich in negative impressions of Russia and Slavs in general. His research for the novel would certainly have rekindled these impressions.

Vampirism, Russia, and the Slavs

In preparing to write *Dracula*, Stoker consulted a number of relatively contemporaneous documents about the geography, peoples, and customs of Eastern Europe.[1] Excerpts from most of these sources are available in Clive Leatherdale's *The Origins of Dracula: The Background to Bram Stoker's Gothic Masterpiece*. Among the books "written by British official servants—soldiers, administrators, or their wives" (97) that Stoker consulted, William Wilkinson's *An Account of the Principalities of Wallachia and Moldavia: with various Political Observations Relating to Them* of 1820 gave Stoker the material for Dracula's racial and ethnic identity, an identity with pronounced Russian and Slavic antecedents. Wilkinson writes that toward the end of the seventh century,

> a nation, known under the names of Slaves and Bulgarians, came from the interior of Russia to that part of Maesia, which has since been called Bulgaria. Soon after a great number of Slaves [. . .] crossed the Danube and settled in Dacia, where they have since been known under the name of Wallachs. [. . .] The modern Wallachians, however, exclude it altogether from their language, and call themselves "Rummunn" or Romans, giving to their country the name Roman-land, "Tsara-Rumaneska" [92].

Thus Stoker learned that in their inception, the Wallachians,[2] and by association the Moldavians, the predecessors of the modern Romanians, descended from Slavic peoples immigrating to the region from Russia and sharing close blood relations with the Bulgarians.

Dracula's genealogy reveals marked vestiges of Wilkinson's text. But more importantly, Dracula's heritage suggests clear Russian and Slavic antecedents. According to the count, in his "veins flows the blood of many brave races," especially that of the "Ugric tribe," who "bore down from Iceland the fighting spirit which Thor and Wodin gave them, which their Berserkers displayed to such fell intent on the seaboards of Europe [. . .] Asia and Africa." So fierce were they that their victims believed "that the werewolves themselves had come." In an explanatory footnote to this passage, Leonard Wolf points out that in the "early stages of the superstition in Eastern Europe, werewolves and vampires were closely akin." But more importantly, he comments that the Ugric tribe "denotes an ethnological group that included [. . .] related people of western Siberia" (*D* 40), a region conquered by Russia during Stoker's life. Although critics have for the most part rejected his having educated Stoker in vampire lore, Arminius Vambery, Stoker's friend and arch Russophobe, may have contributed something to Stoker's vision of the count's heritage, as well. In the opening chapter to *The Coming Struggle for India*, he writes that the "Russians were at the beginning only a small number of Slavs, grafted upon Ugrian, Turko-Tartar, and Finnic elements" (2–3).

Among his progenitors Dracula also claims Attila the Hun, who descended from "those old witches [. . .] expelled from Scythia" (*D* 40). Once again in a note to this passage, Leonard Wolf indicates that Scythia refers to "a region in southeast Europe and Asia lying north of the Black and Caspian seas" (*D* 40), an area that included Russian Armenia and bordered on the Crimean peninsula, site of Russo-Turkish hostilities and British anxieties in 1895. Wolf does not investigate, however, the associations to Russia suggested by Dracula's Scandinavian heritage. The word Russia is derived from *Rus*, a corrupted form of *Ruotsi*, a Finnish term—Vambery's "Finnic"—describing the Varanger, the Vikings, the "Berserkers"[3] (*D* 40) who settled in conquered towns and villages along the Volga beginning in the ninth century (Pares 28). Furthermore, the Vikings have been credited with organizing the first Slavic state in Russia, and the first Russian Chronicle glorifies the exploits of the Viking prince of Novgorod, Rurik (Pares 19 and Columbia *History of the World* 470).

The Huns further connect him with the Slavs in general and Russia in particular. Bernard Pares, the noted Western scholar of Russian history, has shown that in the course of his conquests in the West, Attila subjugated much of the territory that comprises modern day Russia and the Balkans. Furthermore, Attila incorporated many Slavic people in the Hunnish Empire. When Attila's short-lived empire broke up in 453, the Slavs coalesced into a united group. Their original homeland occupied most of the arable lands from the Carpathian Mountains in the south to the Dnieper River in the north, extending west to the Elbe River and east to the Vistula River (*Columbia History* 461). From this central location, the Slavs would eventually spread their domain throughout what is now Eastern Europe, the Ukraine, and Russia, from the Baltic to the Balkans (Pares 11–12). Castle Dracula, it should be noted, sits, conspicuously, within this Slavic zone of expansion.

Stoker situates the castle "in the extreme east [. . .] just on the borders of three states, Transylvania, Moldavia, and Bukovina" (*D* 3) near the conjunction of the Pruth and Seret rivers (*D* 417). This specific location suggests further allusions to Russia. First, it describes a disputed area at the border of Wallachia, Moldavia, and Bessarabia,[4] a territory that Russia won from Turkey in 1812. After the Crimean War, England and France forced Russia to return the tract to Turkey. Russia subsequently recovered the territory from Turkey after the war of 1878 only to lose it later that same year when the Congress of Berlin—a great power conference dominated by England, France, and Germany—demanded that Russia cede the land to newly independent Romania (M. S. Anderson). Thus Castle Dracula rests not only on a site of many ancient "battles" (*D* 38) but also on a source of prolonged Russo-Turkish and Anglo-Russian hostility. As late as 1895, Vambery notes that by mid-century from "the Isker in Siberia to the banks of the Pruth, all became Russian," a position of strength that now allows Russia to focus her ambitions south, toward India (4–5).

Moreover, at the location of Castle Dracula a significant event in the career of Peter the Great occurred. Pares describes him as "a barbarian in his habits, direct and practical in his insistence on knowing everything that was to be learned, and with the kind of genius which consists in extraordinary quickness of thought" (198). What Peter most wanted to learn was the military and bureaucratic practices of the West. So in

1697 he began a "journey of education to Europe" (Pares 197), taking in the secrets of the Swedish fortress at Riga and working incognito in the shipyards of Amsterdam and London so as to master modern shipbuilding theory, all the while trying to hire the best experts in the military and practical sciences each country could provide (Pares 198). Equipped with this new knowledge, he proceeded upon his return to prosecute successful wars of expansion on his neighbors to the north, west, and south. Fortunately for Europe, Peter was not always victorious, and one of his most famous defeats came at the hands of the Turks at the Pruth River, in the vicinity of Castle Dracula, in 1710 (Pares 206).

This defeat at the Pruth is but one parallel between Dracula and Peter, however. Dracula's reasons for sojourning to England are also very similar to Peter's, but much more sinister. According to Jennifer Wicke, Dracula journeys to "London to modernize the terms of his conquest, to master the new imperial forms and to learn how to supplement his considerable personal powers by the most contemporary understanding of the metropolis" (487). However, Dracula visits England not, as had Peter, to export innovation and expertise, but as an invader who plans to conquer and stay. Thus, as Stephen Arata suggests, Dracula educates himself to be "the most 'Western' character in the novel" before commencing on his trip:

> No one is more rational, more intelligent, more organized, or even more punctual than the Count. No one plans more carefully or researches more thoroughly. No one is more learned within his own spheres of expertise or more receptive to new knowledge [637].

Stoker, who at age twenty-five was elected auditor of the historical society at Trinity (Ludlam 24), was much too thoughtful a student of history to have been unaware of Peter's exploits in England, exploits that resonate in his evil Eastern count.

Since the 1970s, scholars have contended that in his research for *Dracula*, Stoker happened upon Vlad Dracula, a Wallachian prince whose cruelty in battle earned him the sobriquet Vlad the Impaler, and modeled Dracula after him. Although this assertion is now a matter of scholarly debate,[5] Stoker may well have drawn inspiration from another infamous impaler. In his first major study of the novel, *Dracula: The Novel and the Legend, A Study of Bram Stoker's Gothic Masterpiece*, Clive Leatherdale suggests that Stoker could have drawn a connection between the historical Vlad Dracula and Ivan the Terrible. According to Leatherdale, after reading of Vlad Dracula's penchant for impaling his victims, both domestic and foreign, Stoker added staking to the list of measures for killing vampires. Further investigations of the subject would have shown that within a century of Vlad's death,

> his impaling exploits [were] seized upon by Ivan the Terrible in Russia. Vlad had shown himself to be a hero of the Orthodox faith and a model of the harsh, autocratic ruler. As such he was taken to justify Ivan's supposed divine right to tyranny and sadism [216].

Felix Oinas, a student of Slavic folklore, lends support to Leatherdale's argument, for he reports that tales of Vlad Dracula's cruelties "were especially popular in Russia, since the Russians associated him with the person of Ivan the Terrible" (115). Oinas goes one step further in establishing a correspondence between vampires and Russia by arguing that vampires are a predominantly Slavic and Russian phenomenon:

> There are clear indications that the beliefs in vampires have deep roots among the Slavs and obviously go back to the Proto-Slavic period. These beliefs are also well documented among the early Russians. The term "vampire" (*upyr*) appears as the name of a Novgorodian prince (Upir Likhyi) as early as 1407 and resurfaces in 1495 as a peasant name. This term has also been recorded in western Russia as both a personal and place name. The previous existence in Russia of a vampire cult is illustrated by the fight clerics waged in encyclicals against sacrifices made to them [113].

Furthermore, Oinas shows that the vampire's ability to assume the form of a bat appears first "among the Slavs" (109).[6] It is well within the realm of possibility, then, that Stoker would have uncovered much of this information about the vampire tradition among the Slavs and in Russia during his research and incorporated it into his novel.[7]

Stoker's inherited antipathy to Russia combined with the links he very possibly discovered between Eastern vampire myths and Russia could account for the prominent allusions to Russia and to Slavic vampire folklore that the author placed in or considered for what some scholars believe to be the original opening chapter of *Dracula*.[8] Although eventually excised from the novel, the chapter was published separately by his wife after his death under the title "Dracula's Guest." The chapter contains close parallels with the vampire legends among the Russians, Bulgarians, Romanians, and Serbians enumerated by Oinas. For example, Oinas records that among the Slavs, vampires

> are believed to lie in their graves as undecayed corpses, leaving at mignight [*sic*] to go to houses and have sexual relations with or suck the blood of those sleeping, or to devour their flesh, sometimes causing the death of the victims. If the grave is opened, the presence of a vampire can be recognized by finding the body in a state of disorder, with red cheeks, tense skin, charged blood vessels, warm blood and growing hair and nails; in some cases the grave itself is bespattered with blood, doubtless from the latest victim [109].

Similarly, in "Dracula's Guest" Jonathan Harker learns from a carriage driver that in a deserted village near their route

> that long ago, hundreds of years, men had died there and been buried in their graves; and sounds were heard under the clay, and when the graves were opened, men and women were found rosy with life, and their mouths red with blood [448].

Later in the novel after Lucy Westenra has become a vampire—a "*nosferatu*, as they call it in Eastern Europe" (*D* 261), says Van Helsing—she is described in her coffin as "more beautiful than ever [. . .]. The lips were red, nay redder than before; and on the cheeks was a delicate bloom" (*D* 245). When he next encounters the vamped Lucy, Dr. Seward notes that her "lips were crimson with fresh blood, and [. . .] the stream had trickled over her chin and stained the purity of her lawn death-robe"(*D* 257).

Also like the Eastern European vampires described by Oinas, Lucy becomes sexually active after her vamping. Just before she is staked, the "undead" Lucy attempts to seduce her fiancé, Arthur Holmwood, later Lord Godalming, in language fraught with sexual allusions:

> "Come to me, Arthur. Leave these others and come to me. My arms are hungry for you. Come, and we can rest together. Come, my husband, come!" [*D* 257].

Such behavior violates Victorian sexual mores, characterized by "male-initiated and male-dominant genital intercourse" (Cranny-Francis 65). Lucy, therefore, elicited horror as a vampire victim and as a sexual predator, "the nymphomaniac or oversexed wife who [threatens] her husband's life with her insatiable erotic demands" (Showalter 180).

"Dracula's Guest" features a significant direct reference to Russia as well. Harker becomes intrigued with the driver's story and asks to be shown the village in question. When the driver refuses to accommodate his wishes, Harker sends the driver back to Munich and proceeds alone on foot. Once Harker reaches the deserted town, a sudden snow storm breaks, forcing him to seek refuge in the only available refuge, "a great massive tomb of marble" (451). As he enters the structure, a sudden flash of lightning reveals "a beautiful woman, with rounded cheeks and red lips, seemingly sleeping on a bier" (452). Before he can investigate further, however, an unseen force hurls him back out into the storm, he loses consciousness, and when he awakes, he discovers a giant wolf gnawing at his throat. Fortunately, he is saved by a group of mounted troopers. What makes this scene significant, other than the obvious allusions to Slavic vampire myths, is that before entering the tomb Harker notices a most unusual inscription on its back, "'The dead travel fast,'" a message "graven in great Russian letters" (451).

The chapters with which Stoker eventually did open the novel feature similar references to Russia. Chapter one places the castle, as has already been shown, well within the Slavic realm and the sphere of Russian influence. Likewise, Dracula's description of his heritage, also examined above, occurs in chapter four. Chapter two provides another, perhaps more concrete connection with Russia. To explain his intense desire to master spoken English, Dracula says to Jonathan Harker,

> Well, I know that, did I move and speak in your London, none there are who would not know me for a stranger. That is not enough for me. Here I am noble; I am boyar; the common people know me, and I am master. But a stranger in a strange land, he is no one; men know him not—and to know not is to care not for [28].

In a note to the passage, Wolf comments that *boyar* originally signified "a member of the old Russian nobility" with estates in Russia or conquered territories (28); Leatherdale further elucidates, stating that "In Russia, *boyar* referred to the higher Russian nobility, below the rank of prince" (*Dracula Unearthed* 55). According to Pares, the boyars had a long history "in the service of Moscow and had contributed to build up her power" (96) from the twelfth century on.

Unquestionably, then, Stoker uncovered a great deal in his studies for *Dracula* that would have made him particularly conscious of the role of the Slavs and the place of Russia in the myths and folklore surrounding vampirism. I further believe that his choice of a setting for the Count's fortress had as much to do with his perceptions of Russia and the Balkans as with the tradition of Eastern European vampires. Certainly, the references to Russia and the Balkan Slavs already mentioned are more than just coincidental. However, more conclusive proof of specific, intentional references to Russia and the Balkans can be found if the novel is interpreted as a fictional narrative that attempts to resolve, if only in the popular imagination, a host of fears and anxieties that entered the English consciousness as a direct result or indirect consequence of long standing Russophobia, England's participation in the Crimean War, and the ongoing imperial struggle known as the "Great Game" in Central Asia.

Dracula and Late Victorian Anxieties

The Crimean War, it should be remembered, precipitated a number of far-reaching changes in English society and left indelible scars on the English psyche. Unlike the forces of the glorious Wellington and Nelson, English arms faltered miserably in the Crimea. Perhaps even more galling to the English public, the long distrusted French saved British forces from utter destruction and finally defeated the Russians at Sebastopol. Aside from those bloodied in combat, the great losers were the British aristocracy. Once the dominant force in the government and the military, the aristocracy after the war were reviled as superannuated, impractical, self-absorbed. The professionals of the middle class had shown that they were better equipped to manage the government, the army, and the emerging *laissez faire* economy that had steadily replaced the aristocratic-controlled agrarian economy of England since the late eighteenth century.

Also called into question after the war was the tradition of English patriarchy. Florence Nightingale, among others, challenged the authority of the male-dominated medical community and army command. Her efforts before, during, and after the war at reforming military health care practices and at professionalizing nursing assured her widespread public acclaim and, conversely, resentment until her death in 1910. Because of her exploits she stood for many as a prominent symbol of what came to be known as the New Woman, an appellation first enunciated by Sarah Grand in her 1894 essay "The New Aspect of the Woman Question" (Chothia x). A phenomenon of the 1880s and 1890s, the New Woman sought equal legal standing—female adultery was considered legally worse than male adultery at that time—greater economic opportunities "in professions such as nursing and in the civil service," political equality, and "sexual emancipation" (Altick 59, 301). In the decade before the publication of *Dracula*, the image of the New Woman was the subject of popular controversy in England. Henrik Ibsen's *A Doll's House* and *Hedda Gabler* were performed in London, respectively, in 1889 and 1891. Conservative critics attacked them as "depraved works" (Chothia ix). In addition to Grand's essay, 1894 witnessed women gaining the right to vote in local elections in England and, ironically, the production of Sidney Grundy's play *The New Woman*, a work in which "Female education, interest in art, questions about the sexual double standard are all held up for mirth" (Chothia xiii–xiv). Although the press organs of the day reflected almost exclusively middle-class male prejudices,[9] toward the end of the century, fewer and fewer Victorian women were content with the supposedly ideal life for women described in Coventry Patmore's "Angel in the House."

Psychologically and intellectually, the English public was forced by the war to recognize the limitations of English military power and to question the validity of the nation's foreign policy ambitions. Like America in the twenty years following her withdrawal from Vietnam, England maintained a similar period of relative isolationism, figuratively licking its wounds while putting its political and military houses in order. Moreover, just as "No more Vietnams" became the rallying cry for conservative elements in the American government and military bureaucracies during the regional wars of the late 1980s and early 1990s and the Iraqi incursions of 1991 and 2003, so too did the memory of failures in the Crimea motivate conservatives in England to institute military reforms that helped to secure colonial victories in Asia and Africa in the 1880s and 1890s.

The Crimean War also fixed in the English conscience the idea of the Balkans as a locus of disease, pestilence, and brutal death. The reporting of subsequent wars between Russia and Turkey would reinforce these notions. George Stoker's *With the Unspeakables*, for instance, confirmed the savagery and barbarism of the Balkan Slavs and their Russian brethren and refocused attention on the horrible diseases common to the Balkans. In the 1880s and 1890s, the waves of Jewish immigrants that descended on England from Russia, Romania, Bulgaria, and other Slavic countries would revive English fears of the East. Though not Slavs themselves, these new immigrants would incur the wrath usually reserved for Russia and her allies and suffer under an intensified anti-Semitism. Although her ambitions in the Balkans and Turkey were temporarily thwarted by the Crimean War, Russia emerged from the conflict a still virulent threat to English commercial interests in Asia and an obstacle to expansion of the empire. As such, Russia appeared to the public and those in power as England's primary enemy on the world stage. Until the Boer War of 1899 and the emergence of a unified, militaristic, and commercially ambitious German state, Russia would continue to fill the role of "enemy number one." She was the raison d'être for increased naval spending, diplomatic legerdemain, and great power solidarity.

As a moderately successful, middle-class professional—both as a lawyer and a professional theater manager—Stoker benefited from the social changes eventuated by the war. But, he also lived with the residual fears and anxieties his society inherited from that conflict. These cares and concerns, I suggest, are at the very core of the narrative in *Dracula*, and Count Dracula should be seen to represent a multiplicity of social and political dangers to Stoker and his ilk. First, as a *boyar*, an Eastern European/Russian aristocrat, he threatens to replace English democracy with an oriental despotism and to undermine middle-class laissez faire capitalism, to return to power an aristocratic class humiliated and discredited during the Crimean War. Furthermore, like the ominous Russian menace dramatized in cinema and fiction in the

1950s and 1960s, Dracula insidiously invades England, following, in cold war terms, a plan for conquest laid out over many years and expedited with the help of "brainwashed" natives. In the course of his assault, he appropriates his enemy's women for his own needs, emulating the behavior attributed to Russians and Bulgarians by George Stoker. Once Dracula has had his fill of them, his female victims themselves threaten Victorian stability, for they have been contaminated, deracinated, and most opprobrious of all, liberated. Finally, as a wandering, pestilential Jew, he visits disease and degradation upon his Victorian hosts.

Dracula as an Aristocratic Menace

For some time, many critics have viewed Dracula as an Old World aristocrat. Malcolm Smith writes that "*Dracula* pits Eastern Europe, tyranny and aristocracy against England, democracy and the middle class" (93). Clive Leatherdale agrees, arguing that "Dracula is the embodiment of the anachronistic land-owning class, seeking to sequestrate the newly-earned privileges of the *nouveaux riches* and reopen the historic struggle between the aristocracy and the bourgeoisie" (*Legend and the Novel* 217). Anne Cranny-Francis moreover deems the Count "an ancient, East European aristocrat" (76). Undoubtedly, then, Dracula is both socially and, as Burton Hatlen believes, "culturally" challenging to the Victorian middle class "values of technology, rationality, and progress" (125).

As a cultural alien, Dracula threatens the liberal, bourgeois democracy of England, which after the Reform Bill of 1832 allowed the middle class ever greater political and economic opportunities. Nicholas Daly attests to the rising influence of the middle class, noting that the dramatic growth of the empire in the latter part of the century "depended upon the existence of a new class of experts," the professional middle class (30). Jani Scandura goes so far as to acclaim that Stoker's working notes indicate that he "hoped to achieve some sort of occupational balance between characters, to create a 'working' portrait of the British middle classes" (1). Dracula militates against this emerging social and economic force, attempting to re-establish the political and economic power of the privileged landed gentry of the past. Even more frightening to Victorian readers, Dracula symbolized the formidable Russian aristocracy, whose hold over the populace was many times more brutal and comprehensive than any exercised by the English aristocracy since the Middle Ages.

As a *boyar*, Dracula has absolute command over his subjects, who live in mortal dread of him. One subject group, the Szgany, is sworn to do the Count's bidding and to protect his person, much like the Praetorian Guard of ancient Rome. Jonathan Harker describes them as

> gipsies [. . .] peculiar to this part of the world, though allied to the ordinary gipsies all the world over [. . .]. They attach themselves as a rule to some great noble or *boyar*, and call themselves by his name [*D* 56–57].

The Szgany, interestingly, have Russian cognates in the Streltsy and the Szlachta. The Streltsy served as the czar's "Palace Guard, officered and partly manned by Russian nobles," while the Szlachta were, in Peter the Great's time, "the gentry of Russia" who composed a "service class" for the czar (Pares 194, 212). As did sitting Russian czars at the time, Dracula can likewise call on the aid and service of various "Slovaks" under his dominion (*D* 68, 413).

Also like the Russian aristocracy, Dracula lives parasitically off the labors of his subjects. Thus Van Helsing appropriately describes him as having a "child-brain that lie in his tomb for centuries, that grow not yet to our stature, and that do only work selfish and therefore small" (*D* 401). David Glover has shown that Dracula's underdeveloped mental capacities reflect notions of degeneracy popularized at the time by Cesare Lombroso and Max Nordau. Glover cites the example of the Manchester economist W. R. Greg, who "bemoaned a civilization in which 'rank and wealth, however diseased, enfeebled or unintelligent,' triumphed over 'larger brains'" (*Vampires, Mummies, and Liberals* 68). Dracula is certainly, then, an anachronism, a type of the ancient aristocrat, a member of a class who consume the fruits of the labors of the dispossessed, who fritter away their lives in vain, childish pursuits while those in thrall to them, to borrow lines from E. A. Robinson, "worked, and waited for the light / And went without the meat, and cursed the bread" ("Richard Cory" 13–14). When Harker records in his journal the appearance of the Count sleeping off one of his nightly debauches, he strikes upon a most apposite metaphor for Dracula and his aristocratic kin, the leech:

> There lay the Count, but looking as if his youth had been half renewed, for the white hair and moustache were changed to iron-grey; the cheeks were fuller, and the white skin seemed ruby-red underneath; the mouth was redder than ever, for on the lips were gouts of fresh blood, which trickled from the corners of the mouth and ran over the chin and neck. [. . .] It seemed as if the whole awful creature were simply gorged with blood; he lay like a filthy leech, exhausted with his repletion [*D* 67].

Although Dracula goes to great lengths to disguise his origins and purpose once in England, he cannot hide his aristocratic origins. The keeper at the London Zoological Gardens recognizes him right away "as a lord" (*D* 178) and instantly dislikes him because of "the airs as he give 'isself" (*D* 177). When he purchases one of his many properties around London, Dracula vainly signs the deed as "Count de Ville,"[10] what Wolf describes as a "generic name for an aristocrat" (*D* 326). Dracula's choice of homes is equally demonstrative of his social pretensions. For example, as his primary base of operations, he acquires an estate founded at Carfax Abbey. Though dilapidated and sorely in need of repair, it still is distinctly aristocratic. Sitting on over twenty acres surrounded by a stone wall, the house is very large and of all periods back [. . .] to mediaeval times, for one part is of stone immensely thick, with only a few windows high up and heavily barred with iron. It looks like part of a keep, and is close to an old chapel or church [*D* 32].

Dracula maintains a smaller yet equally run-down lair in Piccadilly, the most fashionable part of Victorian London, an area where the nineteenth-century gentry kept residences for their stays in town (*D* 318). In whatever apparition, country squire or London dandy, Dracula manifests an aristocratic hauteur out of place in a thoroughly middle-class Victorian England.

Opposing the Count is a diverse group, what Christopher Craft calls the "Crew of Light" because of their struggle to save Lucy Westenra, the light of the West (169). Consisting of a Dutch physician and philosopher, Dr. Van Helsing[11]; an English aristocrat, Arthur Holmwood, later Lord Godalming; three middle-class English professionals—Dr. Seward, a physician; Jonathan Harker, a solicitor; and his wife Mina Harker, a teacher—and an American millionaire, Quincey Morris, the Crew fights to secure "the values of the English professional middle class" (Malcolm Smith 93).[12] Although Van Helsing and Quincey Morris are, strictly speaking, outsiders, they nonetheless serve English interests. Van Helsing, a native of "that other classic homeland of free trade" (Moretti 74), provides "an important ideological bridge," for he is at once a "Westerner [. . .] but enough of a European to be able to understand the exotic world of Dracula" (Malcolm Smith 92). Also as a religious outsider, a "superstitious/idolatrous Catholic," he possesses a knowledge unavailable to the scientific "Anglican Englishmen with their 'matter-of-fact' religion" (Garnett 49). On the other hand, Quincey Morris, who Seward notes "had always been the one to arrange the plan of action" in all their "hunting parties" (*D* 363), provides the know-how of a "pragmatic campaigner," and as the supplier of "military aid in the form of Winchesters," he acts as England's "armorer" (Wasson 22).

The sole aristocrat in the group, Lord Godalming,[13] an outsider by reason of class, renounces his title so as to fit in with the others. This fact is apparent shortly after the death of his fiancée, Lucy. When Van Helsing starts to address him as "Lord," Godalming cuts him off, saying, "No, no, not that, for God's sake!" And he informs Van Helsing and the others that the only title he wishes to have is "the title of friend" (D 212). Godalming, therefore, is an acceptably "tamed" aristocrat (Leatherdale, *Legend and the Novel* 217), what Burton Hatlen sees as a "bourgeois aristocrat" who prefers the company of his middle-class confreres in the Crew "to that of his fellow peers" (121). When the Crew actually draft their plan of attack, the ascendancy of the middle class is evident. Recording the event, Mina writes that

> we unconsciously formed a sort of board or committee. Professor Van Helsing took the head of the table, to which Dr. Seward motioned him as he came into the room. He made me sit next to him on the right, and asked me to act as secretary; Jonathan sat next to me. Opposite us were Lord Godalming, Dr. Seward, and Mr. Morris—Lord Godalming being next the Professor, and Dr. Seward in the centre [D 286].

The Crew is thus headed by a man of science, and sitting to his right, a position of most favored status, sit a solicitor and a teacher. For Daly, this assemblage represents the emergence of a "corporate" hero, an "increasingly fraternal, or associationist, and in specific ways patriarchal, group" (46–47).[14] The marginalization of Quincey Morris and Lord Godalming signifies, Daly further contends, the elevation of the "idea of the heroic professional" over the "older idea of masculine heroism" (39).

Besides protecting female virtue and middle-class political prerogatives, the Crew fights to preserve unfettered *laissez faire* capitalism and free trade against "the vestiges of feudal ideology which continued to exist" (Cranny-Francis 76), especially in Russia. Franco Moretti contends that Dracula threatens to "subjugate [. . .] the liberal era and destroy all forms of economic independence" enjoyed by the middle class (74). As "the aristocrat, the figure of the past, the relic of distant lands and dark ages," Dracula consumes the labor of others but produces nothing in return (74). Judith Halberstam conceives of him as "an image of monstrous anti-capitalism" which interferes with the "natural ebb and flow of currency" (346).

While seeking an escape route from the castle, Harker uncovers evidence supporting these claims. Searching Dracula's bedroom for a key, Harker finds

> a great heap of gold in one corner—gold of all kinds, Roman, and British, and Austrian, and Hungarian, and Greek and Turkish money, covered with a film of dust, as though it had lain long in the ground [*D* 63].

Capitalism dictates that currency "should be used and circulated" (Halberstam 346) to stimulate economic growth and development. The Count, however, apparently refuses to allow his money "*to become capital*," preferring to treat it as an "end in itself," to delight "in its continuous accumulation" (Moretti 75). Dracula has also obviously been stockpiling the coin of the realms with which he has warred in the past and with whom he will engage in the future. Dracula cannot carry out his invasion of middle-class London without money, a fact best exemplified by his actions when surprised by the Crew at his Piccadilly lair. Harker lunges at the Count with a "Kukri knife,"[15] but "the point just cut the cloth of his coat, making a wide gap whence a bundle of banknotes and a stream of gold fell out." When Harker strikes again, Dracula "swept under Harker's arm, ere his blow could fall, and, grasping a handful of the money from the floor, dashed across the room, threw himself at the window" (*D* 364). Ultimately, Dracula knows that he must have funds to further his ambitions in England. In terms of my argument, the monies that Dracula accumulates are further significant. Except for the Roman coins, the others have been taken from countries hostile to Russia at one time or another during Stoker's lifetime.

Money for the Crew of Light, conversely, must be put into circulation so as to expel the Count—i.e., the aristocratic Russian threat—from England and to track him down and to kill him in his homeland. Thus, money performs a "moral" service (Moretti 75). Mina makes this point clear when she writes "of the wonderful power of money! What can it not do when it is properly applied; and what might it do when basely used" (*D* 420). She is referring here specifically to money spent lavishly by Godalming and Morris to pay for travel and accommodations, to bribe foreign officials and natives, and to purchase the implements necessary to defeat the Count. Underlying the statement, however, is the middle-class notion, justified by social Darwinism, that wealth accrues to those who most deserve it by dint of personal effort and that it makes possible the ultimate expression of Victorian society, the middle-class home. It is only appropriate that both this home and England itself should be saved from destruction at the hands of a despotic, feudalistic Eastern European aristocrat by a group pledged to uphold the middle-class virtues of the day.[16]

Dracula as a Russian Invader

In 1966, at the height of the Cold War, the first essay to treat *Dracula* as a political document appeared, Richard Wasson's "The Politics of *Dracula*."[17] Wasson argued that

> the novel represents those forces in Eastern Europe which seek to overthrow, through violence and subversion, the more progressive democratic civilization of the West [19].

A little over twenty years later, Rhys Garnett wrote that the "role" of the Count is that of an imperial "rival to and potential conqueror of Britain and its empire" (36). Although Wasson and Garnett refer only to some unspecified, generic Eastern menace, I suggest that Stoker envisioned Russia and her Slavic allies in the Balkans endangering English democracy and empire, thereby anticipating by almost fifty years cold war relations between England and Russia. A close examination of Dracula's invasion of England will, I contend, corroborate this assertion.

Much like Peter the Great, Dracula assimilates as much knowledge as he can about the language, people, government, and military of England before launching his invasion of the West. By conversing with Jonathan Harker, Dracula hopes not only to improve his English but also to learn the idioms of English law and customs, thus his request that Harker "shall stay with [him] a month" (*D* 45). Moreover, at Castle Dracula, Jonathan Harker stumbles across evidence of the Count's studies and well-laid plans. Looking for diversion in the library, Harker to his "delight" discovers "a vast number of English books." What appears on first sight to be merely the reading material of a conscientious tourist turns out to be the homework of a potential invader:

> The books were of the most varied kind—history, geography, politics, political economy, botany, geology, law—all relating to England and English life and customs and manners. There were even such books of reference as the London Directory, the "Red" and "Blue" books, Whitaker's Almanack; the Army and Navy Lists, and—it somehow gladdened my heart to see it—the Law List [*D* 27–28].

A tourist would have no need to know the names of "all persons serving or pensioned by the state" contained in the Red Book or the parliamentary acts published in the Blue Book (Wolf 28). Someone planning a detailed invasion scheme, however, would wish to know the whereabouts of all those with government service as well as the list of personnel serving in the Army and Navy. A historical figure who closely resembles this description of the Count was none other than the arch Anglophobe Count Nikolai Ignatiev. While serving in London, the debonair count masked his anti-British sentiments behind a pleasant demeanor, but when a London map seller reported to the Foreign Office that "he had been discreetly buying up all available maps of Britain's ports and railways," he became the subject of constant surveillance (Hopkirk 295–296).

Later Harker comes across an atlas opened at a "much used" map of England. On closer inspection, he notices

in certain places little rings marked [. . .] one was near London on the east side, manifestly where his new estate was situated; the other two were Exeter, and Whitby on the Yorkshire coast [D 32–33].

Situated along the eastern seaboard, these are all ideal invasion sites. Whitby, where the count debouches on English soil, would provide a convenient staging area in northern England for forces descending out of the Baltic, whereas vessels sailing north out of the Mediterranean would find Exeter, where Jonathan Harker lives and works, suitable for debarking. The Count's estate at Carfax, in Purfleet, moreover, is not only well to the east of London near the more navigable entrance to the Thames, but it is also strategically located near a number of government arsenals, such as the one at Woolwich, and the important Royal Victoria, Royal Albert, and King George V docks.[18] Furthermore, Dracula arranges to have crates of his native soil, his war materiel, preshipped to Newcastle, Durham, Harwich, and Dover (D 44), all ports on the eastern seaboard or sites located on waterways with easy access to the North Sea.

When he launches his assault, Dracula sails from Varna, in Bulgaria. During the Crimean War, it should be remembered, Varna played an important strategic role as a staging area for British naval and army forces. Varna was also the site of the first epidemics[19] to lay waste the forces, prompting Russell's initial published condemnations of the government and high command. In her 1859 official, but unsigned, report to Parliament, *A Contribution to the Sanitary History of the British Army During the Late War with Russia*, Florence Nightingale describes the encampments in and around Varna as pestilential killing fields:

In June, 1854, the army, as already mentioned, went to Bulgaria, an undrained uncultivated country, at all times suffering more or less from malaria, and consequently rendering its inhabitants, but especially strangers, remarkably susceptible to attacks of any epidemic disease which may happen to prevail, altogether apart from the occurrence of what are commonly called sanitary defects. Judging from the experience of the shipping, the influence of this malarial atmosphere extended out to sea. In such a region, part of the army was encamped in a district so unhealthy that it had attained the Turkish name of the Valley of Death. Cholera soon appeared . . . [8].

Later during the siege of Sebastopol, she reports that scorbutus, "a blood disease" that usually produced "diarrhoea, dysentery, and fever," contributed mightily to the decimation of British forces (8). George Stoker recorded similar scenes of pestilence and death in Varna and Bulgaria a generation later in *With the Unspeakables*. Plus, in George's account, Varna is the scene of many Russian and Bulgarian abuses of the Turks. Thus Varna's associations with cholera,[20] the Crimean War, and his brother's stories of Russian brutality might well have fixed the location in Stoker's mind as a particularly fertile image of the port of debarkation for an Eastern/Russian menace.

The vessel that carries Dracula to English shores is, appropriately, a Russian one, the *Demeter*. Devendra Varma interprets the ship's name as an allusion to the myth of Persephone:

> In *Dracula*, *Demeter* is a coherent choice for the name of the schooner that brings the vampire count from the Black Sea to the shores of England because of the goddess Demeter's connection, by her daughter's marriage, with the King of the Underworld ("Dracula's Voyage" 208).

Wolf's footnote about the ship echoes Varma's assumption. However, I would suggest that Stoker has a Russian allusion in mind as well. As Belford notes, Stoker took the name for the wrecked vessel from an actual ship washed ashore at Whitby in October 1885 during a terrible storm. The ship was the Russian schooner *Dimitry*, which sailed from Narva on the Baltic carrying a load of silver sand. Because "Stoker loved codes," Belford further contends that Varna, the port from which the *Demeter* sails, is really an "anagram of Narva" (223–224). If true, Belford's assertion is doubly significant. First, Stoker might quite consciously have associated Narva with Varna because both signify important places in Russian history. Varna, as I have already shown, is a significant site in the English experience of the Crimean War and the Russo-Turkish War of 1877–1878. Narva, on the other hand, is the scene of another defeat, like that at the Pruth in 1710, suffered by Peter the Great, this time at the hands of Sweden under Charles XI. So thorough was Peter's failure that Charles had medals struck commemorating the battle, featuring on one side the image of "the flying Tsar" (Pares 200).

The name Dimitry is likewise infamous in Russian lore. In 1604, during the reign of Boris Godunov, Uyrey Otrepyev, the son of a retainer in the Romanov household, tried to take the throne of Russia by claiming to be Prince Dimitry, the rightful heir who had been murdered in 1591. With the assistance of Polish nobles like the Voevode of Sandomir,[21] the pretender raised an army, defeated the forces of Boris, who died at the height of the crisis, and proclaimed himself czar before the people on the Red Square of Moscow (Pares 138–141). Although he reigned only until unmasked and subsequently assassinated in 1606, his memory was immortalized in Pushkin's 1825 historical drama *Boris Godunov*. According to *The Oxford Companion to English Literature*, third edition, the first translation of Pushkin's works appeared in England in 1835. A one-time drama critic and lover of dramatic literature, Stoker could certainly have been familiar with the text. Quite possibly, then, the *Demeter* could quite easily be but an Anglicized version of Dimitry.

Once the vessel arrives in Whitby, the Russian allusions continue to proliferate. Her cargo of "silver sand and boxes of earth" (*D* 109) corresponds almost exactly with the actual cargo of the *Dimitry*, "silver sand from the Danube" (Belford 222). The Danube is fraught with significance. Not only does Dracula traverse the Danube going to and returning from England, but it was at the Danube that the historical Vlad was defeated by the Turks in 1462 (Wolf, *D* 42). Moreover, Russia and Turkey fought over control of the entrance to the Danube from the Black Sea from the seventeenth century on through the nineteenth, and the Danube figured large in peace negotiations after the Crimean War in 1856 and the Russo-Turkish War in 1878.

A clue to Stoker's having these wars in mind here is a passage recorded at Whitby by Mina Harker a week before the wreck. Lucy and she strike up a conversation with a retired sailor, Mr. Swales, a veteran of the Napoleonic Wars, during their daily walk through the cemetery overlooking the harbor. When they ask Mr. Swales if he knew any of the people buried about them, he specifically mentions "Edward Spencelagh, master mariner, murdered by pirates off the coast of Andres, April, 1854, aet. 30," "Andrew Woodhouse, drowned [. . .] in 1777," and "John Rawlings [. . .] drowned in the Gulf of Finland in '50" (89). The Crimean War started in 1854, and Wolf notes that "Andres" refers to "Cape Andreas, at the end of a long narrow peninsula of northeast Cyprus," an island just south of Turkey in the Mediterranean Sea. Wolf further remarks that the "1777" date given by Swales for the death of Andrew Woodhouse should read 1877, during the Russo-Turkish war in which George Stoker served, "since Swales claims to have known the man."[22] Finally, Wolf notes that the "Gulf of Finland" is an "arm of the Baltic Sea, south of Finland" (*D* 89). This last reference is noteworthy because before the Crimean War England and France had "probed the possibility of using their superior sea power to attack Russia in the Baltic" and eventually sent "a formidable naval force into the Baltic that in August 1854 succeeded in capturing Bomarsund, the principal fortress on the strategic Aaland Islands" (Norman Rich 124) located at the entrance to the Gulf of Finland.[23]

The form Dracula assumes to escape undetected from the *Demeter* also has Russian ties. A correspondent for "The Dailygraph" reports that "the very instant the shore was touched, an immense dog sprang up on deck from below, as if shot up by the concussion, and running forward, jumped from the bow on the sand" (*D* 105). The animal in question, however, proves to be a grey wolf. In the same guise, Dracula later entices from its den a large white wolf at the London Zoological Gardens. There too a gardener had mistaken Dracula for "a big grey dog" whom he saw "a-gallopin' northward faster than a horse could go" (*D* 178). When Harker asks the head animal keeper about the incident, he tells Harker that the animal was a grey wolf, for dogs "don't gallop" (*D* 179). In a footnote to this passage, Wolf writes that grey wolves were virtually extinct in western Europe at this time and could only be found in "Russia, and parts of Asia" (*D* 179). Because a vampire can only enter a house if invited, Dracula uses the wolf from the London Zoological Gardens to gain entrance to Lucy Westenra's room. The "Russian consul" in Whitby provides a similar service, for the correspondent reports that he "took formal possession of the ship, and paid all the harbour dues, etc" (*D* 107) and thereby officially invited Dracula into England.[24]

In the course of reporting the story of the wreck of the *Demeter*, the "Dailygraph" correspondent also reveals native English hostility toward Russia. For example, of the first sighting of the *Demeter* out at sea, he writes

> The only sail noticeable was a foreign schooner with all sails set, which was seemingly going westwards. The foolhardiness or ignorance of her officers was a prolific theme for comment whilst she remained in sight, and efforts were made to signal her to reduce sail in face of her danger [*D* 102].

The foolhardy and ignorant officers are none other than a Russian captain and a Romanian first officer. Though it could be argued that the correspondent is unaware of the makeup of the ship's staff at this point and is not purposefully insulting, his later comment that the Russian clerk's translation of the captain's log "must be taken *cum grano*," or, as Wolf notes, with a grain of salt (*D* 109), makes his distrust and contempt for Russia clear.

Once he is safely ensconced on English soil, Dracula does what almost all invaders do, carry away his enemy's wives and daughters. Dracula thus recalls George Stoker's account of Russian and Bulgarian appropriations of Turkish colonial women in Bulgaria after the 1877–1878 Russo-Turkish War. Moreover, the Count threatens to undermine the entire Victorian social and political superstructure by destroying the very foundation of English life, the middle-class home. Citing Dracula's comment to the Crew of Light that "Your girls that you all love are mine, already; and through them you and others shall yet be mine" (*D* 365), John Allen Stevenson contends that the Count is "an imperialist whose invasion seeks a specifically sexual conquest," namely to "take other men's women away and make them his own." However, Dracula poses not just the danger of "miscegenation, the mixing of blood," but something even more sinister and pernicious to the security of England, the eventual deracination of his victims, the production of "new loyalties" in those he vamps (144). When he confronts the undead Lucy, Seward recognizes that she is no longer the ideal Victorian mate of his dreams. So, in an instant, his abject love for her "passed into hate and loathing," for she is now to him just a "thing" which he could kill with savage delight (*D* 257). Only when they have driven a stake through her heart, severed her head from her body, and stuffed her mouth with garlic is she "no longer the foul Thing" but once more the image "of unequalled sweetness and purity" (*D* 264).

Through the subversion of English women—the ostensible justification for the "power and privilege" of the middle-class male (Hatlen 121)—the Count both emasculates Englishmen and, more frightening still, inverts the gender roles underlying Victorian social stability. He performs the latter by creating, as in the case of Lucy Westenra, "sexually aggressive women" (Cranny-Francis 68). Lucy and her ilk thus come to represent the era's greatest challenge "to patriarchal bourgeois society," the New Woman (Cranny-Francis 64). The New Woman of the last two decades of the nineteenth century, writes Carol Senf, sought "financial independence and personal fulfillment as alternatives to marriage and motherhood."[25] The New Woman also "felt free to initiate sexual relationships" (35). As Linda Bowling suggests, for many men and women in Victorian England, the New Woman spelled the coming of social chaos and eventual collapse:

> The New Woman [. . .] was perceived to have ranged herself perversely with the forces of cultural anarchism and decay precisely because she wanted to reinterpret the sexual relationship. Like the decadent, the heroine of New Woman fiction expressed her quarrel with Victorian culture chiefly through sexual means—by heightening sexual consciousness, candor, and expressiveness [qtd. in Senf, "New Woman" 37].

David Glover argues that Stoker "seldom missed an opportunity to excoriate the presumption of sexual equality" (*Vampires, Mummies, and Liberals* 106).

Dr. Van Helsing iterates Stoker's bias toward and fear of the New Woman when he explains that Dracula's strategy is to father "a new order of beings" (*D* 360), a progeny of racially and ideologically different beings who, left unchecked, will destroy from within male-dominated, middle-class Victorian society. Alexandra Warwick has shown that the "trope of infection"[26] became a component of the vampire myth in the nineteenth century only as the increasingly liberated woman came to be viewed as a "source of danger." Most alarming was the "disruption of gender identity" threatened by the vampire's bite, the inevitable consequence of which was the feminization of men and the masculinization of women (203–204). So powerful is this menace that even the staunchly traditional and self-effacing Mina Harker is not safe from infection (impregnation?) by the Count. It takes all of the energy and resources of the Crew of Light, a possible metaphor for England and her commonwealth and commercial allies, to save Mina, by extension English patriarchy itself.

Dracula's strategy is nothing less than genocide via rape, practiced by the Russians of Stoker's time among the Turks and by their Serbian brethren among the Bosnian Muslims in the early 1990s. Dracula symbolizes the possibility of deracination and racial contamination as well as gender inversion. These too may be seen as Eastern European/Russian threats posed by what must have been for many Victorians a disturbing figure. During the 1880s and 1890s, thousands of Bulgarian, Polish, Romanian, and especially Russian Jews immigrated to England either to escape the pogroms which followed the assassination of Alexander II or to avoid state-sponsored anti-Semitism carried out by Russia at home and in her sphere of influence (Colin Holmes 3; Zanger 34). Undeservedly, they were perceived as an "'alien invasion' of Jews from the East, who in the view of many alarmists, were feeding off and 'poisoning'" the blood of the nation (Pick 80). *Dracula*, it will be seen, is to a large extent a projection of these alarmists' fears.

Dracula as an Eastern European/Russian Jew

The word anti-Semitism first appeared in 1879 in a pamphlet written by Wilhelm Marr warning of "the Jewish domination of Germany" (Kushner 2). By the last decade of the nineteenth century, England too witnessed a profusion of anti-Semitic literature. In 1895 one of the most popular plays of the day featured a sinister Jew. Appearing shortly after the Dreyfus affair in Paris, this was none other than Svengali, the villain of Herbert Beerbohm Tree's stage adaptation of George Du Maurier's novel *Trilby*. Jules Zanger suggests that such works as *Trilby* "owed much of their vitality to the way in which they embodied and alluded to a number of popular apprehensions which clustered around the appearance in England of great numbers of Eastern European Jews at the end of the century" (33). In her introduction to *Trilby*, Elaine Showalter argues that Du Maurier capitalized on a deep-seated anti-Semitism in British society, asserting that "his portrait of Svengali as an 'Oriental Israelite Hebrew Jew' created a character who stands

alongside Shylock and Fagin in the annals of anti-Semitic literature"
(ix). Much as Dracula works his evil through a retinue of vamped female victims, "Svengali, the 'little foreign Jew,'" likewise employs
Trilby's "body as a vehicle" to achieve his ends (Showalter xx).[27]

Foremost among the apprehensions surrounding the immigrant Jewish community in England was the belief that Jews spread disease and
contamination. As noted earlier, Robert Sherard fomented the image of
the new Jewish immigrants as a "brutalized race" whose bodies were
"black with filth and red with sores" (qtd. in Colin Holmes 38). Joseph
Banister, in like manner, attributed to the East End Jews of London an
extraordinary lack of hygiene and a concomitant foul smell. He once
wrote that Jews stood out for reason of their odor and

> their repulsive Asiatic physiognomy, their yellow oily skin, their flat feet,
> fat legs and loathsome skin and scalp diseases [qtd. in Colin Holmes 40].

Jews also posed a threat because of their "propensity to carry and
spread disease and thereby infect and weaken other elements of the
population" (Colin Holmes 40). Thus, Banister warned against mixing
English and Jewish bloods:

> If the gentle reader desires to know what kind of blood it is that flows in
> the Chosen Peoples veins, he cannot do better than take a gentle stroll
> through Hatton Garden, Maida Vale, Petticoat Lane, or any other London
> "nosery." I do not hesitate to say that in the course of an hour's peregrina-
> tions he will see more cases of lupus, trachoma, favus, eczema, and scurvy
> than he would come across in a week's wanderings in any quarter of the
> Metropolis [qtd. in Colin Holmes 40].

A fellow anti-Semite, John Foster Fraser, lamented in the *Yorkshire
Post* that England had no provisions for preventing the influx of
"smallpox, scarlet fever, measles, diphtheria" with the "unwashed ver-
minous alien" from Eastern Europe and Russia (qtd. in Holmes 38).

Dracula has unmistakable similarities with Victorian accounts of the immigrant Jews crowding the dilapidated and poorly drained slums of the East End.[28] The Count's residence at Carfax, in Purfleet, for example, is well to the east of downtown London, near the Whitechapel district, the epicenter of the London immigrant community. In addition to its dense Jewish population, Whitechapel was also noteworthy as the scene of the murders ascribed to Jack the Ripper, a figure often represented in newspaper stories and sketches as an Eastern Jew (Gilman 156–160). Further marking Carfax and Dracula's other lairs as Jewish residences is their foul smell. The laborer who delivers Dracula's boxes to Carfax tells Jonathan Harker that one "might 'ave smelled ole Jerusalem in it" (*D* 276). When the Crew subsequently enter the estate in search of the Count, they encounter a "malodorous air" (*D* 302). Even upon stepping into the Count's upscale digs in Piccadilly, Godalming remarks; "The place smells so vilely" (*D* 356).

The Count himself is also markedly Jewish in appearance. Stoker, it should be remembered, was a practitioner of the pseudoscience of physiognomy. According to David Glover, Stoker "regarded physiognomy as an eminently practical form of knowledge, and there are countless references to it scattered throughout his work." Stoker owned a rare five-volume quarto edition of Johann Caspar Lavater's 1789 work *Essays on Physiognomy,* "the book which more than any other had been responsible for the modern revival of this age-old set of beliefs" (*Vampires, Mummies, and Liberals* 71–72). Furthermore, Glover suggests that Stoker was familiar with the nineteenth-century theory of "ethnological physiognomies," which posited that "social identities were [. . .] plainly readable from appearances" and that these "appearances could be used as data from which to extrapolate judgments as to a nation's social and moral well-being" ("Bram Stoker and the Crises of the Liberal Subject" 988–990).

Stoker's fascination with physiognomy appears early on in *Dracula* when Jonathan Harker first meets the Count. Describing Dracula's "very marked physiognomy," Harker records that his face was a strong—a very strong—aquiline, with high bridge of the thin nose and peculiarly arched nostrils; with lofty domed forehead, and hair growing scantily round the temples, but profusely elsewhere. His eyebrows were very massive, almost meeting over the nose, and with bushy hair that seemed to curl in its own profusion. The mouth [. . .] was fixed and rather cruel-looking, with peculiarly sharp white teeth; these protruded over the lips [. . .] [*D* 25].

Harker also cannot help but notice that the Count's "breath was rank" (*D* 26). Additionally, when Harker looks upon Dracula's hands, he is surprised to see that "there were hairs in the center of the palm" (*D* 25). Wolf, in a footnote to this passage, suggests that Dracula's hairy palms affiliate him "with the standard nineteenth-century image of the masturbator." This figure, argues George Mosse, was thought to be akin to "those infected with venereal disease," people who were "pale, hollow-eyed, weak of body and spirit," common stereotypes of the pestilential Jew in the popular imagination (*Nationalism and Sexuality* 11).

According to Judith Halberstam, the description of Dracula bears an unmistakable resemblance to "both other fictional Jews in the nineteenth century and to the Jew as described by the anti-Semitic literature of the time" (*Parasites and Perverts* 122). Corroborating Halberstam's contention, Zanger details a host of similarities occurring between Svengali and Dracula:

> Both figures are aliens among us, and both move from the East [. . .] to the innocent West on missions of corruption. Both are shown possessing supernatural powers of control. Both are physically very like one another [. . .]. In addition to their physical similarities, both are repeatedly linked literally or metaphorically to non-human creatures [. . .] [35].

Among their "supernatural powers of control" is the ability to manipulate the sexual appetites of women. Thus Sander Gilman sees Dracula as a "seducer" and his victims as the "embodiment of the degenerate and diseased female," the prostitute (160). Because it was assumed that Jack the Ripper was "the victim of the prostitute, the syphilitic male, so too were the Jews closely identified with sexually transmitted disease" (163). Not surprisingly, then, after she is assaulted (seduced?) by Dracula, Mina screams "Unclean, unclean! I must touch [Jonathan] or kiss him no more" (*D* 339). Later, when Van Helsing touches the Host to her forehead, she is left with a mark, similar to the syphilis victim's ulcerous skin eruptions, and screams again "Unclean! Unclean! Even the Almighty shuns my polluted flesh!" (*D* 353). The image of the Jew and the prostitute intertwine with respect to money as well as disease.

Gilman suggests that Victorians perceived a monetary relationship between the Jew and the prostitute, for the two "both seek money as a substitute for higher values, for love and beauty." Jews were further thought to treat "money as if it were alive, as if it were a sexual object" (163). Remarkably, here Gilman is describing Moretti and Halberstam's "anti-capitalist" aristocrat. Appropriately, Halberstam suggests that the Count "fits in with the popularly received image of the Jew as the friend to aristocracy" (*Parasites and Perverts* 122) while Zanger contends that to the Victorian conception of the "Jew as Ritual Murderer or as Anti-Christ" the image of "the Jew as Usurer, as Miser" should be added (40). The image of the Count is therefore also in keeping with the rapacious Jewish bankers and money lenders described by William Russell, George Stoker, and, it should be recalled, Bram Stoker himself in *Reminiscences of Henry Irving*. In Dracula, then, coalesces the multiple anti-Semitic notions of the Jew as a "blood-sucker [who] drains health and wealth, [and] feeds on lives and labor" (Halberstam, *Parasites and Perverts* 132).

In his 1908 essay "The Censorship of Fiction," which appeared in *The Nineteenth Century*, Stoker asks

Are we or are we not ultimately to allow fiction to be put forth without any form of restraint whatsoever? The question is not merely a civic or a national one. It is racial, all-embracing, human [qtd. in Halberstam, *Parasites and Perverts* 115].

Although he was an author whose own fortunes rested on the discretion of the "blue pencils" of the Lord Chamberlains Office (Belford 271), Stoker nonetheless saw fit to encourage censorship as a safeguard of the nation's racial inheritance. Residing in a city home to "more Jews than Palestine" (Belford 91), Stoker was quite conscious of the anti-Semitic literature directed toward the new immigrants in London's East End. That he subscribed to the notions of Sherard, Foster, Banister, and others of the same ilk is likewise clear. In an introduction Stoker wrote for a 1901 Icelandic translation of *Dracula*, he "hints at a connection between the vampire killings and the Whitechapel murders of 1888" (Belford 227). Stoker writes,

This series of crimes has not yet passed from the memory—a series of crimes which appear to have originated from the same source, and which at that time created as much repugnance in people everywhere as the notorious murders of Jacob the disemboweller [Jack the Ripper], which came into the story a little later [*Dracula Unearthed* 25].

Thus in the figure of Dracula, Stoker combines Victorian fears of the dangerous, pestilential Jewish immigrant, an image that also calls to mind the loathsome aristocrat of Eastern Europe and Russia. The novel does much more than just distill these anxieties in a fictional menace, however. Rather, it provides a mechanism for restoring "cultural order" (Croley 85) and of reasserting the "'natural' superiority of Englishmen over the 'lesser' races" (Spencer 218) of Eastern Europe. As I will next elaborate, one way in which the novel asserts this superiority is by transforming Britain's failures in the East in 1856 into signal victories.

Crimea Redux: An English Triumph in the East

The 1890s marked the "zenith of European imperial expansion" (Schmitt 30). In England, leading voices in government and commerce promoted the "doctrine of unlimited expansionism as justified by racial superiority, manifest destiny and divine mission" (Garnett 33). Shortly after the publication of *Dracula* in 1897, an expedition under the command of General Horatio Kitchener invaded the Sudan to revenge the death of General Gordon at Khartoum (*Columbia History* 930). By 1898, Gordon's killer had been "finally and ruthlessly crushed by Kitchener," the Sudan fully incorporated into the empire, and the honor of the nation restored (H. C. G. Matthew 508). *Dracula* performs much the same feat. Although English forces failed to effectively blunt the imperial designs of its chief imperial rival with the ease they dispatched poorly armed primitives, the novel may be seen to restore the prestige lost during the Crimean War by wreaking, at least in fiction, the nation's revenge on Russia and her Balkan allies. The novel thus operates much like what Wolfgang Schivelbusch calls a loser's myth. These myths,

> arising from frustrated desires for revenge, are the psychological mechanisms for coming to terms with defeat. Moreover, they are not merely neurotic fictions of the imagination but also healthful protective shields or buffer zones—emotional fortresses—against a reality unbearable to the psyche. Their function can be compared to the coagulation of blood and formation of scabs necessary for wounds to heal, or to the convalescent world of the sanatorium, or lastly (Freud's analogy) to the "reservations" or "natural reserves" in the industrial landscape [26].

As does Sylvester Stallone in the *Rambo* franchise and Chuck Norris in *Missing in Action*, Jonathan Harker and his colleagues assuage national pride and exorcise the social anxieties troubling Victorian society by returning a British force to the Black Sea and Balkans. David Glover, employing the language of the Vietnam war, makes much the same point:

With everyone armed to the teeth, the campaign against the vampire ends in true imperial style with a paramilitary raid, a search and destroy mission into the heart of Transylvania. Beneath the Gothic wrapping lies a tale of buccaneering, an adventure story to raise the cheer of civilians in which the *unheimlich* terrors of home are expelled and then quelled on foreign soil [97].

From the very beginning Jonathan Harker functions as an agent of England's commercial empire. His initial trip to Castle Dracula is, for me, something approximating a reconnaissance mission. What makes Jonathan ideal for this task is that like the famous Green Berets of Vietnam lore, he is one of the best and the brightest. As Troy Boone notes, Jonathan "represents rational English masculinity" (78) because he is at one and the same time "a good specimen of manhood" and a "businesslike gentleman" (*D* 273), the perfect emissary of the middle class. As would any professional commando, he makes a "search among the books and maps" in the British Museum "regarding Transylvania" (*D* 2–3) before departing. However, to his unmistakable disappointment, no "Ordnance Survey" map—"a military map showing the topography of a terrain," according to Wolf—exists for the region (*D* 3). Like the colonial explorer of his time, he is forced to chart a dark region as he goes in preparation for future consolidation.

Alluding to the cultural theories of Edward Said, Cannon Schmitt suggests that Harker "orientalizes eastern Europe" as he travels to Castle Dracula (27). Said argues that the Orient has, among other things, been "the place of Europe's greatest and richest and oldest colonies" and at the same time "one of its deepest and most recurring images of the Other" (*Orientalism* 1). As a place of difference, otherness, the Orient became in the European psyche a likely site "of domination, of varying degrees of a complex hegemony" (*Orientalism* 5).[29] Notions of empire, Said further demands, were popularized by "nearly every nineteenth-century writer" (*Orientalism* 14). I would add Stoker to that list, and I would argue, much as does David Seed, that as Jonathan

Harker travels East, he "constantly tries to normalize the strange into the discourse of the nineteenth-century travelogue" (197) and thereby appropriate it for England. His observations during this first journey out to the East reveal his "Orientalist" (Arata 635), imperialist, tourist perspective, for they provide manifest proof of deeply-held ethnic and cultural prejudices, very much like those evidenced by George Stoker in *With the Unspeakables*.

According to Belford, Stoker never journeyed further east than Vienna (220). She further suggests that the background material for the opening chapters of *Dracula* comes almost exclusively from George Stoker's descriptions of Bulgaria and Turkey (128). David Glover agrees, asserting that "one of several sources for Stoker's descriptions of people and places in *Dracula*" is his brother's book, where Bram found

> the men with their enormous black moustaches and traditional peasant dress consisting of wide baggy trousers and white homespun shirts; the packs of wolves coming down from the hills to terrorize the villagers; and the difficult journeys across snow-clad mountains through precipitous gorges and dangerous ravines [*Vampires, Mummies, and Liberals* 33].

Manifesting his Orientalist attitude toward Eastern Europe, early in chapter one Harker remarks contemptuously "that the further East you go the more unpunctual are the trains. What ought they to be in China?" (*D* 4–5). George, in comparison, has this to say of the trains in Bulgaria:

> The journey by railway from Constantinople to Adrianople occupies about eleven hours, but it might easily be done in half the time; the train only goes about ten miles per hour. The line is badly constructed, and would fall a [*sic*] to bits if it was too much shaken [20].

The Slav natives Harker meets along the way to the castle likewise incur his disdain:

The women looked pretty, except when you got near them, but they were very clumsy about the waist. They had full white sleeves of some kind or other, and the most of them had big belts with a lot of strips of something fluttering from them like the dresses in a ballet [. . .]. The strangest figures we saw were the Slovaks, who are more barbarian than the rest [. . .]. They are very picturesque, but do not look prepossessing. On the stage they would be set down at once as some old Oriental band of brigands [*D* 5].

Moreover, among the unprepossessing Slovaks he notices, with requisite revulsion, that "goitre was painfully prevalent" (*D* 12). The Slavic peasant women here bear striking resemblances to the Bulgarian women described by George Stoker—the women wear "sukhman," highly embroidered dresses complete with "a silver waist-belt, white stockings, and coloured slippers" (*With the Unspeakables* 9). The Slovak men, on the other hand, virtually replicate George's description of the Zeibecks of Asia Minor, who "are great robbers and scoundrels, but are very finely built and extremely handsome men" (*With the Unspeakables* 67).

Most of the accounts Harker gives of the flora, fauna, and topography of the Carpathians are also strikingly similar to what George describes in *With the Unspeakables*. In his ascent to the castle, Harker passes through "an endless perspective of jagged rock and pointed crags"; the "mighty rifts" between the mountains afford a glimpse of "the white gleam of falling water"; and the roadside is dotted with "oak, beech, and pine" (*D* 12–13). On a journey to Bazardjick, a Bulgarian village "4,000 feet" up in the Balkan Mountains, George records a similar scene:

> The road or path that leads to it is a most picturesque but excessively difficult one. It follows the course of a mountain torrent which you are obliged to cross no less than seventeen times. Nothing can exceed the wildness of the scenery. The gorge through which the torrent rushes is shaded by overhanging trees, which grow out of the cliffs on either side, and on a hot day form a most agreeable shade [*With the Unspeakables* 40].

Only later does George reveal that the trees he mentions are none other than the beech and oak (58). Finally, whenever he draws near the Count's castle, Harker encounters ferocious wolves (*D* 17, 65, 439): George might well have supplied Bram with this idea as well, for he recounts an incident of wolves which "had been driven down from the higher mountains by the excessive cold, and were committing sad ravages amongst the scanty herds of the villagers" and amongst the inhabitants themselves in one Bulgarian village (*With the Unspeakables* 45).

As a "scientific, sceptical, matter-of-fact nineteenth-century" traveler (*D* 289), Harker dismisses his carriage mates' warnings about his destination and the strange behavior of the wolves as mere superstition and fancy. However, despite all of his apparent superiority, Harker still falls victim to the Count, the evil of the East. Dracula imprisons him, impersonates him, and eventually leaves him to be the plaything—dare I say blood bank—of three vampiric women. Nonetheless, through pluck, daring, and English determination, he escapes the castle and somehow makes his way to "Buda-Pesth" (*D* 131). After recuperating in a Catholic run hospital, he and Wilhelmina Murray are married there by "the chaplain of the English mission church" (*D* 139).

Harker's finding asylum in Hungary and his subsequent marriage are especially significant. First of all, in an illustration of English chauvinism, their marriage can be solemnized only in the presence of an English clergyman, not a European Catholic. Secondly, though not the equals of their English patient and spouse, the Hungarians are nonetheless acceptable, worthy hosts. In articles featured in the English press just before and during the Crimean War, Kossuth had substantiated Russian brutalities among the Hungarians in 1848 thereby attracting the sympathy of the public and the government. Hungary was therefore viewed as a potential ally against Russia, and by giving Harker asylum and nursing him back to health, the sisters exemplify Hungarian support of English aggression against Russia. The Hungarians even provide the necessary military intelligence required to defeat the Count. It is from Van Helsing's colleague, "Arminius of Buda-Pesth

University," that the Crew learns of Dracula's past, habits, and abilities (*D* 291).

Armed with the intelligence supplied by Arminius and the scouting report of Jonathan Harker, the Crew sets out to capture and execute the Count, who, only appropriately, has retreated from English soil on a ship named the "Czarina Catherine," embarked for, where else, Varna (*D* 375). In strictly military fashion, the Crew formulates a "Plan of Campaign" and provisions themselves "with Winchesters," the most advanced weapon of its day, proven highly effective in subduing savages in the American West (*D* 383). Quincey Morris, who recommends the use of Winchesters, knows from experience the need for such weapons when confronting the Russians. He and Godalming, it turns out, had confronted a Russian foe previously in "Tobolsk," a city in western Siberia, without the benefit of modern weapons (*D* 383). The mention of Winchesters also brings to mind one of the few successes of the Crimean War, the Minie rifle carried by British and French troops. Unlike the highly inaccurate smooth-bore muskets of the Russians with an effective range of only 100 yards, the Minie rifle was deadly up to 1,000 yards (Norman Rich 126).

As the Crew follows the Count's route of retreat, they retrace in almost every particular the path taken by British forces in the advance on and withdrawal from the Crimea, a route that George Stoker also follows in 1877. As in the Crimea, then, their assault begins with an occupation of Varna,[30] where they take rooms at the hotel "Odessus," named after the Russian port of Odessa and, I believe, a symbol of Russian interests in Bulgaria[31] (*D* 393). By means of bribery—it seems that Bram's Bulgarians are no less corrupt than those described by George—they discover that Dracula has moved on in the night. But thanks to telegraphic surveillance provided by Lloyd's of London, they learn that the Count has disembarked at Galatz, modern day Galati, a Romanian Black Sea port located near the confluence of the Seret and Pruth rivers, in the disputed region of Bessarabia (*D* 398). It should be noted here that whereas such technological innovations as the telegraph, Kodak, and steamship failed to insure an English victory in 1856, in *Dracula* they guarantee triumph.

At Galatz a group that evokes images of Russia comes to the Count's assistance. One Immanuel Hildesheim,[32] "a Hebrew of rather the Adelphi Theatre type," a Petrof Skinsky, and a party of "Slovaks" take possession of Dracula's box for transshipment up the Seret to the castle (*D* 412–413). Later, the Count's Szgany join the expedition. Realizing that they face a "strong and rough" though inferior opponent, the Crew adds to their "small arsenal" a steam launch and a team of horses (*D* 418–420). In the manner of combined naval and ground forces, Jonathan and Godalming pursue on water while Quincey and Dr. Seward follow the Count's entourage on horseback. Overseeing the operation as would a command staff, Mina and Van Helsing set up an observation point overlooking the battlefield (*D* 439–440).

As the Crew approaches the castle, a heavy snow commences to fall, prompting Seward to worry that they may be forced to find sledges and proceed "Russian fashion" (*D* 424). When the battle is finally joined, it is set against a frigid landscape resembling combat around Sebastopol in the winter of 1855 described by Russell. The four combatants advance on foot toward the Count's party, who have "formed round the cart in a sort of undisciplined" perimeter. Jonathan Harker boldly dashes into their midst, heedless of possible injury. However, no harm befalls him, for before a determined Englishman, the undisciplined Slavs "cowered aside and let him pass." While Godalming and Seward provide cover with their Winchesters, Jonathan severs the Count's head with his Kukri knife as Quincey plunges a bowie knife into his heart (*D* 442–443). Thus, Dracula dies from wounds inflicted by imperial warriors wielding what Arata terms "weapons of empire" (641).[33]

Though victory is theirs, the Crew's triumph is not without cost. While fighting his way through the ring of Szgany protecting Dracula, Quincey Morris is fatally wounded. Yet even in the midst of his death throes, Quincey musters the strength to utter, "I am only too happy to have been of service!" before expiring in Jonathan's arms, ever the "gallant gentleman," as Mina observes (*D* 444). Quincey's death removes, according to Glover, the "implicit dangers of interimperial rivalry," insuring that the fruits of imperial conquest accrue solely to England (*Vampires, Mummies, and Liberals* 94). Quincey's ultimate act of "service" also guarantees that credit for Dracula's defeat rests with the professional members of the Crew, demonstrating that their skills take precedence over what Daly terms the superannuated "heroic amateur values" of the wealthy American adventurer (39). Daly further opines that Quincey's death is necessary to maintain the "homosocial arrangement of the text," to obliterate any suggestion of sexual deviance, the penetration of man by man, that would call into question the professional, patriarchal, middle-class credentials of the Crew (40).[34]

With the Count's death, "his threat to the progress of Western civilization [is] brought to an end" (Wasson 23), and put back into the bottle with the genie are the anxieties he produced in Victorian society. Erased are the threats posed by the revenant aristocrat and his feudalistic economy; the pernicious, disease-ridden Yid; the tyrannical, despotic czar; and, closer to home, the independent, sexually assertive New Woman. Mina Harker is saved from the contagion which doomed Lucy Westenra because unlike Lucy—who in typically New Woman fashion once asked Mina "Why can't they let a girl marry three men, or as many as want her, and save all this trouble?" (*D* 78)—she renounces independence and fights against the Count's seduction. As Carol Senf has shown, Mina thus represents the "traditional kind of woman" ("Stoker's Response to the New Woman" 37) preferred by Victorian men.

Recognizing that she is but "a poor weak woman" (*D* 390), Mina puts her fate in the hands of men who are "so earnest, so true, and so brave" (*D* 420), the same men who ruthlessly killed an unrepentant Lucy. Because she has a practical "man's brain" (284) and thus knows her place in Victorian society,[35] Mina willingly accepts a subservient position as the secretary for the Crew, helping her husband while remaining "supportively in the background,"[36] and after the battle, she assumes a "woman's traditional role as a mother" (Senf 46). Mina may also be seen to contrast markedly with Florence Nightingale, who waged a "war against medical men" (Poovey 192). Stoker could very well have had Florence Nightingale in mind when he created Mina. For some years, Stoker had endured a loveless relationship with his wife Florence, named after the Crimean heroine. Indifferent to the demands of decorum, Florence went about London with "any number of fascinating escorts" during her husband's frequent absences (Belford 121). Moreover, according to Farson, Florence's "frigidity" after the birth of their son Noel "drove [Stoker] to other women" (234). The dutiful, devoted Mina therefore provided an antidote to the New Woman encoded in the image of Florence Nightingale.

It seems fitting that the novel closes with a note from Jonathan Harker reporting a recent return visit to Transylvania and the birth of their son Quincey, named for all of the Crew.[37] Sounding very much like an old veteran reminiscing over the battlefields of his youth, Harker writes

> we made a journey to Transylvania, and went over the old ground which was, and is, to us so full of vivid and terrible memories. It was almost impossible to believe the things which we had seen with our own eyes and heard with our own ears were living truths. Every trace of all that had been was blotted out. The castle stood as before, reared high above a waste of desolation [D 444].

The old wrong has been redressed, and English pride has been restored at the expense of Russia and her Balkan allies. Moreover, the castle and its environs are now a safe haven for tourists because what Jonathan had once described as "a whole world of dark and dreadful things" (D 422) has been pacified. In terms of what Paul Rich identifies as the "ideology of racial improvement in colonies of white settlement," the Count's homeland is thus potentially a fit "rural and pastoral" site for the "regeneration of a race that was undergoing deterioration in the imperial metropolis itself as cities and industrial conglomerations destroyed the old idea of England as a green landscape" (14–15). Impressions of the countryside that Mina records shortly before the battle suggest just such an underlying intention:

> The country is lovely, and most interesting; if only we were under different conditions, how delightful it would be to see it all. If Jonathan and I were driving through it alone what a pleasure it would be. To stop and see people, and learn something of their life, and to fill our minds and memories with all the colour and picturesqueness of the whole wild, beautiful country and the quaint people! [*D* 424].

Glover further asserts that the novel, published just as "Britain was moving into its last brief climactic imperialist phase," responds to theories of social and cultural degeneration popular at the time, to the concern that an advanced civilization is increasingly incapable of producing "the heroes it needs" to maintain the empire (97). In *Dracula*, at least, Stoker affirms that it can. And, twelve years after the publication of *Dracula*, in his next vampire novel, *The Lady of the Shroud*, Stoker will reiterate his vision of a vital empire when another set of indomitable British subjects once again defeat an Eastern menace and plant a British colony in the Balkans.

From *Bram Stoker and Russophobia: Evidence of the British Fear of Russia in "Dracula" and "The Lady of the Shroud"* (Jefferson, N.C.: McFarland & Company, Inc.): 118-149. Copyright © McFarland & Company, Inc. Reprinted by permission of McFarland & Company, Inc.

Notes

1. In the interview with Jane Stoddard, Stoker singles out two of his most useful sources: "I learned a good deal from E. Gerard's 'Essays on Roumanian Superstitions,' which first appeared in *The Nineteenth Century*, and were afterwards published in a couple of volumes. I also learned something from Mr. Barin-Gould's 'Were-Wolves.'"

2. According to McNally and Florescu, when Stoker was twelve, the union of Mol-

davia and Wallachia as part of a greater Romania occasioned a great deal of publicity in Britain. They contend that this event "was probably his initial introduction to that mysterious part of Europe" (137).

3. Bruce Haley draws attention to the emergence in nineteenth century England of the "'Viking or Berserker' ideal" that grew out of the practice of muscular Christianity. Perhaps the finest expression of this vision in print was Charles Kingsley's 1866 novel *Hereward*, whose title character is a "muscular wonder" and "also Christian" (217). He is "stronger, cannier, and superficially nobler" and less "decadent" than the "Normans, Franks, or Frisians" (218–219) that he battles. David Glover also points out that "Stoker often gives his heroes some kind of Viking genealogy," but draws a distinct difference between the Count and the "moral Viking" Quincey Morris. Quincey earns the appellation of "moral Viking" as opposed to "berserker" because, unlike the primitive Dracula, he understands the need for civilized self-restraint in the midst of adversity: "To bear oneself like 'a moral Viking' is precisely to display a measure of self-control conspicuously absent among those bellicose peoples who have not yet evolved out of the past. In short, the sublimation of human aggression requires the right combination of birth and upbringing if the march of human progress is to continue" (*Vampires, Mummies, and Liberals* 74).

4. Wilkinson observes that descendants from the original Slavs "went to the lower part of Dacia lying between the rivers Olt and Danube, where they fixed their habitations. They formed themselves into a nation, and chose for their chief one Bessarabba [. . .]. Their general system, however, consisted in making war against the Romans of the lower empire, in which they were seconded by the Slaves and Bulgarians of Maesie, whom they looked upon as their natural allies" (qtd. in Leatherdale, *The Origins of Dracula* 92–93).

5. Elizabeth Miller, echoing Clive Leatherdale, categorically refutes the assumption, advanced most famously by McNally and Florescu, that Vlad Tepes (aka Vlad the Impaler) was Stoker's model for Count Dracula. In *Dracula: Sense and Nonsense*, she writes, "To state this as fact is irresponsible. All we know for certain is that Stoker borrowed the name 'Dracula' and a few scraps of miscellaneous information about Wallachian history from William Wilkinson's *An Account of Wallachia and Moldavia* (1820). Out of such a mole-hill, mountains have emerged" (180).

As with her refutation of Vambery's pivotal influence on Stoker in crafting the Count, Miller rests her argument on the absence of any reference to Vlad Tepes or Vlad the Impaler in Stoker's working notes for the novel.

6. The illustrators at *Punch* would scarcely have known of this fact, but their repeated depictions of the czar adorned with the wings of a bat suggests at least the possibility that in the popular imagination, vampires, bats, and Russians might well have been lumped together.

7. McNally and Florescu contend that when Stoker read Joseph Sheridan Le Fanu's novel *Carmilla* in the 1870s, "he began thinking about writing his own Vampire tale." Additionally, they remark that "Le Fanu's description of how a person becomes a vampire is also based upon folk belief in Eastern Europe" (139).

8. Clive Leatherdale in the introduction to his definitive annotated edition of the novel, *Dracula Unearthed*, contends that of "all the popular misconceptions surround-

ing Dracula, none seems more entrenched as the idea that 'Dracula's Guest' is the excised opening chapter" (14). He rests his argument on the differences in the styles, narration, and characterization of Jonathan Harker between the two works. Leatherdale believes that "Dracula's Guest" was originally intended to be one in a set of three scenes taking place in Munich during Harker's trip east. Its excision from the final published novel means that it "fell under the author's or editor's axe," most likely the later, for "whole chunks of the early part of the novel were removed at a very late stage, after the manuscript had been submitted to the London publishers" (15).

9. Jean Chothia, in her introduction to *The New Woman and Other Emancipated Woman Plays*, describes the typical reaction in the press to the New Woman: "Throughout the 1890s, *Punch* both reflected and considerably shaped the habit of addressing female emancipation and educational success as subjects for glorious mirth, while, in September 1894, *The Idler* ran an Advanced Woman number with advice on how to court such creatures and invited eight women of different persuasions to comment on the species. Although much of the humour might seem feeble now, its omnipresence suggests that it answered a need" (x).

10. Clive Leatherdale posits that "Dracula's choice of alias has delicious irony, since the first five letters spell 'Devil.'" He goes on to state that Dracula "presumably reasons that, like Arthur, his title opens more doors than it closes" (*Dracula Unearthed* 375).

11. According to Nicholas Daly, Van Helsing is the embodiment of the new middle-class professional: "Van Helsing is the professional ne plus ultra [. . .]. In addition to his qualifications as a doctor and a scientist, we also learn he is a qualified lawyer [. . .]. Thus it is that this super-professional is the natural leader of this new social group composed largely of professional men" (39).

12. Daly argues that works such as *Dracula* should be "termed popular *middle-class* fiction, insofar as it was produced by, broadly speaking, middle-class writers for a middle-class reading public" (5). He further believes that the novel as well as its brethren "embodies the fantasies of this emerging professional group, whose power is based on their access and control of certain forms of knowledge" (8).

13. Of Holmwood, Daly writes, he "is the team's equivalent for the 'Sir John Paxton, the president of the Incorporated Law Society' who appears by proxy at Hawkin's funeral: his presence confers a suitable air of dignity and respectability on the business in which he is engaged, in this case the hunting of Dracula" (38).

14. Dracula, in Daly's thinking, threatens the corporate heroes of the novel because he represents "archaic or traditional individualism" that is at odds with "the emergence of monopoly capital, in the specific form that takes in the professional monopolies." The novel, he suggests, should be read to promote "the professional ideology of the self-regulating organization of experts, but also the more general collectivist ethos of the late nineteenth century" (43–45).

15. Both Leatherdale (419) and Wolf (364) note that the Kukri knife is the weapon of choice of the Gurkhas of Nepal, the most trustworthy and ferocious native troops in the imperial British army in India. Not only does the use of a Kukri knife reinforce the imperial overtones of the novel, but it also may be seen to signify the importance of India, described to no small extent by Vambery, in the British economy.

16. Jani Scandura argues that Dracula might also be said to resemble an undertaker, a marginalized professional often lumped in with "Jews and 'sexual inverts'": "The undertaker, as embalmer, literally sucks blood from the vessels of corpses, literally creates a corpse resistant to decay, literally obscures distasteful signs of death. And he survives on 'blood money,' income garnered by this pursuit. Gothic, androgynous, parasitic, the undertaker is a vampire without metaphoric disguise" (10).

The unsavory aspects of the profession do not solely make it repellent to other middle-class professionals, but, as Scandura writes, it is that the undertaker "represents a socially and economically aspiring Other who scales the slippery façade of free enterprise, an Other whom members of the established bourgeoisie cannot readily distinguish from themselves" (26).

17. Daly wryly notes that contemporary readers may find it "easy to smile at this . . . overdetermined reading," one "which tells us more about cold-war America than about Stoker's novel" (34).

18. In *Dracula Unearthed*, Clive Leatherdale notes that "Purfleet at the time was dotted with worn-out chalk quarries and the riverside was dominated by huge gunpowder magazines housed in reinforced silos. This high-security government arsenal, with attendant barracks, presented an ominous spectacle from the river, but provided work for much of the local population" (59–60).

19. In the two-volume *Medical and Surgical History of the British Army Which Served in Turkey and the Crimea During the War Against Russia in the Years 1854–55–56*, produced on order of Queen Victoria by Andrew Smith, Director-General of the Army Medical Department, and presented to both houses of parliament in May of 1858, Varna is prominently mentioned as a site where "Diarrhoea acquired considerable prevalence, Cholera soon appeared, and committed great ravages, and Fever and Dysentery were diseases of common occurrence" (1: 1).

20. According to Belford, Stoker was especially fearful of the disease because as a child he had often heard the gruesome tales of the cholera epidemic that swept through his mother's hometown of Sligo in 1832 (18).

21. In 1956, Bacil F. Kirtley posited that the original source for Dracula was the fifteenth-century Wallachian ruler Vlad Tsepesh. Kirtley bases this belief on parallels existing between Van Helsing's descriptions of Dracula and those of Vlad Tsepesh found in a little-know[n] monastic manuscript. Kirtley notes that in "the monastery at Kirill-Belozersk, in northern Russia near the Finnish border, was found a manuscript which dates from the year 1490 and which is a copy of a document originally penned in 1486. The manuscript relates the story of Dracula (Rumanian for 'devil'), which is the name bestowed in horror by monkish chroniclers upon Vlad Tsepesh, Governor of Wallachia from the years 1456–1462 and again in the year 1476. The material of the Kirill-Belozersk manuscript was widely circulated among the monasteries of the Eastern Slavs, and by the middle of the 16th century had reached as far as Germany, a fact attested by the appearance of the Dracula story in the vernacular edition of Sebastian Munster's *Cosmographia universa* in 1541 (Latin edition, 1550)" (13).

Vlad Tsepesh's title as governor was "Voivod of Wallachia" (14). Also of interest is the fact that in *The Lady of the Shroud*, the narrator, Rupert Sent Leger, journeys to the

Balkans to assist the ruler of the Land of the Blue Mountains, the Voivode Peter Vissarion.

22. According to Leatherdale, Stoker's working notes reveal that he took all five names from tombstones at Whitby (*Dracula Unearthed* 120).

23. In *The Struggle for Asia: 1828–1914*, David Gillard describes actions considered and taken by the British and the French in the Baltic in preparation for a strategic assault on St. Petersburg. These included a planned blockade of the Gulf of Finland that would preclude "some thirty Russian ships of the line from commerce raiding in the North Sea" and induce the Russians to shift forces away from the Black Sea theater of operations. In preparation for this move, British and French forces bombarded the Aaland Islands and "Sveaborg, in the Gulf of Finland" (92).

24. Leatherdale notes that Russia had no consulate in Whitby and that Baltic trade with London was conducted through an office in London (*Dracula Unearthed* 140). In a footnote a few pages later, he explains why Stoker, who was usually quite fastidious about such details, contrived a Russian consular in Whitby: "Stoker needs a Russian-speaker in Whitby, otherwise the captain's log would not be translated. The Russian consul employs a clerk, who lends his services to the press and doubtless puts a pro-Russian slant on his translation. Russian ships, Russian log, part-Russian crew, Russian consuls and clerks. The Russian subtext in *Dracula* is extensive" (142). As regards this study, the last sentence is extraordinarily significant.

25. Warwick writes that the "mother/child relationship is often picked up in the vampire fantasies to focus monstrosity of the women; the children become the victims of their mothers' or other women's infection. Where Dracula concentrates his attention on fully grown adults, the women turn to children" (212).

26. According to Warwick, the "metaphor of venereal disease is consolidated" in *Dracula* "by its origins 'abroad'" in "Eastern Europe" (210).

27. Belford suggests that the parallels between Svengali and Dracula are intentional. In 1890 the Stokers and Du Maurier were vacationing in Whitby at the same time. A *Punch* illustration that year, drawn by Du Maurier and titled "A Filial Reproof," depicts Bram, Florence, and their son, Noel, relaxing at a garden party. Belford notes, "Du Maurier was completing his second novel, *Trilby* (published in 1894), which introduces the mesmerist Svengali, an enduring mythic character to rival Dracula. Surely the two writers had tea at the Spa and discussed their protagonists as the band played softly. Was Dracula born from Svengali, as critic Nina Auerbach suggests, with his powers still further extended over time and space? There are striking parallels between the two novels. Both deal with the fear of female sexuality and the loss of innocence, and with brave men who rescue the mother figure from a foreigner's embrace. Trilby O'Ferrall has three suitors, Taffy, Sandy, and Little Billee; Lucy Westenra also has three. The tone-deaf, weak-willed Trilby becomes a great singer when hypnotized, and Lucy becomes voluptuous when bitten. Both books illustrate the male-bonding novels popular in the late 1880s, novels such as H. Rider Haggard's *King Solomon's Mines* (1885) and Arthur Conan Doyle's *A Study in Scarlet* (1887)" (228).

28. Leatherdale writes that his association "with Jews made Dracula yet more despicable to the average 1890s reader. Stoker was typical of his time when it came to

anti-Semitism, the prevalence of which is observable in Major Johnson's *On the Track of the Crescent*, listed among Stoker's source books" (*Dracula Unearthed* 473–474).

29. Joseph Boone has shown that the Orient, especially the Arab world, became "the psychic screen on which to project fantasies of illicit sexuality and unbridled excess." He also discusses the investigations of Sir Richard Burton, travel writer par excellence and Stoker's friend, into the sexual relations between men in the region. Burton contended that the vice spread east out of its original "Mediterranean 'belt'" to the Far East and the Americas and that it even gained a foothold in "our modern capitals, London, Berlin, and Paris" (93). Although Boone does not draw the connection, it is not untenable to suggest that Burton's ideas regarding the Orient may well have influenced Stoker's depiction of Dracula as both a physical (Jewish-borne blood contagion) and moral (gender inversion and sexual license) threat.

30. George Stoker suggests a triumphal return by England to Varna in the following passage: "It was after dark when we arrived in Varna, and I fear the peaceful inhabitants must have thought another Crimean war was about to commence. An 'Italian from Cor-r-r-k,' who afterwards distinguished himself at Plevna, favoured us with 'The Wearing of the Green;' and to counterbalance the rebellious sentiments therein expressed we all sang, or rather howled, 'God save the Queen'" (*With the Unspeakables* 13).

Not only has Varna been occupied, but a subversive Irishman put in his place as well.

31. Kaplan describes the profound affinity that came to exist between Bulgaria and Russia as a consequence of the Russo-Turkish War: "A Russian army swept through Bulgaria in 1877 and 1878, liberating Bulgaria from Ottoman subjugation in order to create a pro-Russian, Bulgarian buffer state against the Turks. Although the 1878 Treaty of Berlin forced newly independent Bulgaria to cede Thrace and Macedonia back to Turkey—triggering a renewed outbreak of guerrilla war—Bulgarian gratitude to the Russians never entirely dissipated. The Russian liberation was one of the few happy moments in Bulgaria's history since the Middle Ages. Construction of the Aleksandar Nevski Memorial Church began in 1882, to honor the 200,000 Russian soldiers who died during the war" [206–207].

32. Here is another example of the anti-Semitic overtones of the novel. Hildesheim is described as having "a nose like a sheep" (*D* 413). Leatherdale notes that the "nose has always been a cultural indicator of inferiority or barbarity" (*Dracula Unearthed* 473). It should be remembered that Dracula has a similarly large and hooked nose.

33. As with Jonathan's Kukri knife, here is another example of imperial weapons at work, in this instance a weapon made famous by a former British colony and a contemporary ally.

34. Leatherdale echoes this view: "Stoker may have felt uncomfortable at the homoerotic idea of Dracula being phallically staked by men and then writhing and screeching in his orgasmic death-throes" (*Dracula Unearthed* 509).

35. Glover defines Mina's role thusly: "Ironically, it is only by becoming a man that the woman can ever come to deserve parity of esteem or cease to be other than a problem; but one condition of phallic womanhood is that it is almost immediately abandoned for the over-feminized maternal" (*Vampires, Mummies, and Liberals* 97).

36. Daly contends that Mina "may be seen as a soldier in the army of cheap (here,

free) female labor that sustains the group." Although she "resembles a New Woman in her skills," she exhibits "no desire for equality" (40).

37. The choice of the name Quincey signifies, for Glover, a "form of hierogamy which subordinates American energy to the triumph of British breeding" (*Vampires, Mummies, and Liberals* 94).

Vampires, Mummies, and Liberals:
Questions of Character and Modernity_____

David Glover

Indeed, everything comes alive when contradictions accumulate.

Gaston Bachelard[1]

"In obedience to the law as it then stood, he was buried in the centre of a *quadrivium*, or conflux of four roads (in this case four streets), with a stake driven through his heart. And over him drives for ever the uproar of unresting London!"[2] No, not *Dracula* (1897), but the closing lines of a much earlier nineteenth-century work, Thomas De Quincey's bleakly ironic essay "On Murder Considered as One of the Fine Arts" (1854). De Quincey is describing how in 1812 the London populace dealt with the body of one of his prize exhibits, a particularly grisly serial killer who had escaped the gallows by hanging himself in his cell at dead of night. Yet it is difficult for us to read this gleefully chilling passage today without thinking of Bram Stoker's classic vampire novel. The quirky Christian symbolism, the mandatory staking down of the monster to keep it from roaming abroad, the sense of a busily self-absorbed London unaware of its proximity to a murderous presence that haunts its most densely populated byways: together these features seem virtually to define a basic iconography for the vampire Gothic as it achieved canonical status in *Dracula*.

In the half-century that separated Stoker from De Quincey the punitive assumptions behind the old suicide laws may have become little more than a barbaric memory, but the subsequent attempts to view suicide medically as mental illness, redefining it as an instance of "moral insanity," offered no easily civilizing consolation. Thus what unites these two otherwise historically distinct writers is their menacing use of the buried past to interrogate the present. In Stoker's work the twin poles of past and present make their appearance through a strangely paradoxical and crucially modern trope, that of the spectator forced to confront a horror whose very existence seems to compromise any possibility of securing the line between the modern and the premodern. This troubling of modernity's own historical self-consciousness is perhaps especially marked in *Dracula*, which comes replete with the latest in late-Victorian consumer goods, many of which function as a means of recording the structure of appearances and hence permit a precise memorializing of the past: cameras, phonographs, and portable typewriters. "It is nineteenth century up-to-date with a vengeance," as one of Stoker's characters so aptly puts it (*Dracula*, 49).

At the same time, in *Dracula* the past extends across space into those zones of arrested development which modernity has not fully reached, where the trains do not yet run on schedule or where the railway lines have come to an abrupt halt. Though no farther from home than a rural Hampstead churchyard, it can be profoundly "humanising" to gaze upon the lights of London and to hear "the muffled roar that marks the life of a great city," despite the knowledge that the capital is simultaneously a site of depravity and danger (*Dracula*, 251). For the routes of communication out of the metropolis may also bring terrifyingly archaic elements back into it, as in that eerie moment when Count Dracula is seen hailing a hansom cab near Hyde Park or when, in *The Jewel of Seven Stars* (1903), the presence of an ancient Egyptian mummy in a house in Notting Hill begins to have strange effects upon everyone who comes into contact with it. Such frightful encounters are imagined as tests of character in Stoker's supernatural romances, moments of truth that will purge the self of its secret weaknesses, ascertaining a person's intrinsic worth in the face of a plethora of social and psychic complications and providing a center of stability in a dangerous world of flux. Hall Caine, the novelist and dedicatee of *Dracula*, once defended the genre of romance as a type of writing that shows "what brave things human nature is capable of at its best."[3] But in Stoker's work, the protagonists are forced to confront their worst, before they can really know what their best might be.

If tests of character are endemic to modern adventure narratives,

Stoker's Gothic novels mark a growing sense of difficulty with the notion of "character" itself, a term that was intimately linked to late-Victorian views of modernity. At its most straightforward, "character" designated the self-reliant private individual whose ability to take control of his (quintessentially his) own destiny was the cynosure of social and national progress. This was the brand of individualism espoused by moralists like Samuel Smiles, for whom the display of character was proof that one was living a truly dutiful life. At the same time, in the language of politics, character indicated the rational citizen, the individual property owner of classical liberalism who, by Gladstone's era, was increasingly expected to rise above his own narrow self-interest. What united these different emphases was the belief that character was essentially a function of human willpower, a disciplined effort called into play by the idiosyncrasies of the self and the vagaries of one's situation.

But it was never entirely clear to what extent character was the product of circumstances not of our own choosing. Thus John Stuart Mill, whose *On Liberty* (1859) was the finest defense of the sovereignty of the individual, was also a proponent of "ethology" or "the science of the formation of character."[4] The antinomies of Mill's philosophy are a reminder that throughout the nineteenth century we find arguments in favor of free will and determinism side by side, frequently operating within the same body of thought. Not surprisingly, these inner contradictions helped to make character a thoroughly protean concept, whose meaning could shift radically as it came into contact with newly emergent or smartly revamped systems of knowledge. From the 1880s onward, the assault on the autonomy of the individual subject in fields as various as scientific physiognomy, degenerationism, mental physiology, criminal anthropology, and "psychical research" made the classic liberal idea of character as individual self-mastery harder and harder to sustain. As a corollary, this classic idea began to disappear from liberal political theory during the same period, to be replaced by a new view of character which justified state intervention to actively promote the ideal of individual self-fulfillment by removing the social and material barriers to its realization.[5] For with the expansion of the democratic franchise and further demands for its extension to hitherto excluded groups like women, the question of the moral fitness of a new or aspirant citizenry became a crucial political question. In this chapter I want to argue that one of the remarkable features of Stoker's work lies in the way in which he attempts to hold on to the older notion of character, while being completely transfixed by the findings of the modern sciences and parasciences. This is particularly true of his two most influential novels, *Dracula* and *The Jewel of Seven Stars*, whose narratives press the relationship between science and character toward its most remote epistemological latitudes.

Material Facts

As I have already noted, *Dracula* is a novel that is very much concerned with modernity's strengths and weaknesses, and, understandably, some of Stoker's contemporaries were uneasy with this aspect of the book. In the *Spectator*, for example, one anonymous critic dismissed *Dracula*'s modern-day trappings, suggesting that the novel would have been "all the more effective if [Stoker] had chosen an earlier period" as his setting, particularly given the essentially "medieval methods" by which the vampire is laid to rest.[6] And, of course, the reviewer has a point, corroborated by no less an opinion than that of Jonathan Harker, the first character to fall into Count Dracula's clutches. Harker innocently worries that "the old centuries had, and have, powers of their own which mere 'modernity' cannot kill" (*Dracula*, 49). The mixture of curiosity and fear recounted by Harker at the opening of the novel as he makes his journey to Count Dracula's castle in order to finalize the mysterious aristocrat's purchase of property in London is a very modern young Englishman's sense of shock at slipping into a premodern world. It is a world that is all too vivid. On his coach ride through Transylvania—his first trip abroad—Harker is fascinated by the sight at "every station" of "groups of people, sometimes crowds . . . in all sorts of attire." "Strangest" of all are the Slovaks, "with their big cowboy hats, great baggy dirty-white trousers, white linen shirts, and enormous heavy leather belts, nearly a foot wide, all studded over with brass nails. . . . On the stage they would be set down at once as some old Oriental band of brigands" (*Dracula*, 11). Harker's nervousness is intensified by the "hysterical" reactions that the news of his final destination provokes among the local people. When an old lady offers him a crucifix from her own neck, he hardly knows "what to do, for as an English Churchman" he had been "taught to regard such things as . . . idolatrous" (*Dracula*, 13).

This powerful historical pull back into the past becomes even stronger upon Harker's arrival at his final destination. Thomas De Quincey once observed that the gift of total recall "must be the next bad thing to being a vampire," but it is clear that in *Dracula* total recall is partly what makes the Count who or what he is.[7] Once ensconced at the castle, the newly accredited solicitor hears the Count expatiate with immense pride on his family lineage, tracing it back to Attila the Hun and conceiving time as an endless series of battles and invasions. Harker records that the Count "spoke as if he had been present at them all," his lyrical nostalgia barely disguising the pure immediacy of the good old days (*Dracula*, 40). In a sense, then, Harker must unlearn what he already knows, since *Dracula* is essentially a tale in which Protestant Englishmen and Englishwomen with a healthy respect for facts come to see that, far from being "idolatrous," "such things" as holy wafers, missals, wild garlic, and the rosary are a vitally necessary means of self-defense—despite their medieval provenance.[8] At first glance, the book could be described as a kind of conversion narrative, a return to ancient beliefs motivated by an occult, and truly oscular, dread. From this perspective, *Dracula* can be read as a modern novel that is largely dominated by the stories and specters of the past.

Nevertheless, Stoker's novel does insist upon a very different temporality, a continuous present that is constituted jointly through the procedures of law and science. Jonathan Harker's detailed notes from his Transylvanian journey reflect both his own recently completed legal training and the ethnographic travelogues of the period. If, in purely literary terms, *Dracula* draws heavily upon the legal narratives associated with Wilkie Collins, whose book *The Moonstone* (1868) imagined the novel as a collection of depositions, Stoker's work also invokes more practical nonfictional sources like his own exhaustive compilation of *The Duties of Clerks of Petty Sessions in Ireland* (1879). Written while the author was still employed as a civil servant in Dublin, this handbook was designed to enhance bureaucratic effectiveness throughout "the whole British Empire." In an ambitious attempt to rationalize the mass of "facts and theories resulting from the operations of the last twenty-seven years," Stoker itemized the formal requirements in preparing evidence for use in court proceedings in words that echo those of *Dracula*'s prologue. Thus, "each Information should contain a full and simple statement of all material facts to which the witness can depose" and "should be taken as nearly as possible in the witness's own words, and in the first person."[9] Empirically, therefore, Stoker's novel pretends to the status of "simple fact," assembling an impressive variety of sources, predominantly journal or diary entries, but also including newspaper articles, letters, fragments from a ship's log book, and an alienist's case notes (*Dracula*, 8).

But in *Dracula* "simple fact[s]" are never simple. They are a constant problem for the various professionals who make facts their business. The same opening chapters which depend upon a lawyer's observations also reveal to us the law's fallibilities. After encountering a pack of wolves on his coach ride, Harker confesses that it "is only when a man feels himself face to face with such horrors that he can understand their true import" (*Dracula*, 23). Yet, in truth, it takes him some time to recognize the gravity of his situation. Mesmerized by the vampire's business acumen and reassured by the presence of the Law List among the other English reference books in the castle's library, Harker is unprepared for the Count's nocturnal activities, which include spreading false evidence by putting on the solicitor's own clothes as a disguise.[10] Harker's visit to Transylvania has placed him beyond any legal redress, turning him into "a veritable prisoner, but without that protection of the law which is even a criminal's right" (*Dracula*, 59). One of the lessons to be drawn from Harker's misperceptions is the need for a thorough scrutiny of the experience of our senses if the true facts are to be known. This gives scientific investigation a special place within the novel.

Insofar as it stands for the accumulation and rigorous testing of evidence, science ultimately provides the key to the novel's construction, offering a master discourse that orders and organizes the disparate empirical knowledges and variously inflected voices contributed by a succession of narrator-witnesses. Still, this investigative stance is not without its difficulties. Private memoranda are not always readily assimilable into publicly intelligible scientific frameworks and there is often an unmanageable residue of testimony that somehow fails to fit. The alienist Dr. Seward's notes on his "life-eating" patient R. M. Renfield, recorded on phonograph cylinders, merge imperceptibly into the doctor's own personal journal (*Dracula*, 90). Thus, when played back on his "wonderful machine," the heart-wringing tones of Seward's narrative sound so "cruelly true" that its objectification as typescript becomes a way of editing out its emotional expression and protecting the privacy of his suffering (*Dracula*, 266). Such all-too-human data threaten to overwhelm the explanatory resources available to us, presenting real problems of interpretation. Jonathan Harker's inconclusive speculations as to what makes the "idolatrous" crucifix such a potent force founders precisely on the uncertainty of its ontological or factual status, for he is unable to tell whether "there is something in the essence of the thing itself," or whether the cross "is a medium, a tangible help, in conveying memories of sympathy and comfort" (*Dracula*, 40). But both of these examples suggest that scientific objectivity is essentially a humanistic ideal. Building upon statements "given from the standpoints and within the range of knowledge of those who made them," science seeks to bring nature under the full control of the human subject (*Dracula*, 8).

This humanistic focus is epitomized by the quizzically encyclopedic utterances of Professor Van Helsing, "philosopher," "metaphysician," and "one of the most advanced scientists of his day" (*Dracula*, 137). An austere and sententious figure, he embodies the uncompromising authority of the scientific voice and is therefore the man best fitted to lead the struggle against Count Dracula. "You reason well, and your wit is bold; but you are too prejudiced," he complains to his former pupil and colleague, Dr. Seward. "You do not let your eyes see nor your ears hear, and that which is outside your daily life is not of account to you." And he follows this observation with a baffling list of what the puzzled Dr. Seward rather desperately calls "nature's eccentricities and possible impossibilities" (*Dracula*, 229–31). Science may run counter to the everyday, but the only significant objects of study are tangible, "positively" or directly ascertainable realities, and for Van Helsing—as for the positivist philosopher Auguste Comte—scientific theory is rooted in "the coordination of observed facts."[11] But *Dracula*'s "possible impossibilities" point to scenarios both of advancement and of backwardness, revealing an unusually close relationship to the aporias and hesitations of late-Victorian positivism. Van Helsing's supplementary credentials as a "metaphysician" provide an additional safeguard against the unmanageability of these contradictions.

Like Edward Dowden, his intellectual ally and mentor at Dublin's Trinity College, Stoker was gripped by the explanatory sweep of positivist system-building and strongly attracted to the universalizing "power, authority and philosophic certitudes of modern science," even when it threw the traditional claims of "humane culture" into doubt.[12] An avid, if ambivalent, reader of Comte and Spencer, Dowden tried to give "the Positivist in me a fair chance," though as a conventionally devout Victorian he always believed that "in the end that limber transcendentalist in me should take the other fellow by the throat and make an end of him."[13] Dowden's internal struggle highlights one of positivism's key features: its consignment of speculation divorced from observation to the domain of unreality or illusion, a dismissal that for Dowden worked as an incitement to metaphysical revenge.[14] It is precisely this demarcation between the real and the unreal that is at issue in *Dracula*, despite Van Helsing's question-begging complaint against Dr. Seward which amounts to accusing him of not being positivistic enough.

Perhaps because of his training in science and mathematics, Stoker was far more prepared than Dowden to explore and take seriously the outer reaches of positivistic science and to contemplate its starkly problematic edges.[15] Running in and out of science's official claims to steady incremental progress, Stoker descried another, quite discontinuous history of knowledge in which undisciplined and often self-interested experimentation repeatedly confronted the sober, legislative tests of mature theory. Writing of Franz Anton Mesmer, whose "system" combined an unscrupulous manipulation of his patients with genuine scientific discovery, Stoker noted that "true medical science has always been suspicious of, and cautious regarding, empiricism," and therefore slow to recognize and take up its achievements.[16] From this standpoint, the link between scientific theory and practical knowledge was often problematic and frequently marked by anomalies and gaps, discrepancies which *Dracula* opens up and exploits in ways disturbing to positivist and transcendentalist alike. Coming at a critical juncture in positivism's grand sociopolitical narrative, Stoker's novel seizes hold of that moment and weaves a romance around it, turning it into an adventure story.

Ideologies of Degeneration

"By the late nineteenth century," Josep Llobera has argued, there were an increasing number of European writers who were "expressing serious doubts about the blessings of Western industrial civilisation," doubts that came to be "articulated around the ideas of race, of the crowd, of violence and of selectionism." Often using "perversions of

---

scientific or pseudo-scientific concepts," these discourses parodied or inverted positivism's normative theory of history.[17] While England was hardly the epicenter of this general movement, it too saw a "sustained and growing pessimism in the 1870s and 1880s about the ramifications of evolution, the efficacy of liberalism, the life in and of the metropolis," and "the future of society" generally.[18] During the 1890s when Stoker was planning and drafting *Dracula*, the human sciences were heavily preoccupied with the pathologies of natural selection—what we might call a case of Darwinism and its discontents. Jonathan Harker's ethnographic diary of Transylvania, the home of "every known superstition in the world" (*Dracula*, 10), offers a foretaste of this discourse which ran across medicine and biology into psychology and social theory.

This fear of a slide back down the evolutionary chain influenced intellectuals at every point on the political spectrum, while posing special problems for those Liberals who had held a strong belief in social progress. By the 1890s the idea of sterilizing the unfit or at least of preventing their reproduction had become a commonplace and "the virtual absence of any protest on liberal or humanitarian grounds" suggests that degenerationism could even be embraced by progressive thinkers who were concerned to set society back on the right course.[19] Consequently Liberals like the political scientist Graham Wallas or the young John Maynard Keynes were not alone in advocating the adoption of eugenic measures, and throughout the Edwardian period there was an extensive debate as to the size of the degenerate population and its likely prognosis. It was, argued the Liberal journalist and future politician Charles Masterman, nothing less than a "blasphemous optimism" to fail to see how "the modern city . . . has choked so many innumerable human lives: a mob moving who are dead."[20]

In the previous chapter I argued that *Dracula*'s elaborately racialized opposition between heartland and hinterland was in part a distinctively Anglo-Irish response to the vicissitudes of the Liberal Party's policy on Ireland. Where *The Snake's Pass* had sought to effect an idealized reconciliation between the two countries, *Dracula* visits a nation that appears to be beyond the pale, a place that seems somehow dangerously close to home yet largely impervious to the appeals of modernity's rational-legal order, at least in its British form. There is a strange duality about Transylvania, "a lovely country . . . full of beauties of all imaginable kinds" that is also "so wild and rocky, as though it were the end of the world" (*Dracula*, 429, 432). At the same time, it is important to remember that *Dracula*, like its author, has a foot in the camps of both colonizer and colonized, and that the terrors and delights of country and city, of periphery and center, are always changing places and identities in the novel, giving rise to phantasms that cloud the confident administrative vision of the imperial agent.

As we have seen, Stoker seems to have had a lively sense of the conjectural theorizing going on in the sciences of his day, and it is remarkable just how thoroughly pervasive the language of degeneration is in *Dracula*, including specific references to such well-known writers on the subject as Max Nordau and Cesare Lombroso.[21] Certainly contemporary portraits of the degenerative condition were key referents for Stoker's depiction of the vampire. For example, the list of identifying traits enumerated in Nordau's controversial book *Entartung* (1893) seems peculiarly applicable to what we know of the Count. In his morbid mix of energy and lassitude Dracula alternates between *extreme passivity*—that "abhorrence of action" which Nordau likened to a state of reverie—and *over-stimulation*, leading to "love of the strange, bizarre, evil, loathsome, and ugly, and to sexual perversions," a condition tantamount to "moral insanity."[22] However, it is important to recognize that *all* the characters in *Dracula* are placed in relation to the conceptual field of degeneration theory. Thus, if the Count displays his deviant nature anatomically through his "thin nose and peculiarly arched nostrils," "his eyebrows . . . very massive, almost meeting over the nose," and his "mouth . . . under the heavy moustache . . . fixed and rather cruel-looking, with peculiarly sharp white teeth" (*Dracula*, 28), Professor Van Helsing's moral fitness can be discerned from his physiognomic juxtaposition to Dracula: the "face, clean-shaven, shows a hard, square chin, a large, resolute, mobile mouth, a good-sized nose, rather straight, but with quick, sensitive nostrils that seem to broaden as the big, bushy eyebrows come down and the mouth tightens" (*Dracula*, 218–19).

Yet while the ideology of degeneration supplies a semantic matrix for much of the novel's characterization and action, its effects are also complicated by the instabilities inherent in this mode of thinking. "Degeneration" was never a unitary concept, but instead consisted of a relay of representations loosely inscribed in a whole cluster of professionalized disciplines and cultural practices. Because its objects were nowhere consistently or satisfactorily defined, we might best see the various attempts at theorizing degeneration as a set of overlapping hypotheses competing with each other to define the true dimensions of the culture's crisis, its sources and parameters. Hence their broad and often uncertain scope, ranging from worries about the dissipation of natural talent, through narratives of the rise and fall of nations, to moral panics about disease and infection.

Somewhat schematically, these hypotheses and their proponents can be grouped into two general categories. The first group perceived a real decline at the upper end of the social scale, especially though not exclusively within the ranks of the aristocracy: "the tainted offspring of forefathers beggared in their bodies by luxury and riotous living, and of fathers who sapped their manhood in vice," as one moralizing tract put it.[23] Charles Darwin's cousin, the scientist and sometime Spiritualist Francis Galton, provides an exemplary instance of this tendency. "We know how careless Nature is of the lives of individuals," Galton wrote in his 1869 book *Hereditary Genius*; "we have seen how careless she is of eminent families—how they are built up, flourish, and decay: just the same may be said of races and of the world itself."[24] From this postulate Galton argued that inherited titles were no guarantee of innate ability since this tended to decline over the course of several generations, suggesting that, at best, the evolutionary process was prone to breaks and discontinuities. In a subsequent study *Natural Inheritance* (1889), "prompted by questions about traits of notable European families," he developed a statistical model or measure of racial decline which he had initially termed the coefficient of "reversion," later (and less neutrally) referred to as the "regression toward mediocrity," better known today as the "regression toward the mean."[25] Like the Manchester economist W. R. Greg, Galton "used the idea that society could be divided between the 'fit' and the 'unfit' to attack aristocratic privilege and landed property."[26] And Greg, for his part, bemoaned a civilization in which "rank and wealth, however diseased, enfeebled or unintelligent," triumphed over "larger brains."[27] Symptomatically, the reduction of Count Dracula to manageable criminological proportions in the later part of the novel hinges upon the realization that this decadent European aristocrat is "not of man-stature as to brain" (*Dracula*, 406).

At the same time, Galton also espoused a second perspective on degeneration, most fully typified by the writings of the psychiatrist Henry Maudsley and the zoologist E. Ray Lankester, both of whom were chiefly preoccupied with the threat to the nation emanating from the lower reaches of society. This specifically urban-industrial focus amounted to a kind of rear-mirror Darwinism in which a rapid deterioration in the racial stock was believed to result from the pressure on workers to adapt themselves to a degraded environment, posing formidable problems of social control as the numbers of criminopathic paupers steadily grew. Galton wrote of his distress at encountering "the draggled, drudged, mean look of the mass of individuals, especially of the women, that one meets in the streets of London," "the conditions of their life" destroying any semblance of common humanity.[28] Predictably, Galton took a keen interest in the developing "science" of criminal anthropology and was one of the few British intellectuals to attend the international congresses organized by the Italian criminologist Lombroso. In the same year that *Dracula* was published, Galton presented to the fourth (1897) congress his most enduring contribution to modern policing, a newly devised scheme for classifying fingerprints that was to revolutionize the methods of social control.[29]

Stoker's familiarity with these ideas can be traced to the early 1890s when, in a short story called "The Secret of the Growing Gold" (1892), he writes of "the causes of decadence" in both their "aristocratic" and their "plebeian forms."[30] Despite the manifest differences between them, the one nervous of the traditionally well-to-do, the other fixing its fears upon the new poor, these two accounts of degeneration do find a point of intersection in the threat they each posed to the security of respectable middle-class society, precisely the world of doctors, lawyers, and teachers that is under siege in *Dracula*. Stoker's depiction of vampirism draws upon and draws together these twin fears of degeneration, fusing them into a single potent compound. Though the Count incarnates a powerful image of aristocratic decadence, falling into a long line of melodramatic rakes and villains, it is crucial that his preferred theater of operations is the heart of the Empire, "the crowded streets of your mighty London, . . . in the midst of the whirl and rush of humanity" (*Dracula*, 31). Both Jonathan Harker and his wife Mina speak of the threat to "London, with its teeming millions" (*Dracula*, 67 and 215), yet it soon becomes apparent that the danger lies not merely in the size of London's population, but in the uneasy coexistence of its social strata, signaled in the novel by the juxtaposition of standard English and demotic or vernacular speech. When the Count's first victim Lucy Westenra has been transformed into a vampire, she is known as "the bloofer lady" among the "grubby-faced little children" on whom she preys, an indication that established social boundaries are being breached (*Dracula*, 213). *Dracula* imagines the Victorian bourgeois family as trapped in a sort of vise (the Count's grip "actually seemed like a steel vice"), under strain from both extremes of the social hierarchy (*Dracula*, 24). Or, transposed into the theoretical idioms of European positivism, the choice of pathologies is between Nordau's "highly-gifted degenerates" and Lombroso's "atavistic criminals."

By vividly dramatizing the horrors of degeneration and atavism, the figure of the Count underscores the sexualized threat that lay at their core, the assumption of "a sexual 'instinct'" capable of turning to such perverse or precocious forms as "homosexuality" or "hysteria." Instructively, in his *History of Sexuality* Michel Foucault traced "the opening up of the great medico-psychological domain of the 'perversions'" in the mid-nineteenth century, showing their interrelation with new ideas about "heredity" and "dégénérescence."[31] His argument suggests that the task of establishing the distinction between normality and pathology required one to work across several different levels.[32] That is to say, the medical expert's attention would move from the minutiae of the sexual act to the classification of various maladies and diseases, and from there to the future disposition of the species, before returning to the sexual act again. In this way the diagnostic treatment of the human body could be connected to a program for administratively regulating hereditary traits, paving the way for the extension of state activity into modern eugenics.

Dracula typically follows the same bio-political trajectory, but in a necessarily more anxious key. Thus Jonathan Harker's temptation in a remote wing of the Castle Dracula—one of the earliest episodes in the book—insistently raises the problem of his "biological responsibility," his "obligation to preserve a healthy line of descent."[33] Captured and captivated by "three young women" who cast "no shadow on the floor," Harker finds their "deliberate voluptuousness . . . both thrilling and repulsive" and, though he is unnerved, he is nevertheless consumed with "longing." This ambivalence is heightened by his feeling that one of the "ladies" seems uncannily familiar to him, though he is unable to bring this elusive memory to consciousness. Yet the racialized contrast that triggers his aborted recollection is familiar enough: the woman Harker thinks he knows is "fair, as fair as fair can be, with great, wavy masses of golden hair and eyes like pale sapphires," while her two companions are "dark" with "high aquiline noses, like the Count's, and great dark piercing eyes." Significantly, the role of this blonde Aryan woman is to initiate Harker's fatal seduction, attempting to betray him to the corruptions of the flesh and cut him off forever from respectable domesticity. In "delightful anticipation" of other women later in the narrative, she represents "the enemy within," a source of male hysteria and demoralization, a "dreamy fear" of sexual chaos (*Dracula*, 51–52). But Harker's rude awakening from this trance promises a different order of terror as the Count interrupts the erotic scene by staking his own unspeakable claim: "This man belongs to me!" (*Dracula*, 53).

The progenitive powers of the perverse are also at stake in one of the most dramatic episodes in the novel, in which the Count is disturbed while taking possession of Dracula's heroine, Harker's newly wedded wife Mina. The enormity of this scene is all the more intensely rendered by a double narration: once objectively, as an appalling discovery by the four male protagonists Van Helsing, Dr. Seward, the Hon. Arthur Holmwood, and Quincey Morris; and once subjectively, through Mina's own horrified memory. The Count has broken into the Harkers' room and, usurping their marriage bed by reducing the stupefied Jonathan to complete passivity, he has taken Mina by the scruff of her neck, "forcing her face down on his bosom" like "a child forcing a kitten's nose into a saucer of milk to compel it to drink" (*Dracula*, 336). The extraordinarily dense web of associations evoked by these descriptions—of castration, rape, fellatio, sadomasochism—is held in place by the vampire's bizarrely composite persona, simultaneously that of rake and mother, a patriarch who gives birth to monsters. Of all the scenes in the book this was undoubtedly the one which caused most commotion. For some male readers it offered a fantasy of sexual arousal, a rape that was secretly desired, while for others it was the kind of passage which went against all decency.[34] *The Keighley News*, in an otherwise fairly favorable notice, primly stated that "the nature of Count Dracula's adventure may not be hinted at in this domestic column."[35]

Dracula is a novel which excels in reversals of Victorian convention: men become sexually quiescent, women are transformed into sexual predators who cannibalize children, madness seems ready to overwhelm reason, and all of this is charged by a ceaselessly fluctuating economy of blood and desire. But even so, Mina Harker's violation by the phallically maternal Count signals a remarkable development in the vampire's powers. Certainly this episode explodes once and for all any hierarchically gendered division of the cultural field according to which "in one set of works (Poe, Hoffmann, Baudelaire: 'elite' culture)" vampires "are women," whereas "in another (Polidori, Stoker, the cinema: 'mass' culture) they are men."[36] For it demonstrates once again that in *Dracula* it is matter out of place that matters, the contamination and dissolution of the pure and sacred that counts, the transgression of boundaries and borders that is the ultimate horror, just as in theories of degeneration it was the impulsive, the unstable, the unfixed, and the nomadic that were held to be the sign of the savage and the barbarian—those like the gypsies Harker sees at the castle in Transylvania, "almost outside all law" (*Dracula*, 56).[37] In both cases, anxiety around the question of boundaries is always also a demand that there *be* a boundary.

Faces, Skulls, and the Unconscious

For Stoker, as his contrasting portraits of Count Dracula and Dr. Van Helsing make clear, the "science" of physiognomy served as one of the primary means for making sense of the mutable world of developmental possibilities unleashed by degeneration theory. Physiognomy often figured as a convenient method for ascertaining and depicting character in nineteenth-century novels and, like phrenology, it had been given a widespread currency as a progressive science in such middle-class cultural institutions as the literary and philosophical societies.[38] But in Stoker's fiction its use is unusually explicit and far-reaching. From the inception of his career as a writer, Stoker regarded physiognomy as an eminently practical form of knowledge, and there are countless references to it scattered throughout his work. It has a foundational status in his writing, locating and attempting to stabilize the lines of difference and danger by marking out a highly deterministic order in which some agents can be shown to be so totally other that they pose a threat to human progress. Notwithstanding physiognomy's loss of influence in such diverse fields as painting and medicine once scientists like Charles Bell and Darwin had begun to replace it with a proper psychology of human expression, Stoker continued to be a "believer of the science" and at the time of his death he still owned a five-volume quarto edition of Johann Caspar Lavater's *Essays on Physiognomy* (1789), the book which more than any other had been responsible for the modern revival of this age-old set of beliefs.[39]

In Lavater's exposition, physiognomy emerges as a practice poised somewhat equivocally between the old and the new, an ancient art that he is bringing forward into the modern age by setting it on a proper scientific footing. In true Enlightenment style, Lavater constitutes "Man" as "a grand and interesting subject of investigation," one which can be definitively known through sense-impressions perceptible to "a sound eye." By his own admission, however, Lavater's actual achievements fall short of this lofty ideal. He is able to offer only "a few simple Essays," "*Fragments* which . . . never can compose a Whole."[40] Nevertheless, it is modernity itself which has made this return to the intellectual models of antiquity particularly pressing. Lavater defines his proposed science of surfaces as a necessary form of practical judgment for societies whose basis is changing from inherited status to impersonal contract. As buyers and sellers encounter each other in the market as relative strangers, Lavater argues, they learn how far to extend their trust by reading the characters of prospective business partners from their faces. Physiognomy thus comes to scrutinize and regulate the probity of transactions in a social order increasingly organized on legal-commercial lines.[41]

However, the survival of Lavater's eighteenth-century codification of physiognomic doctrine into the late Victorian era was only possible because of certain crucial but unacknowledged modifications to his original ideas. Without resorting to explicit criticism, later writers changed the whole face of physiognomy by breaking with their founder's virtual silence on questions of race. In predictable pre-Darwinian fashion, Lavater had emphatically denied that there could be any continuity between monkeys and humankind, even in the case of the "savage." Though he had occasionally indulged in idle speculation as to whether "the soul of Newton" could still "have invented the theory of light" if it had "been lodged in the skull of a Negro," Lavater's general working assumption had been that "all men" were created "of one and the same blood."[42] This was a line of reasoning deeply at odds with the focus upon establishing physiological pedigrees of class and nation that was uppermost during the second half of the nineteenth century. From Beddoe to Macnamara, or from Mayhew to Galton, "race" increasingly became a readily identifiable entity both within and between national boundaries, so that by the early 1880s members of the Anthropological Institute could refer to "ethnological physiognomies" or "national physiognomies," terms which would undoubtedly have been quite unintelligible to Lavater himself. But however far their work departed from that of their eighteenth-century exemplar, Victorian physiognomists—including Stoker himself—typically continued to refer to Lavater's treatise as their point of departure.

Despite Stoker's indebtedness to Lavater, the world of *Dracula* is very much a world of "ethnological physiognomies" in which racial identities are assumed to be plainly legible from appearances and can even be used as data from which to extrapolate judgments as to a nation's social and moral well-being. Jonathan Harker's troubled physiognomic description of the Count is immediately confirmed when Dracula tells him "the story of his race" early on in the novel. By proclaiming that "in our veins flows the blood of many brave races who fought as the lion fights, for lordship," the Count is revealing the impurity of the Transylvanian dynasty, as well as that of his "polyglot" state (*Dracula*, 14, 41). His declarations are fateful in another sense, for they also invoke the warrior races of a feudal past in rueful counterpoint to the degraded present, "these days of dishonourable peace" when "the glories of the great races are as a tale that is told" (*Dracula*, 42). The Count's "story" moves rhetorically between stern lamentation and defiant rebuke, telling his own coded tale of degeneration and concluding by asking "where ends the war without a brain and heart to conduct it?" (*Dracula*, 42)—a critical question for those concerned with the preservation of a nation's "fighting spirit" (*Dracula*, 41).

The vampire's chronicle helps to elucidate another closely run antithesis in the novel, that between the use of the term "moral Viking" (*Dracula*, 209) in connection with the American Quincey Morris, the boldest, most adventurous of the book's band of heroes, and the association of Dracula himself with the Berserker hordes (even the Norwegian wolf that the Count spirits away from the London Zoological Gardens is named "Berserker"). Stoker often gives his heroes some kind of Viking genealogy, but nowhere else in his work is this attribute so carefully qualified.[43] Quincey's moral fortitude marks the essential difference between these two frontiersmen, one Texan, the other Transylvanian. Significantly, the phrase "moral Viking" is invoked by a doctor (the alienist Dr. Seward) to describe Quincey Morris's strength of character at the funeral of one of Dracula's principal victims, Lucy Westenra. "If America can go on breeding men like that," confides Seward, "she will be a power in the world indeed" (*Dracula*, 209). To bear oneself like "a moral Viking" is precisely to display a measure of self-control conspicuously absent among those bellicose peoples who have not yet evolved out of the past. In short, the sublimation of human aggression requires the right combination of birth and upbringing if the march of progress is to continue.[44]

But if the battle lines in Stoker's fiction could consistently be reduced to quite such simple melodramatic binaries, Dracula's anxieties about appearances would be much reduced. For this is also a text beset by the difficulties that haunted physiognomy, the fear that things are not always what they seem. In *Dracula*, sleeping virgins may really be monsters, dogs may be the agents of demonic powers, and, despite his vivid presence, the Count himself often seems to occupy a space that is virtually beyond representation, an unmirrorable image, a force able to assume a multiplicity of forms, physiognomy's true vanishing point. It is profoundly comforting to place the Count among the classifications mapped out by Nordau and Lombroso—a verdict given toward the end of the novel—since this identification confines him safely within the categorical boxes of one of the most influential brands of medical and sociological positivism. By contrast, the real horror of seeing the Count in broad daylight in Piccadilly on a hot autumn day stems from the realization that so blatant a criminal might not look unusual or remarkable enough to be singled out as he blends with the London crowd. Far from being foolproof, the Lombrosian project of tabulating the various kinds of criminogenic body was coming under increasing strain during this period, even as these ideas were being popularized in England through the publication of Havelock Ellis's *The Criminal* in 1890 and were beginning to be scrutinized by the Home Office. By the nineties, Lombroso's concept of "the born criminal"—the notion of a natural criminal type recognizable through physical stigmata—was shriveling under a growing weight of evidence, and the criminal anthropologist was forced desperately to modify his theory out of all recognition. Yet, despite this retrenchment, Lombrosian criminology remained influential, its deterministic structure finding echoes even in the alternative aetiology based on "inferior weight, stature and mental capacity" developed by its most incisive English critics.[45]

Just as there were contradictions between Lavater's physiognomy and the newer forms of racial thinking, so the incorporation of physiognomic ideas into criminology came into conflict with established Victorian ideas of individuality and character. In his 1872 letter to Whitman, Stoker perhaps unwittingly put his finger on the root of the problem, by allowing that one's outer appearance and inner life may fail in some ways to meaningfully correspond. After giving a physical description of himself which dwelt upon his facial characteristics, and remarking upon his temperament and disposition, Stoker announced that he was also "naturally secretive to the world," an intensely private self who could choose not to reveal himself to others.[46] Paraded as an advantage here, and idealized in Victorian culture as the character trait of "reserve" or "reticence . . . a quality which a strong man always respects" (*JSS*, 211), this divorce between the inner and the outer caused the author no end of intellectual trouble and led to some curious disavowals. In the book he wrote—and in a sense could not help but write—on *Famous Impostors* (1910), Stoker revealed a fascination with deception and disguise while also denying its efficacy in some of its "commonest forms." Thus he argued that the impersonation of men by women was "so common that it seems rooted in a phase of human nature," though oddly he then rather inconsistently tried to explain away this phenomenon by relating it to the "legal and economic disabilities of the gentler sex." However, he was also at great pains to deny that men were ever really taken in by this kind of cross-dressing, claiming that the "common dangers" experienced at war or at sea, settings which he took to be typical sites for male impersonation, generated a generous, comradely loyalty that forbore to expose concealed gender differences.[47]

Lavater too had recognized the problem wanton and deliberate secrecy had posed for his system of physiognomy, which, after all, was intended as a highly deterministic science eschewing "arbitrary causes." His ingenious solution was to argue that "the art of dissimulation" was also "founded on Physiognomy" since it was for precisely this reason that "the Hypocrite endeavour[s] to resemble the . . . honest Man."[48] Furthermore, though one might be deluded by the mobile expressions that pass across the face, their interpretation was the province of the adjunct science of pathognomy and therefore a trained physiognomic observer would rarely be deceived. Nevertheless, the question remained as to how one could bracket off the pathognomic component in so complex a signboard as the human face. Lavater suggested a number of remedies: the profile or silhouette was one, and visiting the prison or asylum was another, a proposal which would have gladdened Lombroso's heart, since it was based on the claim that the inmates of these institutions were such visibly marked subjects that the "masks and vizors" of dissemblance would either be altogether absent or completely ineffectual. But the perfect solution was to observe the face after death. For then the features settle and become fixed and the barriers to interpretation are removed. According to this reasoning, in *Dracula* the Un-Dead are especially to be feared because they are able to evade the certain knowledge that death brings, creating a falsely appealing presence in order to lure their victims. Conversely, once a vampire like Lucy Westenra has been exorcised and restored to full humanity, we see her in her coffin "as we had seen her in life, with her face of unequalled sweetness and purity," including all "the traces of care and pain and waste," traces that "marked her truth to what we knew" (*Dracula*, 259).

Stoker's use of physiognomy comes with its historical baggage of contradictions and fallibilities, one of whose effects is to call into play a radically different set of concepts, which serve as a reminder that originally physiognomy performed many of the functions of a scientific psychology. If, by the turn of the century, physiognomy was becoming a far less secure discipline than it once had been, psychology was becoming an increasingly well-established specialism, and selected ideas and technical terms were beginning to filter into ordinary, educated discourse. One of the most widely cited phrases from the nineteenth-century psychological lexicon was "unconscious cerebration," derived from the work of the noted professor of physiology W. B. Carpenter.[49] The term crops up in such otherwise rather oddly assorted texts as Henry James's *The Aspern Papers* (1888) and H. G. Wells's *The Island of Doctor Moreau* (1896), and it appears in *Dracula* too, as well as some of Stoker's other novels. Puzzling over the strange obsessions of his patient Renfield, Dr. Seward obscurely senses that their solution is "growing" from a "rudimentary idea in my mind" by "unconscious cerebration" and will soon mature into a fully conscious "whole idea" (*Dracula*, 88). And later, even Renfield himself shows signs of this subterranean process working "through the cloudiness of his insanity" (*Dracula*, 321–22).

These references to Carpenter's notion of "unconscious cerebration" again show Stoker borrowing from the human sciences, at a point where these overlap with contemporary medicine. And again his use of them brings us up smartly against their limits. The most complete account of "unconscious cerebration" is to be found in Carpenter's *Principles of Mental Physiology* (1874), a text which is a rich historical resource in pinpointing the changing conceptions of the self as agent during the late Victorian period, particularly as these bear on the moral notion of "character." The *Principles* offers both an analysis of the workings of the mind and a "study of its morbid conditions," those barriers to personal autonomy which also define the disturbing mental landscape inhabited by *Dracula*. Carpenter's book was in many respects a polemic, and it is striking that his treatment of the question of free will and determinism takes the form of a dual critique directed with equal ferocity against materialist and Spiritualist views of mental phenomena. Against the materialists, he insisted that "our Moral Nature" (p. 7) was such that human beings ought not be reduced to mere automata whose thoughts and behavior were caused by factors entirely beyond their control. On the other hand, Carpenter attacked nineteenth-century Spiritualists for failing to grasp that the mind could never be wholly divorced from the body, and he believed that their claims to the contrary were largely based on outright fraud.

As his title suggests, Carpenter's *Principles* aimed to demonstrate that the mental faculty was embodied in an economy of nerves and muscles, so that he often used the term *mind* as a synonym for *brain*. In his discussion of unconscious cerebration, for example, Carpenter located the nub of the process in sets of "impressions transmitted along the 'nerves of the internal senses' from the Cerebrum to the Sensorium" (p. 517) or center of consciousness, from which point they could "excite muscular movements" (p. 517). Though we are ordinarily aware of such impressions, there is always the possibility that they may be delayed or stalled and so become lost to "*conscious* memory" but with the result that they subsequently "express themselves in *involuntary muscular movements*" (p. 524). There is, of course, no theory of repression at work in this psychology, but what is evident is a shift toward a heteronomous model of mental life in which the hidden levels or dimensions of the mind can hold surprising consequences for our conscious selves. When he tried to explain away such Spiritualist phenomena as planchettes and tableturning, for example, Carpenter referred to "the records of old impressions, left in the deeper stratum of unconsciousness" which "disclose their existence through the automatic motor apparatus" (p. 525) in a manner entirely opaque to their agent.[50] Carpenter was by no means the only psychologist of this period to arrive at this kind of mental topography; others, like the "psychical researcher" Frederic W. H. Myers, devised far more radically "multiplex" accounts of mind and personality.[51] What makes Carpenter's work so fascinating is that his virtual decentering of the subject occurred almost by default as he attempted to move between different principles of explanation, despite his best intentions.

On one level, Carpenter placed a high premium on individual independence and self-command, cleaving to a view of the will overtly influenced by the liberal philosopher John Stuart Mill (though, revealingly, he also sometimes cited Mill in support of several of his physiological concepts, including that of "unconscious cerebration"). However, his stress upon what is involuntary and unrecognizable in human action seems to diminish the scope of the will considerably and drew him back toward the materialistic argument he sought to avoid. Thus, because of "the degrading influences of the conditions" in which they found themselves, he denied that "those heathen outcasts of whom all our great towns are unhappily but too productive" could ever be considered "morally responsible" (pp. 9–10)—an argument which gave a new specificity to his assertion that the mind could never be "independent of its Material tenement" (p. 7). More confusingly still, elsewhere in his treatise Carpenter suggested instances in which the operation of the will may lie, paradoxically, quite outside conscious deliberation. In his chapter "Of Sleep, Dreaming, and Somnambulism," for instance, he stated that the somnambulist "differs from the ordinary dreamer in possessing such a control over his nervo-muscular apparatus, as to be enabled to execute . . . whatever it may be in his mind to do" (p. 591). By extension, hypnotism is to be understood as "artificial somnambulism" (p. 601), a relay of impressions and bodily movements which also bypasses the conscious decision of the mesmerized subject.

Hypnotism, somnambulism, trances, unconscious cerebration: these, just as much as a physiognomically grounded "philosophy of crime" or "study of insanity," are the materials from which *Dracula* is constructed (*Dracula*, 405). In their different ways, physiognomy and "mental physiology" were both bodies of knowledge which attempted to put the idea of "character" as it appeared in Victorian social thought on a scientific footing, but because they constantly foregrounded difficult questions of voluntarism and determinism the meaning of the idea continued to be problematic. So, when Carpenter tries to elucidate the concept of "character" in his *Principles* the result is noticeably inconclusive, since at the same time he depicts it—following Mill—as instantiating an individual's "self-directing" powers, he also presents it as part of a physiologically based causal model, conceiving of character as the "*proportional* development" of "particular *sequences of thought and feeling*" (p. 250).[52] This division was the product of the sharp discontinuity Carpenter had always assumed between the cerebrum as the site of such essential features of the mind as perception, reasoning, intelligence, and will and the lower, automatic sensory-motor centers which are ultimately subordinated to it, a split which replicated the classic mind-body dualism inherited from philosophy.[53] If *Dracula* is positioned on this same fault line, occupying some of the same conceptual space as late-nineteenth-century mental physiology, the instabilities of that paradigm helped to produce a number of incommensurable forms of knowledge, whose emergence can be glimpsed within the novel itself. When Seward fancies that his study of lunacy "might advance my own branch of science to a pitch compared with which Burdon-Sanderson's physiology or Ferrier's brain knowledge would be as nothing" (*Dracula*, 90), he is on the brink of a new view of cerebral functioning—a "knowledge" based upon experimental research carried out within the asylum itself—that was starting to displace many of the old philosophical categories.[54] Alternatively, however, Seward and Van Helsing's interest in Charcot points elsewhere, precisely toward Freud and the study of hysteria, a tradition that would soon leave strictly somatic accounts of mental disorder behind, uncoupling the links with degenerationism which Charcot always tried to maintain.

The "moral Viking," a phrase precisely designed to consolidate the notion of character, in fact teeters on the brink of hysteria. In the case of Quincey Morris, the American's noble demeanor at Lucy Westenra's funeral belies the grief a sensitive observer knows he must be feeling, since, as Seward points out, this disappointed suitor "suffered as much about Lucy's death as any of us" (*Dracula*, 209). Van Helsing's own reaction at the burial, visibly "putting some terrible restraint on himself," underscores the proximity of psychic breakdown, for once the two doctors are "alone in the carriage he gave way to a regular fit of hysterics" (*Dracula*, 209). As I noted in the previous chapter, Stoker is in part attempting to reconcile two ideals of masculinity that had generally become dissociated by the 1890s, creating a bridge between the expressive man of sensibility and the strong, steadfast man of action; and I suggested that this rehabilitation can be read as a kind of Anglo-Irish defense of Celtic emotionalism. Here, however, I want to qualify this argument by stressing the extent to which this sympathetic view rests upon the male subject's vulnerability to forces beyond manly self-control, a vulnerability which can never be entirely free of risk. "King Laugh," observes Van Helsing, is no respecter of persons or occasions—"he come when and how he like"—so much so that Seward feels impelled to pull down the blinds to hide the embarrassment of his colleague's tears and mirth (*Dracula*, 210).

If such open displays of feeling betoken a lack of propriety or respect, in other cases they may be condemned as dangerous signs of effeminacy, a morally reprehensible weakness of the will and a departure from the heterosexual ideal.[55] This fear of being "unmanned" (by men and by women) underlies the "wild feeling" which engulfs Jonathan Harker when he finds himself trapped in the Castle Dracula at the beginning of the novel (*Dracula*, 39). After narrowly escaping the Count's advances, and subsequently being reduced to a condition of sexual passivity at the hands of "those weird sisters" (*Dracula*, 64), Harker chooses to brave the castle's precipice and risk falling to his death in his bid to escape, since "at least . . . at its foot man may sleep—as a man" (*Dracula*, 69). Ultimately, by artfully negotiating the line between the conscious and the unconscious, and between the voluntary and the involuntary, Stoker recuperates the male hysteria to which both Harker and Van Helsing in their different ways fall victim. In the midst of his terrifying captivity, Harker is surprised to pass an untroubled night of dreamless sleep. "Despair has its own calms," he realizes upon waking (*Dracula*, 57). But, though the male unconscious seems to possess a self-regulating capacity to return the psyche to a state of balance or equilibrium, its workings remain mysterious, as unfathomable as they are uncertain.[56] "It may be that nerves have their own senses that bring thought to the depository common to all the human functions" (*The Lady of the Shroud*, 178), speculates the hero of one of the later novels, producing a kind of muddled pastiche of Carpenter's own scientific language. But the point is that this is something he simply does not know for sure.

In the light of Stoker's highly syncretistic amalgam of conflicting accounts of human behavior, accounts which were themselves internally conflicted, it is hardly surprising that one finds no resolution of these discrepancies in his writings. As a result, the languages of freedom and determinism are always inflected by a variety of accents and sometimes fall into a confusion of tongues. Thus *Dracula*'s heroes, "our little band of men" (*Dracula*, 449), possess "powers" that "are unfettered" at least "so far as [they] extend" (*Dracula*, 285), while, in a curious parallel, the vampire "is not free" since it must "obey some of nature's laws—why we know not" (*Dracula*, 287). Nevertheless, this unnatural creature that "seems predestinate to crime" (*Dracula*, 405) may exercise a "limited freedom" at "certain times" (*Dracula*, 287). It is the indeterminacy of agency, human and nonhuman alike, the obfuscation of its capacities and limits, that is so fateful for the novel's protagonists. The precariousness of Lucy Westenra's "unconscious struggle for life and strength" is, for example, as much a consequence of the unknown terms and scope of that struggle as it is of the delicately poised balance of power between good and evil (*Dracula*, 192). Reflecting upon Mrs. Westenra's relative calm in the face of "the terrible change in her daughter," Dr. Seward wonders (along classical laissez-faire lines) whether this propensity for self-preservation is not an unintended by-product of "the vice of egoism" that naturally exists in all of us, resulting in "an ordered selfishness" with "deeper roots for its causes than we have knowledge of." Our understanding of "spiritual pathology" and its defenses is far from complete (*Dracula*, 147).

From *Vampires, Mummies, and Liberals* (Durham, N.C.: Duke University Press, 1996): 58-81.

Copyright © 1996 by Duke University Press. Reprinted by permission of Duke University Press.

Notes

1. Gaston Bachelard, *The Poetics of Space*, trans. Maria Jolas (1958; Boston: Beacon Press, 1969), p. 39.

2. Thomas De Quincey, "On Murder Considered as One of the Fine Arts", in D. Masson, ed., *The Collected Writings of Thomas De Quincey*, 14 vols. (Edinburgh: Adam and Charles Black, 1890), 13:124.

3. Hall Caine, "The New Watchwords of Fiction," *Contemporary Review*, 57 (1890): 479–88.

4. See John Stuart Mill, *The Logic of the Moral Sciences*, intro. A. J. Ayer (London: Duckworth, 1987), ch. 5. This text reprints the sixth book of Mill's *A System of Logic* (1843).

5. See Andrew Vincent, "Classical Liberalism and Its Crisis of Identity," *History of Political Thought* 11 (Spring 1990): 143–61, and Stefan Collini, *Liberalism and Soci-*

ology: L. T. Hobhouse and the Political Argument in England 1880–1914 (Cambridge: Cambridge University Press, 1979).

6. *Spectator*, July 31, 1897, pp. 150–51.

7. Thomas De Quincey, quoted in J. Hillis Miller, *The Disappearance of God: Five Nineteenth-Century Writers* (Cambridge, Mass.: Harvard University Press, 1963), p. 64.

8. In *The Snake's Pass* Protestantism and skepticism are explicitly linked in the character of the "hard-faced" McGlown, who "much prefer[s] the facs" and who prefers a story told by someone "old enough till remember the theng itself" to any legend (*The Snake's Pass*, 23).

9. Bram Stoker, *The Duties of Clerks of Petty Sessions in Ireland* (Dublin: John Falconer, 1879), pp. v–vi and 27.

10. The Law List is a directory of English professional lawyers, whose ranks Jonathan Harker is about to join. The other volumes in the Count's collection include reference books containing the names or biographies of the aristocracy, the well-to-do, London businessmen, and members of the officer corps in the army and navy, as well as a plethora of government publications and a compendium of British railway timetables.

11. Auguste Comte, *La Philosophie Positive*, quoted in Jerry Palmer, "The Damp Stones of Positivism: Erich von Däniken and Paranormality," *Philosophy of Social Science* 9 (1979): 145.

12. See Terence Brown, "Edward Dowden: Irish Victorian," in *Ireland's Literature: Selected Essays* (Mullingar: Lilliput Press, 1988), p. 37.

13. See Edward Dowden, *Fragments from Old Letters: E. D. to E. D. W., 1869–1892, First Series* (London: J. M. Dent, 1914), p. 129. This letter dates from 1877. Among the other relevant texts that Dowden mentions and which are likely to have been passed on by him to Stoker are Charles Darwin's *Expression of the Emotions*, Max Müller's *Science of Religion*, and Henry Maudsley's *Body and Mind: An Inquiry into Their Connection and Mutual Influence*. See Dowden's letter of September 7, 1873, in *Fragments from Old Letters: E. D. to E. D. W., 1869–1892, Second Series* (London: J. M. Dent, 1914), pp. 33–34.

14. Roy Foster suggests a less conventional outcome of Dowden's transcendentalism: his interest in Shelley and his circle. According to Foster, "it was Dowden's account of Shelley's experiments with demonic invocation at Eton that inspired Yeats and AE to attempt spirit-raising in the mid-1880s." R. F. Foster, "Protestant Magic: W. B. Yeats and the Spell of Irish History," in *Paddy and Mr. Punch: Connections in Irish and English History* (London: Penguin, 1993), p. 226.

15. On Stoker's continuing interest in mathematics, see Sir Gilbert Parker's letter to him, May 31, 1893 (Harpenden, Herts.), Brotherton Collection, Leeds University Library.

16. Bram Stoker, *Famous Impostors* (New York: Sturgis & Walton, 1910), p. 100.

17. Josep R. Llobera, "The Dark Side of Modernity," *Critique of Anthropology* 8, no. 2 (1988): 71–76.

18. Daniel Pick, *Faces of Degeneration: A European Disorder, c.1848–c.1918* (Cambridge: Cambridge University Press, 1989), p. 180.

19. Michael Freeden, *The New Liberalism: An Ideology of Social Reform* (Oxford: Clarendon Press, 1986), p. 178. See also his essay "Eugenics and Progressive Thought: A Study in Ideological Affinity," *Historical Journal* 22, no. 3 (1979): 645–71.

20. C. F. G. Masterman, *In Peril of Change: Essays Written in Time of Tranquility* (New York: B. W. Huebsch, 1905), pp. 175, 177.

21. Cesare Lombroso (1835–1909) was the Italian founder of positivistic criminology who originally claimed that crime could largely be explained in terms of evolutionary atavism. Lombroso greatly influenced the German physician and journalist Max Nordau (1849–1923), who helped popularize the concept of degeneration by using it as a critical tool to stigmatize developments in the arts. An English translation of Nordau's magnum opus *Entartung* (1893) was published by William Heinemann (later to become Stoker's publisher) under the title *Degeneration* in 1895. This aspect of Stoker's work has attracted increasing attention in recent years, though few studies go much beyond cataloging textual affinities. The best analysis to date remains Daniel Pick, "'Terrors of the night': *Dracula* and 'Degeneration' in the Late Nineteenth Century," *Critical Quarterly* 30, no. 4 (1988): 71–87; but as Troy Boone notes, Pick "does not focus on how these fears are represented in narrative." See Boone's essay "'He is English and therefore adventurous': Politics, Decadence, and *Dracula*," *Studies in the Novel* 25 (Spring 1993): 90. For a useful overview of degeneration theory's relationship to Anglo-American literary culture, see R. B. Kershner, Jr., "Degeneration: The Explanatory Nightmare," *Georgia Review* 40 (Summer 1986): 416–44.

22. Colin Martindale, "Degeneration, Disinhibition, and Genius," *Journal of the History of Behavioral Science* 7 (1971): 177–82.

23. Albert Wilson (1910), quoted in Richard D. Walter, "What Became of the Degenerate? A Brief History of a Concept," *Journal of the History of Medicine* 11 (1956): 422–29.

24. Francis Galton, *Hereditary Genius: An Inquiry into Its Laws and Consequences* (1869; London: Macmillan, 1914), p. 338.

25. See Ian Hacking, "How Should We Do the History of Statistics?" *I&C* 8 (1981): 15–26. See also D. W. Forrest, *Francis Galton: The Life and Work of a Victorian Genius* (New York: Taplinger, 1974), ch. 14.

26. Greta Jones, *Social Darwinism and English Thought: The Interaction between Biological and Social Theory* (Brighton: Harvester Press, 1980), p. 35.

27. W. R. Greg, "On the Failure of Natural Selection in the Case of Man," *Fraser's Magazine* 78 (1868): 360.

28. Francis Galton, *Hereditary Genius*, pp. 328–29.

29. See Daniel Pick, *Faces of Degeneration*, pp. 176–79.

30. Reprinted in the posthumous collection *Dracula's Guest* (1914), "The Secret of the Growing Gold" was originally published in *Black & White*, January 23, 1892. The original manuscript in the Brotherton Collection in Leeds University Library indicates that the story was written between May 28 and June 12, 1891.

31. Michel Foucault, *The History of Sexuality, Volume 1: An Introduction*, trans. Robert Hurley (1976; Harmondsworth: Penguin, 1981), p. 118.

32. Interestingly, part of the challenge the madman R. M. Renfield poses to Dr. Seward's knowledge of the human mind lies in the fact that he is "so unlike the normal

lunatic" (*Dracula*, 78). For an exploration of the replacement of the idea of human nature by "a model of normal people with laws of dispersion," see Ian Hacking, *The Taming of Chance* (Cambridge: Cambridge University Press, 1990).

33. Foucault, *History of Sexuality*, pp. 118–21.

34. See Melville Macnaghten's highly enthusiastic letter to Stoker, June 30, 1897 (Metropolitan Police Office, London), Brotherton Collection, Leeds University Library. Macnaghten exclaims that he has "revelled" in *Dracula* and singles out this episode, noting that Mina's blood is "not unwillingly" taken from her by the Count. At the time of writing Macnaghten was Chief Constable in the Criminal Investigation Department, Scotland Yard. He was knighted in 1907.

35. "London Letter" (syndicated column written by Henry Lucy), *Keighley News*, July 10, 1897.

36. Franco Moretti, *Signs Taken For Wonders: Essays in the Sociology of Literary Forms* (London: Verso, 1983), p. 103.

37. See Galton's suggestion that "there is a most unusual unanimity in respect to the causes of incapacity of savages for civilization, among writers on those hunting and migratory nations who are brought into contact with advancing colonization, and perish, as they invariably do, by the contact. They tell us that the labour of such men is neither constant nor steady; that the love of a wandering, independent life prevents their settling anywhere to work, except for a short time, when urged by want and encouraged by kind treatment." Galton, *Hereditary Genius*, p. 334.

38. On the popularity of phrenology as a naturalistic science of social life, revealing "progress in action in the world," see Patrick Joyce, *Democratic Subjects: The Self and the Social in Nineteenth-Century England* (Cambridge: Cambridge University Press, 1994), pp. 171–73. Joyce stresses its links with popular Liberalism. On the general importance of popular physiology in the early nineteenth century, see Roger Cooter, "The Power of the Body: The Early Nineteenth Century," in Barry Barnes and Steven Shapin, eds., *Natural Order: Historical Studies of Scientific Culture* (Beverly Hills: Sage, 1979), pp. 73–92.

39. On the historical uses of physiognomy, see Jeanne Fahnestock, "The Heroine of Irregular Features: Physiognomy and Conventions in Heroine Descriptions," *Victorian Studies* 24 (Spring 1981): 325–50, and Mary Cowling, *The Artist as Anthropologist: The Representation of Type and Character in Victorian Art* (Cambridge: Cambridge University Press, 1989).

40. Johann Caspar Lavater, *Essays on Physiognomy, Designed to Promote the Knowledge and the Love of Mankind*, trans. Henry Hunter (London: John Murray, 1789), vol. 1, Author's Preface.

41. Ibid., pp. 14–15, 30–31.

42. Ibid., pp. 137, 236–37; vol. 2, p. 423.

43. For example, in *The Man* (1905) the "rough voyages" undertaken by Harold An Wolf's "forebears amongst northern seas, though they had been a thousand years back, had left traces on his imagination, his blood, his nerves!" And a mid-Atlantic storm is enough to reawaken "the old Berserker spirit" (*The Man*, 279–80). Similarly, in *The Lady of the Shroud* (1909), Rupert Sent Leger refers to "the fighting instinct of my Viking forbears" (*The Lady of the Shroud*, 195). Note also that in *Dracula*, when Arthur

Holmwood drives a stake into the heart of his fiancée Lucy, "he looked like a figure of Thor" (*Dracula*, 259).

44. For a discussion of the Viking as a contested figure in English literary culture in a slightly earlier period, see the account of the reception of Charles Kingsley's novel *Hereward the Wake* (1866) in Bruce Haley, *The Healthy Body and Victorian Culture* (Cambridge, Mass.: Harvard University Press, 1978), pp. 216–20. Other examples would include Carlyle's enthusiasm for "the Pagan Norseman" in his book *On Heroes* (1841) and the account of Sir Henry Curtis's "Bersekir" pugnacity in H. Rider Haggard's *King Solomon's Mines* (1885).

45. See Piers Beirne, "Heredity versus Environment: A Reconsideration of Charles Goring's *The English Convict* (1913)," *British Journal of Criminology* 28 (Summer 1988): 315–39. Beirne's careful analysis gives an excellent account of the intricacies of Lombroso's English reception during the late Victorian and Edwardian periods, stressing the ways in which challenges to Lombrosianism moved "in the same operative direction as that initiated by Lombroso himself" (p. 336).

46. Horace Traubel, ed., *With Walt Whitman in Camden*, Vol. 4 (Carbondale: Southern Illinois University Press, 1959), p. 183.

47. Stoker, *Famous Impostors*, pp. 227–29.

48. Lavater, *Essays*, 1: 30–33.

49. William B. Carpenter, *Principles of Mental Physiology, with Their Applications to the Training and Discipline of the Mind and the Study of Its Morbid Conditions*, 4th ed. (New York: D. Appleton, 1884), p. 517; hereafter cited in text. For a useful historical account of Carpenter's career, see Adrian Desmond, *The Politics of Evolution: Morphology, Medicine, and Reform in Radical London* (Chicago: University of Chicago Press, 1989), pp. 210–22.

50. Jonathan Miller has contrasted Freud's "distinctively custodial interpretation" of the unconscious with the "altogether productive" model developed by Carpenter and others, whose "contents are inaccessible not, as in psychoanalytic theory, because they are held as in strenuously preventive detention but, more interesting, because the effective implementation of cognition and conduct does not actually *require* comprehensive awareness." Jonathan Miller, "Going Unconscious," *New York Review of Books*, April 20, 1995, p. 64.

51. See F. W. H. Myers, "Multiplex Personality," *Proceedings of the Society for Psychical Research* 4 (1886): 496–514.

52. Alan Ryan has argued that John Stuart Mill was oblivious to similar problems: "If the external world was to be constructed out of experience of a self which tried out inductive hypotheses about the course of its experience, then this presupposed a unitary self to do the experiencing, and to make the inferences. Yet the atomistic theory to which Mill was attached seemed to rule out any such self." See Alan Ryan, *J. S. Mill* (London: Routledge & Kegan Paul, 1974), p. 226.

53. See Robert M. Young, *Mind, Brain, and Adaptation in the Nineteenth Century: Cerebral Localization and Its Biological Context from Gall to Ferrier* (Oxford: Clarendon Press, 1970), esp. pp. 210–20. For a general survey of Victorian approaches to the will from a literary perspective, see John R. Reed, *Victorian Will* (Athens: Ohio University Press, 1989).

---

54. When David Ferrier's experimental results were first published in 1873, Carpenter erroneously interpreted them as providing support for his own position, a misreading that continued to command assent for at least another decade. Ferrier's work was not incorporated into standard textbooks until 1890. See Young, *Mind, Brain, and Adaptation*, pp. 215–20. Ironically, as Young shows, Ferrier's thoroughly modern localization of sensory-motor psychophysiology can be placed in a line of descent that goes back to the discredited late-eighteenth-century phrenology of Franz Joseph Gall. For a different view of *Dracula*'s relationship to contemporary medical knowledge, see John L. Greenway, "Seward's Folly: *Dracula* as a Critique of 'Normal Science,'" *Stanford Literature Review* 3 (Fall 1986): 213–30.

55. See Janet Oppenheim, "Manly Nerves," in her *Shattered Nerves: Doctors, Patients, and Depression in Victorian England* (New York: Oxford University Press, 1991), pp. 141–80.

56. Given the atmosphere of intense inwardness that pervades the opening chapters, it is hardly surprising that "one of the most consistent interpretations of *Dracula* has been to see it as the projection of Jonathan Harker's unconscious," in which the Count serves as his lascivious double, acting out the clerk's "repressed desires." See Elaine Showalter, "Blood Sells: Vampire Fever and Anxieties for the *fin de siècle*," *Times Literary Supplement*, January 8, 1993, p. 14.

Feminism, Fiction, and the Utopian Promise of *Dracula*_____

Nancy Armstrong

To think utopically is to imagine how that insatiable being known as the modern individual might acquire the means to perfect and gratify him- or herself. A conceptual countermove always accompanies such utopian imaginings, as we must almost immediately devise measures to check the selfish excesses of that individual, lest they encroach on the rights of others. Isn't this the dilemma we confront, for example, in advocating free speech? No sooner do we imagine the possibility of free self-expression, than we also feel compelled to curb speech at the point where it turns into hate speech, permits telemarketers to violate the sanctity of our dinner hour, or puts salacious material in the tremulous hands of children. Economic theory observes the same paradox when it insists that capitalism be left to work according to its own laws but then hastens to define those laws as either "self-regulating" or in need of controls to bring supply in line with demand. Arguments for free sexual expression similarly limit the scope of their application with such qualifiers as "in the privacy of the home" and "between consenting adults." I am interested in the question of when and by what cultural means people came to be soft-wired with this compulsion to imagine utopia in terms of expanding possibilities for individual fulfillment, only, it would seem, so that those same people would feel conversely compelled to limit those utopian possibilities.

I will identify this pervasive cultural paradox with a change in the novel form that occurred during the Victorian period and fostered great expectations. This body of fiction invites us to imagine better worlds, however, only to turn those wishes so sour that we come to prefer the present world, fraught as it is with social inequities. Indeed, my favorite novels turn fantasies of unlimited inclusion and human perfectibility into scenes of dashed hopes and monstrous forms of self-gratification with a regularity that tells me that this is precisely the point. Victorian fiction is out to convince us that partial gratification is preferable to a social alternative that indulges what is presumed to be man's unlimited appetite for more. But like most definitions of realism, the model I have just offered is both too loose in logic and too close in terminology to the very paradox it seeks to describe.

In order to provide some sense of the curious turn of cultural thought this paradox actually performed for Victorian readers and the rhetorical power that it still exercises on us as a result, I will pursue two critical tactics. First, I want to approach this paradox by way of the form it took and what it did and did not accomplish as recent feminist theory appropriated certain narrative strategies from Victorian fiction and used them to argue for new reading procedures and a more inclusionary literary canon. Presumably, readings informed by feminist theory sought to make it easier for educated people to imagine both a more diverse faculty and a more democratic social world. Naomi Schor reminds us that feminism's interrogation of power in the academy expressed a "perhaps utopian longing for a different university, a university of differences" ("The Righting" 72). Victorian fiction provides the occasion and material for mounting this argument, I believe, because recent feminist criticism sought much the same objective as Victorian novelists once did. Given that feminism's success in the literary disciplines has not made it any easier than Victorian fiction did to imagine expanding the means for self-expression without simultaneously limiting those possibilities, it should be instructive to find out why both fiction and feminism failed to get beyond this paradox. We stand to learn how this feature of Victorian culture continues to inflect our political thinking. After pointing out what feminism shares in this respect with the Victorian novel, I will then try to reverse the critical undertow that accompanies modern utopian thought and consider where a reading of *Dracula* might lead us politically were we to identify with the vampire in rejecting the limits of a realism designed to maintain the autonomy of nation, family, and individual.

What Women Lack

Until the 1980s, when feminism emerged as a major force in novel studies, scholars and critics by and large read novels novelistically. By reading novelistically, I mean that one identifies a lack in the protagonist that someone or something else must supply. Once the protagonist is supplied with the missing element—e.g., Robinson Crusoe with land, Tom Jones with a patrimony, or Edward Waverley with British identity—that individual can overcome the obstacle that keeps him from improving his position in life and achieve recognition within the community whose order and vigor he consequently renews. The protagonist's lack defines the magic ingredient that both enables self-fulfillment along with social empowerment and creates a reader who feels that lack of social recognition and wants to see it fulfilled. Self-fulfillment so defined calls for nothing less than a seismic shift in the prevailing social order. The small shock of incorporating a Pamela Andrews, Tom Jones, Fanny Price, or Jane Eyre throws open imaginary doors to individuals with the energy, wit, and desire to occupy positions formerly closed to them. The novel was born as authors gave narrative form to this wish for a social order sufficiently elastic to accommodate individual ambition.

Feminist literary theory made a swift and telling intervention in this way of reading British fiction when it created a reader willing to consider what a female protagonist lacked and how that lack could be satisfied. Feminists identified the feminine lack in terms of "agency," by which they usually meant the authority enabling men to effect some kind of social change, however local and temporary. But, taking their cue from fiction, these same critics rarely sought a masculine remedy for this lack in terms of property or position. Instead, feminists established a specific verbal performance as the precondition for achieving authority. Novels from Defoe's to those of Virginia Woolf indicate that an author-heroine has to represent herself as rational, consistent, durable, and personally resourceful before she can argue against some form of bias, do what that bias would not let her achieve, and gain recognition within a community that appears progressive for thus extending the limits of acceptable feminine behavior. This move convinced a generation of readers that acquiring a "voice," or what might be called cultural agency, can compensate for the forms of property that traditionally authorized the rights-bearing citizen.[1]

Thus, for example, in their groundbreaking study *The Madwoman in the Attic*, Sandra Gilbert and Susan Gubar ask us to read novels authored by women as the author's way of gaining compensation through the speech of a fictional surrogate for what she lacked in economic and political terms. They claim that

> by projecting their rebellious impulses [. . .] into mad or monstrous women [. . .] female authors dramatize their own [. . .] desire both to accept the strictures of patriarchal society and to reject them. What this means [. . .] is that the madwoman in literature written by women is [. . .] in some sense the *author's* double, an image of her own anxiety and rage. (78)

Guided by this model, the reader feels the author/protagonist's lack but refuses to accept it as something she lacks simply because she's a woman. Like Jane Eyre, that reader projects her lack of political agency onto a madwoman who enacts the outrage of every woman's dependency and confinement within a masculine culture. But as the novel detaches action from the heroine and displaces it onto a debased surrogate, the speech act itself acquires a form of power superior to action, a form of power that consequently authorizes not only Brontë's narrator and Brontë herself but also those critics who identify her lack with their own as members of a masculinist discipline. By shifting responsibility for this lack from the natural condition of being female to the cultural institutions that reserve power and privilege for men, feminism clearly made a move in the right direction.

During the 1980s, this way of reading changed which novels were read and taught in British and American classrooms as well as the imagined relationship between individual and nation that compels one to identify with a protagonist. Feminist critics began to read Daniel Defoe's *Moll Flanders* in place of his *Robinson Crusoe*, Samuel Richardson's *Pamela* for Henry Fielding's *Tom Jones*, and Jane Austen's *Emma* rather than Walter Scott's *Waverley*. Because *cultural* authority, as feminism had defined it, depended on a lack of *political* authority, however, this argument left a new generation of feminists with the difficult task of overcoming their lack of political authority without losing the rhetorical power that very lack had given them. Wendy Brown explains this dilemma as a version of what Nietzsche termed *ressentiment*—the claim that because power corrupts truth and compromises moral authority, those without power are especially qualified to speak. To move from a position of lack to one of power, according to this logic, feminism would have to let go of the lack of power, or injury, on which it has based its claims to occupy the moral high ground, and explore alternative ethical possibilities (45). The solution rested on reattaching voice, or cultural power, to politics. Instead of saying that men have what women lack and use that power to prevent women from having it, feminist scholars of the late eighties and nineties, myself included, identified the feminine difference itself as a positive source of authority, though not the same authority reserved for men.[2] Others argued that their exclusion from the public sphere made it possible for women writers to develop new and interesting ways of displaying psychological breadth and subtlety.[3] Before long, still others noticed that eighteenth-century novels used women as the source of feelings that united those individuals in a community of sensibility whom acquisitive individualism would otherwise put asunder.[4] During the 1990s, literary criticism consequently looked to sentimental fiction as the imaginary seedbed of a more inclusive nation, increased class mobility, and aesthetic innovation.

The publication of Judith Butler's *Gender Trouble* simultaneously validated and demolished the premise that voice could compensate women for the lack of the forms of political power that men came by naturally.[5] Where Foucauldian historicism had seriously undermined the naturalness of gender and placed women on the same cultural playing field with men, Butler's notion that identity was no more nor less than a performance effectively turned the tables on the primacy of the unmarked term, or universal masculinity. Butler made the marked or excluded term—woman, queer, and ultimately drag queen—into the model for all identities, including "straight men." As she famously put it,

> the "presence" of so-called heterosexual conventions within homosexual contexts as well as the proliferation of specifically gay discourses of sexual difference [. . .] cannot be explained as chimerical representations of originally heterosexual identities. [. . .] The replication of heterosexual constructs in non-heterosexual frames brings into relief the utterly constructed status of the so-called heterosexual original. Thus, gay is to straight not as copy is to original, but, rather, as copy is to copy. (31)

According to Butler's model, the individual begins as a mix of possibilities and acquires a gender as he or she drops either feminine qualities or masculine qualities from his or her performative repertoire to become masculine or feminine, respectively. The lack of masculinity is both something women acquire from their culture and the very basis of their identity. Acquiring such an identity is no giddy one-night stand, but a lifetime commitment to repeat performances. With this model, one can read novels as culture's way not only of naturalizing, stigmatizing, and updating categories of identity, but also of setting the standard for an individual performance: Which performances must a protagonist repeat and which discard? What categorical violations can a heroine get away with and which must she eschew as foreign to her very being? Fiction should have shown us that interiority comes from an external source (i.e., writing) and that repeated performances have over time wrought significant changes on our culture's standard for gender difference. Informed by the understanding that performance— or, for my purposes, fiction—produces identity, feminism might have hijacked certain narrative strategies and reworked them to imagine an order whose authority depended on its responsiveness to the needs and desires of disenfranchised and dependent groups rather than to the protection of property. Let us consider what kept us from doing so.

Mother of False Utopias

In recuperating the softer side of femininity, I will argue, critics and scholars repeated that event in the history of the European novel known as the inward turn. Georg Lukács identifies 1848 or thereabouts as the moment when the novel abandoned its attempts to imagine a more flexible and inclusive social order.[6] After the mid-century mark, even such consummate novelists as Dickens and Flaubert fill what they define as lacking in the social world not through some small shift in social relations but through a change of heart, the excesses of sentimentalism, escapes into exoticism, and the pleasures of domestic life. Herbert Marcuse's analysis of this moment puts Lukács's disappointment into useful historical perspective. In "The Affirmative Character of Culture," Marcuse describes the moment of the novel's inward turn as a rupture in modern culture that caused an ideal domain of the mental and spiritual to break off from the rest of culture. The decisive characteristic of this new domain is, he claims, "a universally obligatory, eternally better and more valuable world that must be unconditionally affirmed: a world essentially different from the factual world of the daily struggle for existence, yet realizable by every individual for himself 'from within,' without any transformation of the state of fact" (95). Marcuse identifies this displacement of material gratification onto a purely cultural plane as the liberal solution to the problem of economic inequity. The idea is that each individual is responsible for finding within him- or herself emotional, spiritual, or aesthetic compensation for whatever forms of gratification he or she may lack in material terms. Marcuse's account of the inward turn also goes a long way toward explaining how the utopian imagination came to be stalked by a disingenuous counterpart in the form of nostalgic reincarnations of precapitalist communities that were notably powerless to transform the world defined by realism. As he explains, "[t]he truth of a higher world, of a higher good than material existence," became the means of concealing "the truth that a better material existence" might actually be achieved (121).

The novel performed its own version of the inward turn, as it used a class-specific model of the household to displace the ideal of civil society as the collective body on which one depended for care and protection. In so doing, the novel made that household *the* model for imagining social relations. Over two decades ago, Nancy Chodorow explained in *The Reproduction of Mothering* how this peculiar apparatus—peculiar, that is, to capitalist economies—produces gendered individuals, each differentiated from the other in terms of traits specific to a social stratum more or less determined by the mother. The household so conceived not only serves as the primary means of interpellation in relation to which we continue to individuate ourselves through repeated acts of compliance to or deviance from familial norms; the modern household also provides the reward one receives for meeting those norms. This household is formed and perpetuates itself on a principle of exogamy that compels us to find a partner outside the maternal household with whom we can reproduce something very much like that household, with the result that it appears both natural and available to everyone.[7]

The formation of a community at the end of *Jane Eyre* encapsulates the cultural-historical process that I have in mind:

> My Edward and I, then, are happy: and the more so, because those we most love are happy likewise. Diana and Mary Rivers are both married: alternately, once every year, they come to see us, and we go to see them. Diana's husband is a captain in the navy: a gallant officer, and a good man. Mary's is a clergyman: a college friend of her brother's; and, from his attainments and principles, worthy of the connexion. (Brontë 501)

Why Charlotte Brontë must strain to create difference between households that are almost indistinguishable from the heroine's should be obvious. She has her protagonist describe the formation of a new society as the reproduction of the private sphere through a set of marriages that mimic and normalize Jane's marriage to Rochester. Contrary to our expectations, Brontë does not even try to assemble this social ideal out of the heterogeneous population that her protagonist encounters during the course of the novel. On the contrary, she begins with Jane's blood relatives—cousins Mary and Diana—and so implies that civil society is made of men whom such women deem "worthy of the connexion." The novel consequently leaves us with a social order that has been renovated one household at a time, until all other forms of kinship have been banished either to the colonies or to Catholic Europe.

As it slowly but surely exiles or kills off those characters who dare to exist in alternative living arrangements, *Jane Eyre* universalizes a radically restricted notion of kinship based on the married couple and their biological offspring.[8] In this respect, the novel offers a prolepsis of the formal development of nineteenth-century British fiction itself. After Austen, the exemplary protagonist rarely grows up to become a member of civil society. The Dickensian hero, for example, enters a household that displaces any semblance of the complex and fraught social world he has successfully negotiated. At this point, the limits that the novel has set on his happiness miraculously vanish, along with the fact that such happiness is an exception to the social rule. It is by means of this move, when repeated countless times over, that one class established its own ethnic practices as the national norm and ensured their reproduction in future generations.

If "the family" in this precise cultural-historical sense served as the mechanism by which the novel cancelled out its own democratic mission and naturalized the gendered division of labor and political authority, then why did feminist theory and criticism fail to perform a sustained critique of such literary behavior? Unless we can challenge what happens at the level of literature, what chance do we have in political terms? Yes, feminism has produced important examples of anti-familialism over the course of the movement's history. But when examined in a harshly critical light, most such political critiques end up replacing a household composed of the heterosexually monogamous couple and their biological offspring with another version of that household that can in fact do little to change the way a nation distributes goods and services to its population.[9] Judith Butler confronts this problem in an essay on gay marriage, when she refuses to say whether extending the legitimacy of "the family" to lesbian and gay couples would threaten or authorize traditional marriage.[10] This is the way with hegemonic formations, I would suggest; deviations at once threaten and maintain what culture has defined as nature.

The Return of the Repressed

Once novelists displaced the expanded and renewed society imagined by their Enlightenment predecessors with a constricted and idealized household, anyone who tried to imagine a different model of social relations had to grapple with the family first. This, I believe, is how Victorian fiction painted modern utopian thinking into a corner, where it either had to come up with a genuine alternative to the modern family or else offer readers a reformed version of the status quo. At the same time, however, that same fiction banished nonfamilies to a domain resembling the one that Freud would later identify with the uncanny—a domain that asserts itself in literature and life by suspending realism and common sense, thus undermining our taken-for-granted relation to the real. I would go so far as to say that uncanny experiences are fundamentally collective—involving not only a confusion of the difference between inside and outside but a dissolution of the difference between individual and aggregate as well. Freud's essay on the uncanny labors to separate the thinking of primitive people—always implicitly collective—from the queasiness a modern individual feels when suppressed fantasies well up and overpower the categories on which he or she relies for understanding people, things, and their behavior. But, as Freud himself admits, it is virtually impossible to maintain this difference even in theory.[11] And if that difference cannot be so maintained, I would argue, then the fantasies peculiar to the uncanny provide one way of understanding what our relationships to one another might be like were we not to undergo the separations, identifications, and abjections that turn us into modern individuals. If, as Freud's difficulty in maintaining the boundary between individual and group at the level of the uncanny suggests, modern individuals are first collective and only secondarily individual human beings, then when and how were such individuals made to feel that their very existence would be threatened if they failed to form a nuclear family?

The problem, as I see it, begins as Victorian fiction offers its readership a glimpse of alternative kinship practices only to demonstrate spectacularly that such alternatives dissolve gender differences and so produce monsters. Hence Emily Brontë's incestuously similar Catherine and Heathcliff, Mary Shelley's parthenogenetic monster, and Robert Louis Stevenson's Jekyll internally split into Jekyll and Hyde. This, I am suggesting, is the job of the nineteenth-century gothic: to turn any formation that challenges the nuclear family into a form of degeneracy so hostile to modern selfhood as to negate emphatically its very being. Where the great tradition of Victorian fiction saw modern consciousness as the means to resolve the widening gap between self-fulfillment and what was socially permissible,[12] popular romance took an outward turn. Rather than struggle to keep the Victorian gentleman on the same developmental timeline with his savage forebears, the better to justify the dominion of the West over the rest, Stevenson converts these contraries into a contradiction. In his famous story of 1886, he has Mr. Hyde periodically take over Dr. Jekyll's body and occupy his place in time. Although springing from a single origin, this story proves, the pair can no more live as one than it can live as two independent beings. With the publication of *Dracula* in 1897, Bram Stoker pushed this logic of monogenesis past the breaking point. Rather than the same ontology with the entirely different temporalities that we encounter in Stevenson, self and other confront each other in Stoker's novel as competing varieties of human being between whom the production of some compromise formation is no longer possible. This is the full-blown logic of polygenesis at work, rendering phobic the idea of humanity as a single family, autonomous, relatively self-sufficient, and dedicated to caring for all its members.

Clearly marked as imaginary, vampire practices represent precisely that notion of kinship as one that reproduces itself at the expense of the human species. Natural reproduction is hardly the issue, however. In one of the more peculiar bedroom scenes in modern literature, Stoker identifies the threat posed by the vampire as primarily cultural, as Dracula systematically undoes the naturalized relations of the modern family:

> On the bed beside the window lay Jonathan Harker, his face flushed and breathing as though in a stupor. Kneeling on the edge of the bed facing outward was the white-clad figure of his wife. By her side stood a tall, thin man, clad in black. His face was turned from us, but the instant we saw, all recognized the Count [. . .]. With his left hand he held both Mrs. Harker's hands, keeping them away with her arms at full tension; his right hand gripped her by the back of the neck, forcing her face down on his bosom. Her white nightdress was smeared with blood, and a thin stream trickled down the man's breast which was shown by his torn-open dress. (362–63)

Were we to stop reading here, we could anticipate the unfolding of a classic pornographic scenario. But Stoker adds one sentence more to quell such eroticism: "The attitude of the two resembled a child forcing a kitten's nose into a saucer of milk" (363). This statement transforms the metonymic chain linking man to woman and woman to man into a set of metaphoric substitutions that reverses the dynamic of normative desire.

The facts that Dracula must keep her hands "away with her arms at full tension" and force "her face down on his bosom" tell us that something like a rape is in progress. Her husband's flushed face and heavy breathing indicate that he is in something like a postcoital "stupor." Kneeling before Dracula, Mrs. Harker's position may suggest fellatio, but she is actually subject to an act of maternal aggression performed by a male who has already enjoyed her husband. By thus usurping the positions of wife, mother, and lover, Dracula strips these figures of their meaning in nineteenth-century porn and subjects them to another libidinal economy. This is a radically overwrought scene: a menstruating male—his bodice ripped; a polluted female—her nightgown stained; a castrated father and a phallic mother. For a flickering instant of iconographic confusion before the final sentence reasserts the difference between what this strange man is doing to a woman and how an impatient child might feed a kitten, the rapist behaves as a mother, the lover is truly bisexual, and oral gratification prevails. Against the tide of recent critical opinion, I want to argue that this passage is not using sex to render intolerable the foreigner, the Jew, the Oriental, or the immigrant, the features of which Dracula certainly bears. This novel uses the foreigner, the Jew, the Oriental, and the immigrant to render intolerable all social groupings hostile to the family.[13] What then are these antifamilial rules of kinship?

The novel begins by proposing an ideal family and concludes with a family that has incorporated certain qualities of the vampire. This family is detached from geography. Jonathan Harker is the real-estate agent responsible for the transaction that allowed Dracula to invade England in the first place. The hybrid child whom he fathers contains some of Dracula's blood, along with the blood of the other men who supplied transfusions to combat the vampire blood within Mina's body. This group forms a polyandrous community to care for one quite ordinary woman and their collective child. Thus here, at the end of the nineteenth century, the family still shapes the community. Finding no safe haven in the English countryside, however, this family requires an international community of experts to secure its reproductive capability.[14] The cast of experts in turn lacks something that it must have before it can perform this service and revitalize a society in decline. This cast of experts overcomes that lack only as it incorporates certain features of the vampire. By thus absorbing certain residual cultural elements, the modern middle class adapts to and endures through changing historical conditions.

Still more important to my argument than the forms of aggregation that can be incorporated into a new and less individualistic ruling-class ethos are the gothic elements that cannot be so subsumed in Stoker's family. Topping my list of such elements is the curious formation of the heroine that inverts the formation of earlier domestic heroines. Initially Mina Harker is one of those secondary characters born to serve as man's helpmate. Once bitten she takes over center stage and becomes the focal point and purpose of the labor carried out by her entourage of masculine types—a doctor, a scientist, an American capitalist, and a member of the English gentry, as well as her husband, a real estate agent. In contrast with conventional heroines, Mina is full of information that she has copied from and synthesized for members of the community. Her synthesis blurs the distinction between fact and fiction along with the difference between masculine and feminine labor. As the scientist Van Helsing puts it, "She has a man's brain—a brain that a man should have were he much gifted—and a woman's heart" (302). Mina provides the means of transferring certain qualities of vampire culture to the masculine half of her community. By incorporating and then being purified of the very qualities that modern men lack—a common object of desire, collective thinking, and so forth—she comes to embody that lack. In order to become the traditional reproductive woman, she ceases to manage information and leaves the work of cultural reproduction to men.

In ridding the world and Mina's body of Dracula, the novel eliminates the possibility that individual identity can be formed according to the principle of addiction, which was understood by Victorian medical science as the invasion of an individual's mind and sensibility by a foreign substance capable of overriding that individual's natural desire.[15] While under Dracula's spell, Mina's desire comes from elsewhere and belongs to someone else. Contrary to the domestic novel—which pits a desire that wells up from within the self against the limits imposed on that individual by her social position—the culture of the vampire acknowledges that all identity is cultural at base, therefore external in origin, especially sexual appetite. In Mina's case, however, to say that the individual's desire is not her own but that of someone external to herself does not mean that she is enacting someone else's desire—not if the entire group is made of individuals no different from herself.

The end of individuated desire spells the undoing of any need for fiction to defend the community against excessive individualism, which was, according to Enlightenment versions of the social contract, the main purpose of civil society. With the assumption that individual desire was not only natural but also excessively present in human beings, the idea of property was born—the need to have it as well as the need to protect it. If, however, each individual were to enact the desire of all, then there would be no reason to protect each from all others, thus no need for civil society to defend the autonomy of the home.[16] The same inverse logic holds true for intellectual property. It is one thing for members of a culture of experts to pass around diaries, notes, books, newspapers, and documents. Doing so only reinforces the idea that this printed material arises from thoughts originating in the mind of a specific individual. But it is quite another thing to know what someone is thinking as she thinks it, for this eradicates the boundaries that make her an individual. Having no individuality, Dracula can mimic virtually anyone, male or female, man or beast, including English gentlemen. He automatically assimilates many different forms of knowledge garnered from disparate sources and puts them to work satisfying a desire that is by definition that of a group. For any member of the group to carry all that group's knowledge, especially if that member happens to be female, is to render the very notion of the expert as absurd as the notion of an author. In a sense, then, we can say that vampire thinking reverses the gendered division of intellectual labor that Mina Harker was predisposed to violate anyway.[17] Rather than hoarding information for herself, she recasts it so as to create the big picture necessary for the group's strategic control of battlefield and institution. Like the desire she feels, the ideas that Mina produces come from and rightfully belong to the group.

But the novel makes Dracula's penetration of her mind less shocking than his melodramatic usurpation of the rights of the Harkers' marriage bed, a violation that overtly eradicates sexual difference. The figure of the breast-feeding male cancels out the categorical distinctions between man, woman, and child maintained by the family, a cancellation represented in and produced by the vampire's needy, all-consuming, and yet inseminating mouth. This organ affords Stoker the means of challenging the natural difference between family and civil society, the one expressing woman's nature and the other man's.[18] Wendy Brown's analysis of the symbolic weight that modern cultures place on the gendered difference between public and private spheres provides a sense of how much, besides sex, is at stake in the difference between man and woman. As she explains,

> [T]he autonomous liberal subject is a fantastic creature, born into and existing wholly in the realm of civil society, who disavows the relations, activities, and subjects that sustain him in civil society from their sequestered place in the family. This creature is not only fantastic, however, but ultimately dependent: the "autonomous" subject depends on the subjection of [his dependents] for emotional and physical sustenance. (158)

Dracula's bite may cancel out the principle of difference that inevitably subordinates a marked term to an apparently universal term, as in the difference between woman and man, but the figure of the breast-feeding male makes Stoker's vampire disturbing in another respect as well. Contradicting his traditional role, which is to drain an individual of the humanity that restrains his most basic, presumably bestial impulses, here Dracula performs as the bad breast incarnate to infuse the world with the infectious otherness of foreign blood, along with desires hostile to the reproduction of the human species as modern culture defines it.[19] Where such a novel as *Jane Eyre* allowed the family to eclipse civil society as the symbolic means of resolving social contradictions, *Dracula* turns the tables and allows a radically inclusive community to render the family obsolete, along with the liberal individual.

Negating the Negative

Although Stoker's novel makes it all but impossible for us to see the demise of the nuclear family in positive terms, European culture did offer readers the means of doing so. To negate the negative implications of vampire, we might turn to the fantasy of a cosmopolitan world order that lost out and was finally demonized in its struggle with modern nationalism to dominate the modern political imagination. In his 1795 essay on "Perpetual Peace," Immanuel Kant argues that a representative republic is the only state capable of rule by law rather than violence; any other form of government is despotic. Under monarchy, states are ruled by an elite who are not themselves subject to the law but can command the people "to sacrifice themselves for something that does not concern them." To avoid such tyranny, Kant contends, the rule of law must extend beyond national boundaries and embrace, in theory, all of humanity. Thus he asks his reader to imagine an all-inclusive world republic that guarantees to all people, no matter their origin, "the conditions of universal hospitality." Hospitality, as he explains it, depends on "the right of a stranger not to be treated as an enemy [. . .]. It is not a question of being received as a guest," he continues, "it is rather a right of visit, a right of demanding of others that they admit one to their society" (439). Kant assumes that the foreigner will maintain the differences linking him to his place of origin. (Why else would we need laws ensuring someone admission to another country?) The desires of one group will offset another's, he contends, so as to neutralize conflicts that inevitably arise within and among such populations, "if only they are intelligent" (439). By the time Stoker set pen to paper a century later, the situation looked entirely different. The migration of people from metropolitan core to colonial periphery and back again, as well as the cultural circulation among metropolitan centers, indicated that cosmopolitanism would challenge a nation's autonomy and thus the principle of nationalism itself. By running roughshod over national differences, Stoker's vampire transforms the utopian fantasy of universal hospitality into the xenophobic fantasy of a nation that welcomes strangers only to become something other than itself, a colonizer colonized from within.

Writing at the beginning of the nineteenth century, Kant contrasts the European savage to his American counterpart on grounds that "many tribes of the latter have been eaten up by their enemies, while the former know how to make better use of their conquered enemies than to dine off them; they know better how to use them to increase the number of their subjects and thus the quantity of instruments for even more extensive wars" (437). As Stoker renders it, vampirism combines the subhuman behavior of the American cannibal with the more pernicious instrumentalism of the European, thereby collapsing under- and overdevelopment into one another according to the late-Victorian logic of degeneration. For most readers, the categorical violation linking vampirism to cannibalism would be enough to put the final nail in the conceptual coffin I am exploring. Indeed, one might well ask, what new possibilities can be teased from a model where the dead feed on the living? But this question, I must insist, invites another: What if there is no such thing as a new idea? What if new ideas come into being only as we mine history for residual materials and recombine them so as to alter the way we understand our relation to one another?

It is fair to say that Locke and Rousseau did precisely this when each came up with a model of the state that reworked sovereignty in order to imagine each individual as the sovereign of his own private domain.

Two centuries later, Freud argued that the unconscious mind expressed an individual's deepest and most personal needs by similarly reworking the debris of culture, or "day residue" material (4: 165–87). Fast-forward another half century to the last half of the twentieth century, and one finds Claude Lévi-Strauss explaining cultural change as just such a recycling process in which categories congeal out of earlier material, rise into dominance, and then disperse, once the cultural conflict for which they afford symbolic resolution becomes obsolete (269–81). Close on the heels of structural anthropology, Foucault's *Discipline and Punish* turns this process of narrative transformation into a theory of history, as dressage passes from a mere display of horsemanship, or tactic, into a strategy, or method of social engineering essential to the growth and maintenance of the kind of population required for industrial capitalism.

Stoker invites us to listen to the residual, the repressed, the past, the ostensibly dead, much as Freud, Lévi-Strauss, and Foucault do. But in contrast to theories that try to explain how what is outside, past, and dead gets inside our minds and determines what we desire—thus how we imagine the future—Stoker emphasizes the bone-chilling truth that to invite the past in the form of alternative kinship relations into our present may well mean our extinction as liberal individuals. By associating Stoker with twentieth-century theories that lack his apocalyptic edge, I am certainly not implying that he went overboard in making this prediction. I believe he was simply being more forthright on this point than most modern theoreticians. What I *am* suggesting is that there is something important to be gained from a positive reading of what the Victorian novel deliberately abjects as antagonistic to the very terms in which it negotiates the fraught relationship of self to society. To assume a positive form, a genuinely new way of conceptualizing this relationship will necessarily invalidate the gendered categories that support and lend their features to differences among classes, races, sexualities, and ethnicities.

That feminism has brought us to a crossroads in cultural history is clear. The line of argument that rests on the politics of difference leads us indirectly back to the liberal individual and wins us the power accruing to negative rights: the right not to be violated in one's body; the right not to be unrepresented, implicitly, then, the right to speak for oneself; the right to be different within specified limits. It goes against all common sense to undervalue these rights, especially in today's political climate. Another line of argument is poised within literary theory, however, and ready to challenge the prevailing notion of identity based on the differences we maintain within the category of the human.[20] This counterargument inverts the concept of difference so as to emphasize what we all share by virtue of our individual deviations from the cultural norms naturalized by the modern family.[21] During the 1990s, feminist theory and criticism together began to mount an argument for the superior reality of identities designated as marked, specific, or dependent in contrast with that normative masculine individual who *depends* on his family of dependents for a semblance of realism. Dominant and subordinate, universal and marked, are, according to the logic of this model, two faces of the same cultural coin. Feminist theory intuited this fundamental truth when it staked out the undervalued, or marked, term as its own, only to back away from this conviction as a variety of groups challenged the right of "women" to speak as and for all those in such a position.

Feminist literary theory had by this point come to understand "women" as nothing more nor less than a placeholder for just about everyone who did not feel completely at ease within the category of straight white masculinity, including straight white men. A generation of readers informed by Lacan and Foucault understood full well that modern individuals achieve specificity on the basis of how they either fall short or defy the human standard set by the fantasy of the liberal individual. We knew, in other words, that feminism was not about us so much as an argument for the primacy of the marked term itself, an argument potentially capable of destroying that fantasy. As I have tried to show by pointing out the utopian potential in *Dracula*, the trick of formulating a more adequate notion of the human is to find a way of articulating what we lack in positive rather than negative terms—as the sameness we acquire by virtue of always and necessarily falling short of the cultural norms incorporated in and reproduced by the modern family.

Notes

1. Carol Gilligan's *In a Different Voice* offers what was one of the more influential applications of this novelistic move to actual women:

> As we have listened for centuries to the voices of men and the theories of development that their experience informs, so we have come more recently to notice not only the silence of women but the difficulty in hearing what they say when they speak. Yet in the different voice of women lies the truth of an ethic of care, the tie between relationship and responsibility, and the origins of aggression in the failure of connection. The failure to see the different reality of women's lives and to hear the differences in their voices stems in part from the assumption that there is a single mode of social experience and interpretation. By positing instead two different modes, we arrive at a more complex rendition of human experience which sees the truth of separation and attachment in the lives of women and men and recognizes how these truths are carried by different modes of language and thought. (173–74)

2. See, for example, Armstrong; Davidson; and Sommer.
3. See, for example, Felman; and Schor, *Breaking*.
4. See, for example, Barnes; Johnson; Samuels; Stern; Todd; Tompkins.
5. In *Gender Trouble*, Butler dismantles the fallacy of "agency," namely, the assumption that there is being behind doing. There is, she contends, "no gender identity behind the expressions of gender; that identity is performatively constituted by the very 'expressions' that are said to be its results" (25).
6. In his preface to *Studies in European Realism*, Lukács charges realism with the sacred duty of maintaining "the organic, indissoluble connection between man as a private individual and man as a social being, as a member of the community" (8). In *The Historical Novel*, he argues that fiction abandoned this principle around 1848, even before realism had reached its peak in England and the United States (171–250).
7. Challenges to the exclusive naturalness of kinship based on the heterosexual couple and their biological offspring have proliferated in recent years thanks to the

open formation of gay or "chosen" families and to new reproductive technologies. See, for example, Hayden 173–205; Ragoné 118–31; and Weston 87–110.

8. A number of anthropologists credit Darwin with narrowing down kinship to this very restrictive notion of blood: see, for example, Hayden 177; and Herdt 28–32. I would argue that the novel of the same period did more than science to transform theory into practice, when it took the symbolic order of the so-called facts of life and recast them as many and various individual destinies, the outcome of which depended on marriage and biological reproduction.

9. In *Profit and Pleasure*, Rosemary Hennessy claims, similarly, that alternative "families" do not alter the fact that primary goods and services continue to be distributed to most of the population through the family. Moreover, as she explains, the family ensures that despite "the recruitment of more women into the work-force, the division of labor in the home is not being dramatically effected" (63). "Domestic partnerships and gay marriages that redefine sexuality only in terms of rights for gays" leave unquestioned or even indirectly promote "capitalism's historical stake in the relationship among family, labor, and consumption" (67).

10. See Butler, "Is Kinship Always Already Heterosexual?"

11. In his essay on "The Uncanny," Freud attempts to explain those moments in their lives when modern adults abandon reason and understand their experience in terms of "the omnipotence of thoughts, with the prompt fulfillment of wishes, with secret injurious powers and with the return of the dead" (17: 247). Such moments not only challenge the limits of individuated consciousness but also expose the fact that those limits are as much a cultural acquisition as the old belief in omnipotent thinking. As he explains,

> We—or our primitive forefathers—once believed that these possibilities were realities, and were convinced that they actually happened. Nowadays we no longer believe in them, we have *surmounted* these modes of thought; but we do not feel quite sure of our new beliefs, and the old ones still exist within us ready to seize upon any confirmation. As soon as something actually happens in our lives which seems to confirm the old, discarded beliefs we get a feeling of the uncanny. (17: 247–48)

Freud mentions the possibility of collective regression as if to dismiss that possibility and get on with an argument in which "the distinction between the two" kinds of uncanny experience is "theoretically very important" (17: 248). But the more he tries to differentiate the feeling we get when repressed material wells up within us from the feeling we get when only old collective thought modes can explain the world, the more Freud undermines the difference between the individual's internal nature and the culture external to that individual, until, he admits, his argument "no doubt extends the term 'repression' beyond its legitimate meaning" (17: 249).

12. In *The Great Tradition*, F. R. Leavis describes the Conradian sensibility, for example, as an internally divided one "intimately experienced in the strains and starvations of the isolated consciousness, and [. . .] deeply aware of the sense in which reality is social, something established and sustained in a kind of collaboration" (209).

---

13. In *Skin Shows*, Judith Halberstam links the figure of Dracula to those of the immigrant and Jew:

> Dracula's need to "consume as many lives as he can," his feminized because non phallic sexuality, and his ambulism that cause him to wander far from home in search of new blood mark him with all the signs of Jewish neurosis. Dracula, as the prototype of the wanderer, the "stranger in a strange land," also reflects the way that homelessness or rootlessness was seen to undermine nation. (98)

In *Fictions of Loss in the Victorian Fin de Siècle*, Stephen D. Arata identifies narratives of reverse colonization in which "problematic or disruptive figures come from the periphery of empire to threaten a troubled metropole" (107). Arata considers *Dracula* as a narrative that reflects imperial practices back to the British in monstrous form. In *Alien Nation*, Cannon Schmitt reads *Dracula* through the lens of Orientalism, contending that Stoker's purpose in having "the eastern vampire" threaten "the maternal" is to replace "multiple national identities with a single western one" (144).

14. In *Reproductive Urges*, Anita Levy resists a racialized reading of *Dracula* and instead asks the question, "[W]hat does the figure of the vampire make possible or facilitate?" (158). She responds to this question by reminding us that

> the vampire makes possible [. . .] a revised configuration of the household conjoining in and through the figures of the professional man and the literate woman labors of cultural reproduction with those of family formation and perpetuation. [. . .] What is new in Stoker's representation of the privileged alliance between a middle-class woman and professional men is that the intellectual labor of cultural reproduction is no longer severed from the maternal labor of social and biological reproduction. (168)

In *Modernism, Romance, and the Fin de Siècle*, Nicholas Daly reads *Dracula* "as an origin-tale for a new professional class." The novel "represents the appearance of these new men as the necessary consequence of an external threat that then becomes embodied in the story's female characters. By the end of the narrative the vampire has been defeated, but the team of professional men lives on" (26).

15. For an illuminating explanation of the relation of such theories to *Dracula*, see Margolis 19–37.

16. The one exception to the rule of immediate and unrestrained consumption among the vampires in this novel stands out as a rather transparent device for letting Jonathan Harker know that he is soon to become the object rather than the subject of consumption and so prompts his escape from Dracula's castle. Eavesdropping at his door, Harker overhears Dracula deliver this parodic endorsement of delayed gratification and respect for private property: "'Back, back, to your own place! Your time is not yet come. Wait. Have Patience. Tomorrow night, tomorrow night, is yours!' There was a low, sweet ripple of laughter, and in a rage I threw open the door, and saw without the three terrible women licking their lips" (Stoker 70).

17. In *Vampires, Mummies, and Liberals*, David Glover refers to Mina Harker as a

"double-agent" on grounds that the novel "temporarily recruits a woman into a man's place" only to abandon the parity of esteem accorded to phallic womanhood "for the overfeminized maternal" (96–97).

18. In *Carnal Knowledge*, Stoler explains,

> European women were vital to the colonial enterprise and the solidification of racial boundaries in ways that repeatedly tied their supportive and subordinate posture to community cohesion and colonial security. That contribution was re-inforced at the turn of the century by a metropolitan bourgeois discourse (and an eminently anthropological one) intensely concerned with notions of "degeneracy." Middle-class morality, manliness, and motherhood were seen as endangered by the related fears of "degeneration" and miscegenation in scientifically construed racist beliefs. (62)

19. Melanie Klein's account of the early stages of the Oedipal conflict includes a suggestive description of the confusion of penis and breast overinscribed in this bedroom scene and embodied anatomically in Stoker's vampire. Klein links such confusion to the fact that the formation of the gendered individual entails at once an irreparable separation from the mother's breast and the introjection of the father's penis, a situation giving rise to extraordinary ambivalence toward the mother. This ambivalence takes the form of the breast that can give complete gratification at one moment and withhold it at another, inspiring a deep and abiding destructive fantasy in which the child transforms its own rage outward as a world that provides a source of poison rather than nourishment. See Klein 268–325.

20. In *Modest_Witness@Second_Millennium*, Donna Haraway declared it "time to theorize an 'unfamiliar' unconscious, a different primal scene, where everything does not stem from the dramas of identity and reproduction." In thinking such a thought, she somewhat tentatively proposes, "I think I am on the side of the vampires, or at least some of them" (265).

21. In "Anne Frank and Hannah Arendt: Universalism and Pathos," Sharon Marcus effectively uses Arendt to challenge the opposition of universal to particular as it inflects Holocaust studies. Arendt, according to Marcus, "offers a definition of humanity that is universal, but frees universality from its troubling antipathy to particularity." As she explains, "Arendt defines universal humanity as the conditions of plurality and natality [. . .]. What human beings have in common is the world, which can only exist between people and thus requires, rather than denies, the difference and distance between them; and what each human being represents is natality, the possibility of beginning something new and initiating the unforeseen" (112). Indeed, Marcus maintains, Arendt understands the Holocaust as "an attack on human diversity as such, that is, upon a characteristic of the *human status* without which the very words *mankind* or *humanity* would be devoid of meaning" (269).

Works Cited

Arata, Stephen. *Fictions of Loss in the Victorian Fin de Siècle*. Cambridge: Cambridge UP, 1996.

Armstrong, Nancy. *Desire and Domestic Fiction: A Political History of the Novel*. New York: Oxford UP, 1987.

Barnes, Elizabeth. *States of Sympathy: Seduction and Democracy in the American Novel*. New York: Columbia UP, 1997.

Brontë, Charlotte. *Jane Eyre*. New York: Penguin, 2003.

Brown, Wendy. *States of Injury: Power and Freedom in Late Modernity*. Princeton: Princeton UP, 1995.

Butler, Judith. *Gender Trouble: Feminism and the Subversion of Identity*. New York: Routledge, 1990.

_____. "Is Kinship Always Already Heterosexual?" *differences: A Journal of Feminist Cultural Studies* 13.1 (2002): 14–44.

Chodorow, Nancy. *The Reproduction of Mothering: Psychoanalysis and the Sociology of Gender*. Berkeley: U of California P, 1978.

Daly, Nicholas. *Modernism, Romance, and the Fin de Siècle*. Cambridge: Cambridge UP, 1999.

Davidson, Cathy N. *Revolution and the Word: The Rise of the Novel in America*. New York: Oxford UP, 1986.

Felman, Shoshana, ed. *Literature and Psychoanalysis: The Question of Reading, Otherwise*. Baltimore: Johns Hopkins UP, 1982.

Foucault, Michel. *Discipline and Punish: The Birth of the Prison*. Trans. Alan Sheridan. New York: Vintage, 1995.

Franklin, Sarah, and Helena Ragoné, eds. *Reproducing Reproduction: Kinship, Power, and Technological Innovation*. Philadelphia: U of Pennsylvania P, 1998.

Freud, Sigmund. "The Uncanny." 1919. *The Standard Edition of the Complete Psychological Works of Sigmund Freud*. Trans. and ed. James Strachey. Vol. 17. London: Hogarth, 1973. 217–56. 24 vols. 1953–74.

_____. "The Interpretation of Dreams." 1900. *The Standard Edition*. Vol. 4. 1–338.

Gilbert, Sandra, and Susan Gubar. *The Madwoman in the Attic: The Woman Writer and the Nineteenth-Century Literary Imagination*. New Haven: Yale UP, 1979.

Gilligan, Carol. *In a Different Voice: Psychological Theory and Women's Development*. Cambridge: Harvard UP, 1982.

Glover, David. *Vampires, Mummies, and Liberals: Bram Stoker and the Politics of Popular Fiction*. Durham: Duke UP, 1996.

Halberstam, Judith. *Skin Shows: Gothic Horror and the Technology of Monsters*. Durham: Duke UP, 1995.

Haraway, Donna. *Modest_Witness@Second_Millennium*. New York: Routledge, 1997.

Hayden, Corinne P. "A Biodiversity Sampler for the Millennium." Franklin and Ragoné 173–205.

Hennessy, Rosemary. *Profit and Pleasure: Sexual Identity and Late Capitalism*. New York: Routledge, 2000.

Herdt, Gilbert. Introduction. *Third Sex, Third Gender: Beyond Sexual Dimorphism in Culture and History*. Ed. Gilbert Herdt. New York: Lane, 1994. 28–32.

Johnson, Claudia. *Equivocal Beings: Politics, Gender, and Sentimentality in the 1790s*. Chicago: U of Chicago P, 1995.

Kant, Immanuel. "Perpetual Peace: A Philosophical Sketch." *Kant: Selections*. Ed. Lewis White Beck. Englewood Cliffs: Prentice-Hall, 1988. 430–57.

Klein, Melanie. *The Psycho-analysis of Children*. Trans. Alix Strachey. London: Hogarth Press and the Institute of Psycho-analysis, 1973.

Leavis, F. R. *The Great Tradition: George Eliot, Henry James, Joseph Conrad*. New York: New York UP, 1967.

Lévi-Strauss, Claude. "How Myths Die." *New Literary History* 5 (1974): 269–81.

Levy, Anita. *Reproductive Urges: Popular Novel Reading, Sexuality and the English Nation*. Philadelphia: U of Pennsylvania P, 1999.

Lukács, Georg. *The Historical Novel*. Trans. Hannah and Stanley Mitchell. Lincoln: U of Nebraska P, 1983.

_____. *Studies in European Realism*. Trans. Edith Bone. New York: Grosset, 1964.

Marcus, Sharon. "Anne Frank and Hannah Arendt: Universalism and Pathos." *Cosmopolitan Geographies*. Ed. Vinay Dharwadker. New York: Routledge, 2000. 89–132.

Marcuse, Herbert. "The Affirmative Character of Culture." *Negations: Essays in Critical Theory*. Trans. Jeremy J. Shapiro. Boston: Beacon, 1968. 88–133.

Margolis, Stacey. "Addiction and the Ends of Desire." *High Anxieties: Cultural Studies in Addiction*. Ed. Janet Farrell Brodie and Marc Redfield. Berkeley: U of California P, 2002. 19–37.

Ragoné, Helena. "Incontestable Motivations." Franklin and Ragoné 118–31.

Samuels, Shirley, ed. *The Culture of Sentiment: Race, Gender, and Sentimentality in Nineteenth-Century America*. New York: Oxford UP, 1992.

Schmidt, Cannon. *Alien Nation: Nineteenth-Century Gothic Fictions and English Nationality*. Philadelphia: U of Pennsylvania P, 1997.

Schor, Naomi. *Breaking the Chain: Women, Theory, and French Realist Fiction*. New York: Columbia UP, 1985.

_____. "The Righting of French Studies: Homosociality and the Killing of 'La pensée 68.'" *Bad Objects: Essays Popular and Unpopular*. Durham: Duke UP, 1995. 71–81.

Sommer, Doris. *Foundational Fictions: The National Romances of Latin America*. Berkeley: U of California P, 1991.

Stern, Julia A. *The Plight of Feeling: Sympathy and Dissent in the Early American Novel*. Chicago: U of Chicago P, 1997.

Stoker, Bram. *Dracula*. New York: Penguin, 1993.

Stoler, Ann Laura. *Carnal Knowledge and Imperial Power: Race and the Intimate in Colonial Rule*. Berkeley: U of California P, 2002.

Todd, Janet M. *Sensibility: An Introduction*. London: Methuen, 1986.

Tompkins, Jane. *Sensational Designs: The Cultural Work of American Fiction, 1790–1860*. New York: Oxford UP, 1985.

Weston, Kath. "Forever is a Long Time: Romancing the Real in Gay Kinship Ideologies." *Naturalizing Power: Essays in Feminist Cultural Analysis*. Ed. Sylvia Yanagisako and Carol Delaney. New York: Routledge, 1995. 87–112.

Racialization, Capitalism, and Aesthetics in Stoker's *Dracula*_____

Patricia McKee

Henry Mayhew introduces his survey of *London Labour and the London Poor* (1851) by identifying throughout the world "two distinct and broadly marked races, viz., the wanderers and the settlers." This division also distinguishes, as races, outsider and insider, "the vagabond and the citizen." When he compares the poor in England to "Bushmen," "Lappes," and "Arabian Bedouins," Mayhew effectively locates these "wandering tribes" in imaginary spaces outside the bounds of national life. Mayhew further depicts this vagabond class "preying upon" the nation's citizens, whose movements—as tourists and imperialists, for example—he ignores (1). In *Dracula*, published in 1897, Bram Stoker complicates Mayhew's social order when he suggests that at the end of the century the modern citizen claimed no settled identity, but a mobility even more extensive than that of Mayhew's "wandering races." The vampire Dracula, who in the novel is identified as primitive and alien and who certainly preys upon citizens, is a wanderer, according to the peculiar logic of the "undead." But those in the novel who eventually defeat Dracula are characterized by unsettled behavior as well. Not quite insiders, they comprise a group of Western citizens who belong within no single nation or social class and who are experienced travellers. What endows the movements of these characters with cultural privilege is their power to capitalize upon mobility, to convert changes of place into opportunities for investment.

Dracula has been understood to respond to the fears of late Victorians, due in part to Darwinian thought, that degeneration threatened both the British "race" and the British empire. Stephen Arata points out that, insofar as Stoker's "vampires are generated by racial enervation and the decline of empire," they exploit fears of the genetic and social deterioration that many of Stoker's readers "perceived as characterizing late-Victorian Britain" (115). But the characters who oppose Dracula also learn new means by which to regenerate racial dominance. In an effort to explain this regeneration, my focus here is on the alliance in the novel of a construction of modernized whiteness with the productivity of late capitalism and on how that alliance allows whiteness to claim regenerative powers.[1]

Capitalism faced a crisis late in the nineteenth century because the world's economically underdeveloped territory was seen to be dwindling. Neil Smith has argued that at this time capitalist production of relative space replaced capitalist expansion in absolute space. "It was no longer the case that social and economic expansion were accomplished primarily through geographical expansion" (87). Once "the absolute expansion of nation states and of their colonies came to an end with the final partitioning of Africa in the 1880s," capitalism shifted its aims, from the development of new and underdeveloped spaces to the reproduction of such spaces, providing theoretically limitless potential for growth (87). "With everything it can muster," Smith writes, "this is what capital strives to do: it strives to move from developed to underdeveloped space, then back to developed space which, because of its interim deprivation of capital, is now underdeveloped, and so on" (150). Withdrawals of investment produce the spaces through which capital can circulate as, in effect, it reproduces nature in spaces open, again, to development (150).

In *Dracula*, Stoker articulates the capitalist dimensions of racialization that respond to this shift in the dynamics of empire. Like capitalists in Smith's modernized model of imperial expansion, Stoker's Western characters redirect their energies into symbolic geographies in which they can reproduce both advanced and primitive conditions. A "doubled logic" can be discerned here, similar to the doubled logic of expansion and control that Robert J. C. Young has identified with Victorian racialism.[2] In *Dracula*, racialization becomes part of a productive and growing economy rather than a merely repressive regime, as characters struggling to regenerate racial hegemony learn to reproduce the underdeveloped spaces of the primitive Dracula and make room thereby for an expansion of their own powers. According to this modern abstraction of racialized identity, the place of whiteness is ascribable to no place in particular. Whiteness "belongs" everywhere as a representative power, and whiteness claims as its territory the ever-changing symbolic dimensions through which political and capitalist hegemony can be reproduced.

This is a more extensive and more effective racialization of power than has been often recognized in the novel. In a number of persuasive readings of *Dracula*, critics have argued that Stoker's narrative, failing to provide definitive distinctions between Dracula and his Western enemies, challenges boundaries of race and nation. But despite equivalences between the vampire's "undead" empire and modernity (Arata, Schmitt, Wicke, Day), Count Dracula's resistance to the representative and relativist logic of capitalist expansion means that his "race" (Stoker 43) is also incapable of the regeneration practiced by the West. Whether the vampire undermines particular constructions of otherness—such as primitive versus modern or wanderer versus settler—exerts little effect, I would argue, on the racializing practices of the Western characters whose whiteness is constructed as a claim to the symbolic registers of modern capitalist development and modern disciplinary activity.[3]

This argument parallels some previous commentary on the novel, particularly Gary Day's response to the many readings of sexuality in *Dracula*. Day argues that sexuality needs to be understood as a discursive and disciplinary formation of the modern state, to which the production of abnormalities is as useful as the production of norms (83). I am proposing that racializing practices in the novel be read as disciplinary formations whose extensive institutional affiliations, with capitalism especially, expand power through productions of both difference and identity. The capitalist underpinnings of racial hegemony in the novel require those who overpower Dracula both to repress and to reproduce him. Their victory depends not on putting the vampire to rest but on putting the "horror story" of *Dracula* into circulation, as an entertaining spectacle that reproduces the market logic of Western culture.

Whiteness as Cultural Capitalism

In arguing that Westerners in *Dracula* engage in forms of restless mobility comparable to the movements of vagabonds, I do not intend to contradict Mayhew's claim that travel constitutes a Victorian marker of race. But I do want to address a more complicated racialization of travel in Stoker's narrative. Initially, the opposed tourist practices of Jonathan Harker and Count Dracula enact their racialized differences. But the two men are also positioned in a kind of stand-off. This deadlock has been variously described as the opposition between colonizer and "reverse colonization," by Arata (115), and that between Orientalist and Occidentalist, by Cannon Schmitt (138–42). On his trip to "the East," Jonathan is at first secure in the evidence he observes of the West's superior modernity; east of Budapest, for example, trains do not run on time, and the people are superstitious (Stoker 7). Such distinctions collapse, however, when Jonathan is trapped in Dracula's castle and becomes aware, through his own responses to the vampires, of strange and "primitive" dimensions within himself. Count Dracula, on the other hand, plans his trip to England with the aim of blending in, believing that, as "a stranger in a strange land, he is no one" (31). Observing that Stoker was an Anglo-Irishman, Schmitt has argued that "the creole's fear of racial absorption" may be at work in the novel's "mixed metaphor of vampirism and racialism" (148). Stoker's travellers thus pose two possibilities of racial degeneration of concern to late Victorians: that the Englishman abroad will be absorbed into an alien and primitive culture because of his own internal weaknesses; or that a stronger, more primitive race will invade from without and assimilate the English.

It is through the activities of a third tourist, however, that a hegemonic white culture comes to be regenerated in the novel. Mina

Murray, Jonathan Harker's fiancée and later his wife, appears as the central figure in the abstraction of identity necessary to modernized structures of power. As Dracula's victim, Mina is engaged in productions of new space, and, as the stenographer and typist who records the encounter with the vampire, she reproduces the open spaces necessary to Western expansion. After she is drained of her blood by Dracula, Mina's own body becomes a space in which Western men turn the tables on Dracula. She refigures her body as an open channel, which allows various forms of capital to circulate through her. As the channel through which Western men collect and reproduce knowledge—both because her recollections provide information about the vampire and because, as stenographer and typist, she records others' information—Mina reforms herself into a means of producing the symbolic domain in which the West will reclaim its dominance.

Mina first appears in the narrative as a tourist, visiting, with her friends the Westenras, the town of Whitby, in Yorkshire, while she waits for Jonathan to return from the East. Like Jonathan in Transylvania, Mina records her observations of the place she visits; and like Jonathan, she finds herself in a familiar spot. Along with other tourists from nineteenth-century England who, as Robert L. Herbert says, "carried away images of the pre-modern landscape" from places at which they "arrived with such images already formed in their minds" (1–2), Jonathan sees the East as he saw it at home. He recognizes the superstitious practices that he has read about in the British Museum, as well as picturesque "little towns or castles [. . .] such as we see in old missals" and what appears to be the same peasant costume he has seen at the ballet (9).

Mina also describes Whitby as a place she has already known in other places:

> The houses of the old town [. . .] seem piled up one over the other anyhow, like the pictures we see of Nuremberg. Right over the town is the ruin of Whitby Abbey, which was sacked by the Danes, and which is the scene of

part of [Scott's] "Marmion," where the girl was built up in the wall. It is a most noble ruin, of immense size, and full of beautiful and romantic bits; there is a legend that a white lady is seen in one of the windows. (85)

Here the tourist attraction, unlike Transylvania, is consciously recognized as a symbolic construction, abstracted from its material existence as it is perceived only indirectly, in bits and pieces and in circulating reproductions. Whitby is interesting because of its likeness to pictures, to Scott's poetry, to tourist literature, to romances and legends that Mina recalls from other places and cultural contexts. The actual town is thereby transposed into a simulation of the picturesque, within a technology whereby a traditional culture is reduced to a premodern type and then reproduced and circulated as part of a cultural industry.

The modernization of tourism that occurs in this scene entails a double detachment, a production of distance whereby the tourist sees things, as John Frow says, "as signs of themselves" and becomes self-conscious about their translation into virtual rather than real terms (125).[4] Mina is prevented from absolutely believing the romantic signs because she meets a "local" who is a "very skeptical person" (Stoker 86). Unlike the usual tourist, Mr. Swales refuses to be taken in, as he detaches signs from referents and himself from signs. Like Mina, Mr. Swales enjoys sitting in the graveyard overlooking Whitby harbor; but he has no patience with local legends. "Them things be all wore out. [. . .] They be all very well for comers and trippers an' the like, but not for a nice young lady like you" (87). The stories of ghosts, according to Swales, "be all invented by parsons an' ill-some beuk-bodies an' railway touters to skeer an' scunner hafflin's, an' to get folks to do somethin' that they don't other incline to" (88). From legends of ghosts, Swales turns to the tombstones' legends and doubts their authenticity too. "'Here lies the body' or 'Sacred to the memory' wrote on all of them, an' yet in nigh half of them there bean't no bodies at all" (88), since many of the men were lost at sea. "The whole thing be only lies," Swales insists (89).

Like other Western males in the novel, Swales becomes an interpreter, reading critically the reproductions of his culture as he exercises the freedom to produce multiple possibilities of meaning. Initially perceived by Mina as a picturesque character, he occupies instead the position of the modern citizen under capitalism. Sharing with Mina his critical awareness, he generates an imaginary community with her based on no particular beliefs but instead on his and her common detachment, as distanced and doubting subjects. Swales entertains, with an open mind, multiple beliefs about and interpretations of things. Moreover, he provides interpretations in language that demands a critical listener.[5] His dialect produces, along with local color, a detachment in his listener that allows assimilation or agreement only through self-conscious translation. Swales's discussions with Mina thereby work as a model for the community of detachment and freedom that will later unite her friends within a public sphere that is racialized as a collective construction of whiteness.

According to Swales's and Mina's shared estimation of it, the world is always, on the one hand, assimilable to human construction and always, on the other hand, to be therefore doubted, interpreted, and reconstructed. The production of likenesses and differences in the world can therefore be imagined, at one remove, as an expansive circulation of culture, in which assimilation is always countered by differentiation and in which belief can be invested and withdrawn, like capital, by persons never taken in. In their detachment and mobility, these characters personify the movements and uses of capital as they enter speculatively into representations of different cultures.

This kind of productivity is especially evident in Mina's views of Whitby. Whereas Jonathan sees in Transylvania translations of British views of the place that he does not question, Mina sees in Whitby a collection of reproductions indicating many likenesses that she finds entertaining but dubious. Whitby cannot be for Mina both Nuremberg and the location of Scott's legend; it must be recognized as only *like* both of these. Jonathan observes Transylvanian culture, at least at first, as a museum piece, remembering the description given in the British Museum when he looks at it. But Mina views Whitby as the mental equivalent of a museum collection, as a site at which "beautiful and romantic 'bits'" of Western European culture are extracted from their material identities, viewed as symbolic reproductions, to be recollected and reproduced by a memory organized by the needs of capital.[6] As with collections of art objects or souvenirs, things are removed from local contexts and seen as pieces, which then pile up, like the houses in the painting Mina remembers, in forms aestheticized as picturesque. Doubly detached, this cultural tourism distances the tourist's consciousness from her surroundings and her surroundings from any actual place.

Ideology as Speculation

Western men in Stoker's novel exercise a similar productivity. Able to entertain multiple ideas and beliefs, these characters assert their cultural superiority to "the East" by presuming to have developed open minds capable of reproducing Eastern as well as Western views. Dr. Van Helsing, the Dutchman who spearheads the fight against the vampire, puts this logic of open-mindedness into practice when he insists that what Dr. Seward, Mr. Morris, Lord Godalming, and Jonathan Harker must learn is the validity of phenomena they can neither understand nor recognize. "You are too prejudiced. [. . .] Do you not think that there are things which you cannot understand, and yet which are. [. . .] Ah, it is the fault of our science that it wants to explain all; and if it explain not, then it says there is nothing to explain" (246). Van Helsing wants them "to believe in things that you cannot. [. . .] [T]o have an open mind, and not let a little bit of truth check the rush of a big truth" (249). Eventually, their speculative capacity enables the Westerners to hold multiple beliefs concurrently, and their open-mindedness and self-consciousness allow them both to simulate belief in the vampire and to destroy him.

Not only must Seward and the others entertain beliefs in what they do not know; they must be open to unexpected events. When they are about to leave for Transylvania, Van Helsing tells them all, "We cannot say what we shall do. There are so many things which may happen [. . .] [N]one of us can tell what, or when, or how, the end may be" (328). This kind of open-mindedness—being ready for anything—is also a useful perspective for the modernist interpreter and the venture capitalist, both of which positions these men often seem to fit. Because, moreover, the narrative of *Dracula* is a collective production, composed of various individuals' records, diaries, and testimonies, the identity of these characters and their reproductive practices can never appear merely assimilative. Records are produced by many persons, from many backgrounds. Their various points of view encourage a mobility of perspectives within individuals, even a production of new and different perspectives. Characters learn within their own culture to emulate the mobility and detachment of capital and move into and out of various cultural positions, with investments of belief that reproduce those cultures primarily for the entertainment and profit of Westerners.

By the end of Stoker's novel, Western characters have mastered the reproduction of Transylvania as primitive and underdeveloped space. Jonathan Harker, Mina, and their comrades, seven years after destroying Dracula, return to Eastern Europe as a place they have made safe for tourism:

> In the summer of this year we made a journey to Transylvania, and went over the old ground which was, and is, to us so full of vivid and terrible memories. It was almost impossible to believe that the things which we had seen with our own eyes and heard with our own ears were living truths. Every trace of all that had been was blotted out. The castle stood as before, reared high above a waste of desolation. (485–86)

Despite the history they have experienced as "living truth," these characters see Dracula's castle standing on its "old ground," still surrounded by "a waste of desolation." But that waste is not, as it once was, underdeveloped and unproductive because it is Dracula's domain. Emptied of history, detached from ideology, the castle appears, in its desolate setting, a groundless image of primitive grandeur and isolation.

The detachment of image from grounds moves the landscape into symbolic and speculative dimensions, meaning that subsequent tourists, confronted with a picturesque image, will become free to believe or doubt its authenticity. Similarly, the readers of *Dracula* are licensed to believe what they like, about both Transylvania and the narrators' views of Transylvania. After they return home again, Jonathan and Mina Harker get out the notes and diaries they kept during their struggle with Dracula but find, among "a mass of type-writing," "hardly one authentic document" (486). Yet Van Helsing insists that "'we want no proofs; we ask none to believe us!'" (486). When Jonathan shifts the meaning of "old ground" from the grounds of knowledge to the ground on which the castle sits (which is itself reproducible as a romantic image), he repeats a commutation that has been at work throughout the narrative, transforming truth and knowledge into relativist and reproducible constructions.[7]

To see Dracula's castle as a symbolic reconstruction of a picturesque ruin is for the tourist to participate in the redirection of empire in the novel: away from the absolute or material grounds of nature or history and into what might be thought of as the second nature produced by capitalism (Smith 190). The image signals a degeneration which cannot be attributed to either natural or historical causes or effects. As an entertaining ruin, it is not degenerate but a simulation of what degeneration looks like: an image open to multiple imaginative investments. Thus, the mobility of capital becomes a kind of a model for the ways that white persons travel: at one remove and reproducing even the locations of their own circulation, which occurs within wholly constructed spaces.

Capitalizing on Open-mindedness

While Stoker details an historically localized racialization of white identity, he also clarifies that the power accruing to whiteness depends on its universal claims. "White power secures its dominance by seeming not to be anything in particular," Richard Dyer has remarked in his study of racializations in British and American films (44). Most emphatically in the character of Mina Harker, Stoker indicates that in late Victorian Britain, too, to be white is to be nothing in particular but rather to be "open": open-minded, open to interpretation, candid, and trustworthy.

Apparently inclusive rather than exclusive, a racialized capitalist ideology is put into practice in *Dracula* through characters' openness to new ideas. As Mina demonstrates when visiting Whitby, doubt about the absolute nature of any particular meaning increases possibilities of truth and allows knowledge to circulate and expand. Mina will continue throughout the novel to open up spaces within herself and between herself and others so as to produce opportunities for expanded investment.

But it is not only doubt that is cultivated within the Western collective in *Dracula*. In their detachment, these characters are bound together through trust of one another; Mina Harker is also the central locus and means of production for this trust. Although Franco Moretti's influential reading of *Dracula* identifies the vampire with monopoly capitalism, the trust developed by the Western characters forms the more powerful conglomerate. They monopolize means of production and investment far more extensive in scope than the vampire's reproductive capacity, and they profit also by the apparent moral superiority of their openness and their trust in one another. Doubt opens the mind to differing interpretations of truth; trust is given to persons able to represent various interests with multiple investments. Mina becomes the most trustworthy as she becomes the most representative of Stoker's characters.

How such practices of doubt and trust have been racialized in Western cultures is indicated by David Lloyd, who has proposed a history in which, as in Stoker's novel, whiteness lays claim to representative status and hence moral superiority through a certain internal emptiness. As disinterestedness has become characteristic of European judgment since the eighteenth century, Lloyd argues, the "Subject without properties" (70) has become necessary to the most highly developed aesthetic and political judgment. "Grounding the idea of a common or public sense, the subject of aesthetic judgment supplies the very possibility of a disinterested domain [. . .] through history as the ethical end of humanity itself" (64). This idea "posit[s] the white man as standing closer to the identity of the human which is the telos of history. The white occupies the position of universally representative man within a narrative which we can describe as the narrative of representation itself" (84).

According to this history, practitioners of European common sense can claim to be representative because they reason according to ideal standards about which disinterested people can all agree. In this exercise of common sense, the identity of objects is abstracted from particular objects by persons whose judgment is detached from their particular experiences. Objects become representative objects, and subjects become representative subjects: subjects without any particular properties. Thus, white common sense is universalized, and its ubiquity depends on a kind of typing: the "subordination of difference to the demand for identity" at work in metaphor (71). Racism's "rhetorical structure is that of metaphorization" because, Lloyd argues, racism also "elevates a principle of likening above that of differentiation," attaching to this elevation a moral superiority (71). Colonized persons, identified with what is perceived as an unassimilable "residue" of material from their local cultures, appear different (85). The historical teleology of a representative white culture thereby leaves the colonized person behind (85).

In Stoker's narrative, Western characters assume a representative whiteness but produce a different history of its power, with more explicitly capitalist dimensions than Lloyd considers. Western subjects in

Dracula are assimilated into an identity of moral superiority; the vampire appears incapable of the abstraction and detachment that make whites representative. But the most important distinction between advanced and primitive cultures according to Stoker's narrative is to be seen in their reproductive practices. Westerners circulate capital, which, as a medium of representation, reproduces more rapidly and extensively than any material means of production. Dracula's productivity is limited, however, by his material means; his empire expands through the circulation of blood among bodies in physical contact. The vampire is similarly limited to immediate extensions of knowledge. His "great child-brain" allows him to learn only by experience, like "the little bird, the little fish, the little animal [that] learn not by principle, but empirically" (439). Here likenesses are employed by Van Helsing to severely diminish the assimilative potential of an Eastern culture, seen as incapable of the abstractions that universalize Western knowledge.

It is because the Western culture in the novel learns through ideas that Western citizens can easily reproduce new and strange experience as well as recycle depleted elements of their culture, like those outdated advertising promotions to which Mr. Swales objects. Such worn-out material, like Dracula himself, is not merely residue, to be left behind by historical and moral development. Swales reinterprets both the crude promotions of tourism and the old legends, making of them evidence of his own superior knowledge. Dracula is also simulated as primitive—an animal and a child, for example—as Western characters expand their own knowledge through him. Rather than a teleological aim, racialization in *Dracula* takes a circular aim, as "development" reproduces old as well as new, primitive as well as advanced states.

The central test of the power of white culture in the novel is the reproduction of Dracula as a figure of primitive darkness. At the beginning of the novel, Jonathan Harker observes that the reflection of the vampire does not appear in mirrors, as if Dracula fits no forms of otherness. The vampire's unfitness, Slavoj Zizek suggests, may be seen as his failure to be represented by cultural forms of either sameness or

otherness.[8] While Lloyd locates patterns of racialization in the cultivation of detached aesthetic judgment, Zizek delineates the racialized
character of aestheticized objects, which are beautiful according to
their representability. Any beautiful object must be contained within
the dimensions of a sign.

Racism, Zizek suggests, which identifies persons as ugly, reproduces a fear of closeness; detachment becomes crucial to aesthetics
here too. "The ugly and out-of-place is *the excess of existence over representation. Ugliness is thus a *topological* category, designating an object that is in a way 'larger than itself,' whose existence is larger than its
representation" (165). According to Zizek, then, what is ugly defies reproduction, whereas beauty, lying in the fit of representation, guarantees reproducibility. "'Ugliness' ultimately stands for existence itself—
for the resistance of reality on account of which material reality is
never simply an ethereal medium that lends itself effortlessly to our
molding" (166–67). The vampire, for Zizek, represents one kind of
threat posed by objects that exceed assigned boundaries.

In Stoker's narrative, however, the role of representation in racialization is less clear. In the specific context of late Victorian anxieties
about racial degeneration, the fitness of a race in *Dracula* depends on
its modernity. Westerners in the novel in effect modernize their identity
as they detach their collective identity from biology and nation alike
and realize whiteness as a form of symbolic capital. Staking their whiteness on their representative capacities, these characters can triumph
over Dracula only if they can represent him. Therefore, if Dracula is to
be racialized as inferior to Western whites, he cannot be classed as an
outsider on the basis of his resistance to representation. This would
leave him beyond the reach of Western investment.

In Stoker's narrative, Dracula is racialized as primitive and unfit not
only because he exceeds the space of the sign but because the modernized white characters can produce the space that allows his conversion
to a sign. The vampire becomes reproducible when he makes the mis-
take of invading Mina's body, where space opens up despite his occu-

pation of her and leaves room for her to represent others' interests as well as his own. Nor can Dracula withstand the group of Western men who work against him, once they make mental room among their "previous conviction[s]," as Dr. Seward says (249), to entertain a belief in vampires. The Westerners' open-mindedness eventually allows Dracula, in Zizek's terms, to fit easily among the representations they exchange. Initially impervious to representation and reproduction, Dracula is made to stand for this imperviousness. *Dracula* is entertaining, then, as the representation of a threatening "Other" made into an appropriate, dark double, a mere negation of white culture.

But it is the reproduction of Mina Harker as a figure of pure whiteness that is even more important to Western hegemony in the novel, as proof of the capacity of Westerners to detach value from material history and refigure value in wholly representative terms. In or on Mina, purity and corruption are not bodily effects but signs. After she is drained of her blood by Dracula, Van Helsing touches Mina's forehead with the host and a burn appears, a sign she is "unclean" (381). At the end of the novel, white men are able, by destroying Dracula, to erase this sign; and "the snow is not more stainless than her forehead" (485). Like capitalists reproducing underdeveloped space, the men can reproduce untouched nature on Mina's face because she is identified as a medium of representation rather than as a material body. Victory over the vampire depends on converting his bodily possession of Mina into a sign, an erasable as well as reproducible development.

Mina is pure white insofar as she is "nothing in particular": not because of any material attribute or even any positive sign but because she is open to entertaining any attribute. Mina opens up the spaces of whiteness that detach meaningful phenomena from material bases and convert nature into sign. As a means of reproducing both corruption and purity as signs, Mina confirms that white productivity is abstracted from nature and degeneration, capable of reproducing the full scope of natural history: not in any one direction but in a circulation that precludes completion. Anything that occupies Mina's attention is converted into an entertainable and detachable object, attribute, or practice. She produces space, and especially she reproduces herself as an empty space, an object without properties who enables the desires and the beliefs invested in her to circulate among multiple objects.

Producing White Space

But Mina in fact forms the second front in the war against Dracula that effects his translation into sign. The first battle in which the Western men engage is lost when Lucy Westenra dies, becomes a vampire, and succumbs to ugliness. While she lives, Van Helsing attempts to save Lucy by giving her transfusions of blood, a material replenishment that Dracula simply draws out of her body again. When after her death Lucy becomes a vampire, however, Van Helsing and the other men drive a stake through her heart and effect a symbolic transformation that is permanent and transcendent.

> There, in the coffin lay no longer the foul Thing [. . .] but Lucy as we had seen her in life, with her face of unequalled sweetness and purity. True that there were there, as we had seen them in life, the traces of care and pain and waste; but these were all dear to us, for they marked her truth to what we knew. One and all we felt that the holy calm that lay like sunshine over the wasted face and form was only an earthly token and symbol of the calm that was to reign for ever. (278)

Becoming a sign, Lucy's body, as Elisabeth Bronfen says, "is replaced with a safe, purified memory image," a "semiotic double replacing a somatic double" (319, 321).

As a reflection of Western culture, however, Lucy's image is not fully reassuring. What these men want to see in Lucy are signs that "mark her truth to what we knew." That her truth is conflated with fidelity indicates the cultural relativism that has reformed their knowledge from truth to belief. Restored, Lucy's image represents her return to Western culture, as a reproduction of the way the Westerners see things. Yet she simulates both purity and ruin. And the agreement the men feel about the transcendent form of Lucy's face doesn't last long. Two men remain behind with the corpse when the others leave to "cut off the head and fill [. . .] the mouth with garlic" (279). Once they do this, Lucy is in pieces, a broken reproduction of her own violation.

A semiotic fit, to invoke Zizek's concept of the beautiful, is hard to recognize in a body stuffed, staked, and split in two. But when Van Helsing attempts the second rescue of a corrupted woman in the novel, Mina becomes a more extensive means of cultural reproduction. Her convertibility detaches her from her possessed body and identifies her with a medium of exchange, like money, that can belong to many people. In effect emptied of any necessary contents, she can be filled with Dracula's transmissions or with those of Van Helsing.

Mina proves true to what white men know in a way different from Lucy because, instead of merely reproducing a familiar image, Mina reproduces multiple surfaces and views. Mina enables, that is, the production of metaphor, of likeness. This is strikingly evident in Mina's most spectacular appearance, in the scene in the Harkers' bedroom, shocking to all of the men who see it, when Dracula forces Mina to suck blood from his body. Seward, who reports this scene, breaks down the door to the room with the help of Van Helsing, Quincey, and Godalming.

On the bed beside the window lay Jonathan Harker, his face flushed, and breathing heavily as though in a stupor. Kneeling on the near edge of the bed facing outwards was the white-clad figure of his wife. By her side stood a tall, thin man, clad in black. His face was turned from us but the instant we saw it we all recognized the Count—in every way, even to the scar on his forehead. With his left hand he held both Mrs Harker's hands, keeping them away with her arms at full tension; his right hand gripped her by the back of the neck, forcing her face down on his bosom. [. . .] The attitude of the two had a terrible resemblance to a child forcing a kitten's nose into a saucer of milk to compel it to drink. (362–63)

In what the men "see," as well as in Mina's narration the next day of what happened before they arrived, Mina is a transparent medium through which white men look at things. Her spectacularity fosters the distances that abstract vision from history and open up different points of view.

This extension of knowledge involves a familiarization with the appalling practices of the savage Dracula and, in this, proceeds like an observation of anthropological fact. But Dracula is not only recognizable and readable; he is read variously. Seward's recognition of the child with the kitten and the milk may seem wide of the mark to readers who recognize in the scene something like a forced sexual act. But the recognition of breast-feeding as an important element in this scene, like the recognition of rape, has generated influential interpretations of it, especially those of Joan Copjec and Cannon Schmitt. And the visual reproducibility of the scene—with characters who look like they are doing something else—is crucial both to the characters' and to critics' understandings.

In its recognizability, the scene both fits images already familiar and is available for reproduction as something else. Like racist images of a "black" man in bed with a "white" woman, the renegotiated meanings implemented by the scene work to assimilate it to the terms of a common sense. At the same time, those common terms are marked as partial and abstract. That is, racist cliché, or common sense, is not directly available but can be reproduced if viewers are sufficiently detached from what is before their eyes. This view of things not only fits a familiar form but fits many forms and, even better, places the viewer at a distance at which he is free to see what he thinks, providing yet more meaning. When making Lucy's image fit, by driving a stake through her heart, the men have to work hard to mutilate her body into shape. Here, however, the white men who dash into the room, then stop and stare, remain distanced from the objects they view; they have time to see a lot, despite the violence and danger they witness, before they do anything about it. Not only a reproduction of views but a reproduction of an open public space of common detachment occurs.

The spectacularity of the scene, then, does not lie simply in its visual impact, since the impact of the visual here is to invite interpretation. This marks progress for the characters who are learning to see more in things than they once did. Early in the novel, when Lucy is succumbing to Dracula, little evidence of danger is recognized. Mina looks at Lucy resting against a windowsill, for example, with "something that looked like a good-sized bird" next to her; and this is as far as Mina's speculations go (126). Insufficiently suspicious, or in Van Helsing's terms insufficiently credulous, to believe the bird is a bat and the bat is a vampire, the Westerners see things as usual. But gradually these characters become sufficiently detached from the material world to see it metaphorically.

As an abstracted object of white knowledge—seen more as space than object—Mina is the touchstone that indicates how the emptied space of such detachments can function to constitute culture. Mina is not only the chief means by which the men learn not to believe their eyes and always to read more into things. Both a medium of skepticism and a medium of trust, in a sense, the space of her self is emptied out and filled in variously, as men invest her with and empty her of different meanings. Lucy is both loved by all the men and filled with their blood. But Mina becomes a channel not of sexual or material investment but of information, which circulates through her. Like her typewriter, a means of reproducing and distributing collected representations, Mina is also the medium through which the collective investment pays off, as a kind of trust fund on which the men draw to defeat Dracula. Unlike Lucy, Mina is not, at least at first, directly known to these men. But she is trusted, and she increases their trust in one another because she functions as a representative rather than acting on any absolute or personal grounds.

Seward's as well as Van Helsing's trust in her begins when each reads first Lucy's and then Mina's own diaries. Mina, meanwhile, has read Jonathan's diaries, written during his visit to Transylvania, and recorded her anxieties about his mental health. Dr. Van Helsing, immediately after reading Mina's journal, exclaims that "'this paper is as sunshine. [. . .] I am dazzled, with so much light'" (237–38). Although Mina responds, "'you do not know me,'" Van Helsing insists that he "knows" her through trust. "'Your husband is noble nature, and you are noble too, for you trust, and trust cannot be where there is mean nature'" (238). Morris and Godalming also come to see Mina through an intricately mediated construction of trust. Because Lucy trusted Mina and wrote to her about all these men proposing marriage to her, Mina has that intimate knowledge of them. Because Mina has been trusted with Seward's diary, she also knows about Lucy's brief afterlife and then death as a vampire. With this fund of trust, Mina offers to both Morris and Godalming typewritten copies of both Jonathan's and her own diaries. And after reading these, both men promise Mina lifelong devotion, one as a brother and son and one with "the very words he had used to Lucy" (297) after she refused to marry him and he nevertheless devoted himself to her.

What develops among these characters is an elaborate series of substitutions, through which Mina takes the places of sister, mother, and friend to men who have little more than indirect, written knowledge of her (295–97). She thereby acts as a means not only of trust but of reproducing trust, as she does when using the technology of typing. Mina's use of a typewriter and of Seward's dictation machine is integral to the Westerners' "enlightenment" and to their detachment from material experience. The various journals and diaries are abstracted from individually handwritten or dictated records, for one thing, when reproduced in a common type on the same paper, to be read at virtually the same time. And, whereas the phonograph is "'cruelly true'" (285), recording Seward's emotions as well as his words, Mina's typing erases the intonations that "'no one must hear'" (286). The common knowledge produced on the typewriter is emptied of emotional attachments as well as of other such singular signs as individuals' handwriting or the shorthand Mina uses when she writes. Less true than these, the flow of information for which Mina is responsible is more trustworthy for those whose views are represented in it. It does not give away everything about its sources but represents them only in part. That part is selfless, both in the sense of being disinterested and in the sense of being detached from personal feeling.

But moreover, as neither objectively verifiable knowledge nor a merely partial perspective, the writings Mina reproduces assume the authority of a democratic public sphere in their collective representation of many parts. Recording various views of situations, in newspaper articles and books as well as diaries, the narrative Mina assembles collects together partial views, which achieve comprehensiveness when put together but also remain open to interpretation and to other additions. According to Copjec's psychoanalytic reading of *Dracula*, it is the Western subject's formation of partial objects of desire that is endangered in vampire myths. The vampire, Copjec says, "signals [. . .] a failure of the symbolic reality wherein all alienable objects, objects which can be given or taken away, lost and refound, are constituted and circulate" (26). But Mina compensates for this failure of the symbolic order when she reforms objects of knowledge as well as desire into partial objects and then projects them into circulation within a collective that is never complete but merely representative of many parts.

White Types

As Mina rather than Lucy Westenra becomes the common object of men's desires, the physically beautiful woman is displaced by the representative woman. Once invaded by Dracula, Lucy becomes a fully saturated spatiality, threatening even to invade and occupy the Western men who desire her. Because Mina Harker is self-conscious and self-critical, however, she remains internally divided even after Dracula's invasion of her. Distancing herself in part from the body he occupies, in order to report that experience to her husband and friends, she opens up a space that eludes the vampire's possession.

Thus, despite the fact that she is possessed, Mina allows Van Helsing to reconceive Dracula's entry into her body as a circuit. Van Helsing recognizes that the vampire is able to use Mina against her friends; she involuntarily transmits to Dracula their location as they try to track him down, and he evades them through her. But Mina, practicing the detachment that opens up interpretations, is also able at certain times of the day to report Dracula's activities to Van Helsing. She provides this opportunity for an increased circulation of symbols—a kind of two-way transmission of signs—through her moral rather than physical agreeability. She agrees out of disinterestedness to remain open to multiple constructions. As such, she only represents Dracula and only in part. She continues to represent the Western men as well, speaking in their interests as well as typing their writings.

Her openness means that Mina may reproduce objects of desires that are directed towards others as well as herself. She does this when she represents herself to Arthur, the dead Lucy's fiancé, as *like* Lucy. "'She and I were like sisters; and now she is gone, will you not let me be like a sister to you in your trouble? [. . .] Won't you let me be of some little service—for Lucy's sake?'" (295). As a likeness of Lucy, Mina redirects Arthur's desire towards a simulation, pushing desire into circulation. According to her representations, desire is never absolute but relative; Mina also represents herself as only relative to, but not absolutely, the object desired.

Self-constructed as both agreeable to others and already internally differentiated, so as to be distanced from as well as representative of others, Mina is able to reproduce others' beliefs and take their parts. Her reproduction of type is not only a mechanical construction. At Whitby, Mina modernizes tourism when she recognizes in the town a series of representations. Whitby becomes a typical old and romantic town in comparison to pictures and legends that look alike because they represent only the "bits" of actual towns that correspond to ideal constructions. A similar process is used to type Dracula. The likenesses assigned to him reproduce him as various types of the "primitive" that

Victorian thinkers posited as the modern citizen's opposite: he is a wanderer, he is like an animal, he is like a child.

But whiteness in the novel is typed differently. The typical white person, for one thing, practices self-representation as part of a collective. Whiteness is constructed from the inside and is "seen" not exactly as a type but as a capacity to produce type. Because of this capacity, whiteness can emerge in the novel as a form of capital. Producing multiple parts and entertaining multiple beliefs, and constructing various representations of others, whites reform themselves not merely as representations but as representative. The vampire and Transylvania, represented by whites as types, become themselves means of reproducing the cultural capital of whiteness.

White men's conversions of material history into reproducible space are accompanied by the conversion of white women from means of material and historical reproduction into the raw material of mass media. Mina does have a son before the end of the novel, but she does so only after becoming adept at other, more modern forms of reproduction. A typist even when not using the typewriter, Mina inhabits a symbolic field in which she continually produces the spaces necessary to seeing things in parts and representing them as internally divided. In Mina and through her, spatial production keeps differentiation active, detaching any place or object from what is invested in it or believed about it, so that those investments and beliefs remain partial and temporary.

Mina functions as the raw material of mass media because she converts her body into representation and then types herself and others as broadly representative signs. She is "fit" for this role because she is apparently so selfless as to be already abstracted from her self. Interested more in others, she never expresses personal desire and keeps nothing to herself. It is as if people can see right through her to something else she represents. Thus when her marital infidelity goes on public display, it never occurs to any observer to attach infidelity to Mina personally. Yet Mina's trustworthiness is that of a reliable currency rather than that of a trusted individual; or, she converts trustworthiness into a matter of currency. As sheer medium, with no apparent interest except in reproducing others, Mina becomes an ideal white woman through whom white men can represent anything at all.

Representative White Men

Stoker's white men act as the representative subjects of Lloyd's account of European democracy because they too occupy multiple positions and hold them in common. They are disinterested subjects, defined less by properties than by their shared interests and their cultivation of trust, which have increased over the years as the men have moved around the world together. Bound by neither "blood" nor nationality but in the first place by their travels, Jack, Quincey, and Arthur have shared in various international exploits: "We've told yarns by the camp-fire in the prairies; and dressed one another's wounds after trying a landing at the Marquesas; and drunk healths on the shores of Titicaca" (83). The bonds forged by these adventures allow for common investments of emotion and labor when the men find themselves in England.

Three of the men fall in love with and propose marriage to Lucy Westenra; four of them give blood in hopes of restoring her to health. All five—Jonathan Harker, Abraham Van Helsing, Jack Seward, Quincey Morris, and Arthur Holmwood—devote themselves to destroying Dracula and saving Mina Harker. Collectivized by disinterestedness and trust, their identities seem to be in circulation among themselves, as they take one another's parts and places. Unlike Mina Harker, who is responsible for opening up spaces for the circulation of cultural capital, the collective identity of these men puts them in joint possession of capital and motivates their active investment in and development of the spaces Mina opens up.

Having transformed vagabondage into an adventure of capitalism and empire, the men go on to subsume other "primitive" practices within the collective capacity of modern white culture. The destruction of the vampire requires, for example, material strength as well as open-mindedness. Jack, Jonathan, Arthur, and Quincey engage in a "desperate" pursuit of Dracula, on horseback and with Winchester rifles; then in close combat, armed with bowie knives, they fight the gypsies who guard the Count (482–84). Recalling the "wild west" of North America, the white men in this sensational struggle reproduce the physical fitness believed by late Victorians to belong naturally to people they thought of as primitive. Like tourists who discover in "primitive" places their own "savage" dimensions, these travellers seem called on to develop undiscovered and underdeveloped parts of self. But whereas Jonathan's journey into a primitive interior landscape at the beginning of the novel almost destroys his sanity, by the end of the novel he and his comrades are acting *like* savages as part of their triumphant capacity to simulate underdeveloped persons and cultures.

One British reaction to fears of racial degeneration late in the Victorian period was, as William Greenslade has clarified, a turn-of-the-century physical fitness movement (182–90). In *Dracula*, the Westerners' victory ultimately depends on a representative reach so extensive as to reproduce physical fitness as well as symbolic currency. They claim the places of both vagabonds and citizens, with the mobility of universally representative figures. Such figures, limited to no place in particular, are racialized as white through their capacity to exchange any place or cultural position for another. Read as a narrative of racialization, *Dracula* thereby exposes complicities of capitalism and racialization, in the Victorian period and perhaps in later times too.

Notes

1. Several critics have explored capitalist dimensions of Victorian constructions of whiteness but without considering the specifically regenerative ideology they made possible. See especially Lorimer and Bonnett. The critic who has most influentially considered capitalism within Stoker's novel is Moretti, who argues that the vampire represents the evils of capitalist enterprise. Dracula "threatens the idea of individual liberty" as capitalism threatens it, in monopoly (93, 94). I am arguing that capitalism is not villainous in *Dracula* but rather is a set of practices that, if they are abused by the vampire, are put to use by the West to defeat villainy and to extend the freedom of the West. Another critic who identifies Dracula with capitalism is Wicke, who compares the consumption of the vampire with marketing techniques of modern capitalism.

2. Young argues that "racialism operated both according to the same-Other model and through the 'computation of normalities' and 'degrees of deviance' from the white norm" (181). The production of norms and abnormalities "undid the claim for permanent difference between the races while at the same time causing the boundary territories of the racial frontier to be policed ever more possessively" (180).

3. Valente makes a very different case for "the Symbolic register" in the novel (142). He argues that Stoker's narrative indicates "an effort to break with the pervasive blood consciousness of fin de siècle Britain" (11). This break occurs when "a conversion narrative suddenly irrupts within the conquest narrative of *Dracula*" (131). "In Lacanian terms, the men of Little England have graduated from the Imaginary register [. . .] to the Symbolic register, wherein identity is understood to be the aftereffect of a social relationality inscribed in the signifier. [. . .] Projected onto the geopolitical scale, this shift from an Imaginary of blood to a Symbolic of social articulation or interlinkage represents a theoretical model of the shift Stoker desired and his political hero Gladstone made a Liberal policy goal: from emulous rivalry [. . .] to coexistence within a multinational state" (142). I am arguing that the capitalist dimensions of symbolic activity in the novel indicate that the Western men, rather than "letting go the racialist impetus of their manly ideal," as Valente asserts (143), racialize the symbolic register itself as the domain of whiteness.

4. This means, Frow explains, that "a place, a gesture, a use of language are understood not as given bits of the real but as suffused with ideality, giving on to the type of the beautiful, the extraordinary, or the culturally authentic" (125).

5. Critics tend to see the mix of languages and idioms in the novel as a deconstructive comment on national identity. Wicke argues that "the text relies on pushing at the limits of the common language of English to mark out its national boundary, and controlling the unruliness of speech by technologizing it—typing it—as a print-language of hegemony" (488). Moretti argues that the various patterns of speech in the novel are assimilated into standard English (93–94).

6. Coombes, in her study of late-Victorian museum exhibitions, argues that it was not so much the objects of material culture displayed but the symbolic dimensions of their representation that gave meaning to "Africa" for many British citizens, introducing them "to a symbolic universe with the British Empire at its heart" (214).

---

7. Relativism in the novel is crucial to the freedom of Western characters from the vampire. Christopher Herbert explains that claims of relativism as a form of emancipation from repression were repeatedly made by Victorians. "The relativity movement, even in its most abstract and technically scientific manifestations, has been driven by the imagining of a newly emancipated order of thought amid a context of growing and (its distinctive characteristic) ever more insidious repression" (8).

8. "At the start of the novel the Count occupies a space that is virtually beyond representation," as Glover explains. "But then the inexorable logic of the narrative begins to lay down the conditions of the vampire's increasing legibility, [. . .] a phenomenon amenable to calculation and manipulation like any Other" (258).

Works Cited

Arata, Stephen. *Fictions of Loss in the Victorian Fin de Siècle*. Cambridge: Cambridge UP, 1996.

Bonnett, Alastair. "How the British Working Class Became White: The Symbolic (Re)formation of Racialized Capitalism." *Journal of Historical Sociology* 11 (1998): 316–40.

Bronfen, Elisabeth. *Over Her Dead Body: Death, Femininity and the Aesthetic*. New York: Routledge, 1992.

Coombes, Annie E. *Reinventing Africa: Museums, Material Culture and Popular Imagination in Late Victorian and Edwardian England*. New Haven: Yale UP, 1994.

Copjec, Joan. "Vampires, Breast-Feeding, and Anxiety." *October* 58 (1991): 25–43.

Day, Gary. "The State of *Dracula*: Bureaucracy and the Vampire." *Rereading Victorian Fiction*. Ed. Alice Jenkins and Juliet John. New York: St. Martin's, 2000: 81–95.

Dyer, Richard. "'White': The Last 'Special' Issue on Race?" *Screen* 29 (1988): 44–64.

Frow, John. "Tourism and the Semiotics of Nostalgia." *October* 57 (1991): 123–51.

Glover, David. "'Our Enemy is not Merely Spiritual': Degeneration and Modernity in Bram Stoker's *Dracula*." *Victorian Literature and Culture* 22 (1994): 249–65.

Greenslade, William. *Degeneration, Culture and the Novel, 1880–1940*. Cambridge: Cambridge UP, 1994.

Herbert, Christopher. *Victorian Relativity: Radical Thought and Scientific Discovery*. Chicago: U of Chicago P, 2001.

Herbert, Robert L. *Monet on the Normandy Coast: Tourism and Painting, 1867–1886*. New Haven: Yale UP, 1994.

Lloyd, David. "Race under Representation." *The Oxford Literary Review* 13 (1991): 62–94.

Lorimer, Douglas A. "Race, Science and Culture: Historical Continuities and Discontinuities, 1850–1914." *The Victorians and Race*. Ed. Shearer West. Aldershot, Hants.: Scholar Press, 1996. 12–33.

Mayhew, Henry. *London Labour and the London Poor*. Vol. 1. New York: Dover, 1968.

Moretti, Franco. *Signs Taken for Wonders: Essays in the Sociology of Literary Forms*. Trans. Susan Fischer, David Forgacs, and David Miller. London: NLB, 1983.

Schmitt, Cannon. *Alien Nation: Nineteenth-Century Gothic Fictions and English Nationality*. Philadelphia: U of Pennsylvania P, 1997.

Smith, Neil. *Uneven Development: Nature, Capital and the Production of Space*. Oxford: Blackwell, 1984.

Stoker, Bram. *Dracula*. New York: Penguin, 1993.

Valente, Joseph. *Dracula's Crypt: Bram Stoker, Irishness, and the Question of Blood*. Urbana: U of Illinois P, 2002.

Wicke, Jennifer. "Vampiric Typewriting: *Dracula* and its Media." *ELH* 59 (1992): 467–93.

Young, Robert J. C. *Colonial Desire: Hybridity in Theory, Culture and Race*. London: Routledge, 1995.

Zizek, Slavoj. "Love Thy Neighbor? No, Thanks!" *The Psychoanalysis of Race*. Ed. Christopher Lane. New York: Columbia UP, 1998. 154–75.

RESOURCES

Chronology of Bram Stoker's Life_____

1847	Abraham (known as Bram throughout his life) Stoker born on November 8 in Clontarf, a suburb of Dublin. The third of seven children of Abraham Stoker (a clerk) and Charlotte Thornley Stoker. Lives as invalid until about seven years old.
1864(?)–1870(?)	Attends Trinity College, Dublin. Works as clerk for the civil service, from possibly 1867 through 1877.
1871	Becomes drama critic for *Dublin Mail*.
1876	Father dies.
1878	Becomes acting manager of Henry Irving's Lyceum Theatre in London. Marries Florence Balcombe.
1879	*The Duties of Clerks of Petty Sessions in Ireland* is published. Only child, a son, is born.
1883	Organizes first North American tour for Irving's company.
1886	Publishes lecture "A Glimpse of America."
1889	*The Snake's Pass* is serialized in *The People*.
1890	*The Snake's Pass*, first novel, is published.
1895	*The Watter's Mou'* and *The Shoulder of Shasta* are published.
1897	*Dracula* is published.
1898	*Miss Betty* is published. A fire in the Lyceum's storage area destroys many scenes and props.
1901	Mother dies.
1902	*The Mystery of the Sea* is published. Lyceum closes.

1903	*The Jewel of Seven Stars* is published.
1905	*The Man* is published. Irving collapses and dies.
1906	*Personal Reminiscences of Henry Irving* is published in two volumes.
1908	*Lady Athlyne* is published.
1909	*The Lady of the Shroud* is published.
1910	*Famous Impostors* is published.
1911	*The Lair of the White Worm* is published.
1912	Dies on April 20 in London.
1914	Wife edits Stoker's stories, publishing them as *Dracula's Guest and Other Weird Stories*.

Works by Bram Stoker

Long Fiction
The Primrose Path, 1875
The Snake's Pass, 1890
The Shoulder of Shasta, 1895
The Watter's Mou', 1895
Dracula, 1897
Miss Betty, 1898
The Mystery of the Sea, 1902
The Jewel of Seven Stars, 1903
The Man, 1905 (pb. 1908 as *The Gates of Life*)
Lady Athlyne, 1908
The Lady of the Shroud, 1909
The Lair of the White Worm, 1911 (pb. 1966 as *The Garden of Evil*)

Short Story Collections
Under the Sunset, 1882
Snowbound: The Record of a Theatrical Touring Party, 1908
Dracula's Guest and Other Weird Stories, 1914

Nonfiction
The Duties of Clerks of Petty Sessions in Ireland, 1879
A Glimpse of America, 1886
Personal Reminiscences of Henry Irving, 1906
Famous Impostors, 1910

Bibliography_____

Anolik, Ruth Bienstock, and Douglas L. Howard, eds. *The Gothic Other: Racial and Social Constructions in the Literary Imagination*. Jefferson, N.C.: McFarland & Co., 2004.

Auerbach, Nina, and David J. Skal, eds. *"Dracula": Authoritative Text, Contexts, Reviews and Reactions, Dramatic and Film Variations, Criticism*. New York: W.W. Norton, 1997.

Belford, Barbara. *Bram Stoker: A Biography of the Author of "Dracula."* New York: Knopf, distributed by Random House, 1996.

Bloom, Clive, et al., eds. *Nineteenth-Century Suspense: From Poe to Conan Doyle*. New York: St. Martin's Press, 1988.

Bloom, Harold, ed. *Bram Stoker's "Dracula."* Philadelphia: Chelsea House Publishers, 2003.

Boone, Troy. "'He Is English and Therefore Adventurous': Politics, Decadence, and *Dracula*." *Studies in the Novel* 25 (1993): 76–91.

Carter, Margaret L., ed. *"Dracula": The Vampire and the Critics*. Ann Arbor: UMI Research Press, 1988.

Craft, Christopher. "Just Another Kiss: Inversion and Paranoia in Bram Stoker's *Dracula*." In *Another Kind of Love: Male Homosexual Desire in English Discourse, 1850–1920*, 71–105. Berkeley: University of California Press, 1994.

Daly, Nicholas. "Incorporated Bodies: *Dracula* and the Rise of Professionalism." In *Edwardian and Georgian Fiction*, edited by Harold Bloom. Philadelphia: Chelsea House Publishers, 2005.

Garrett, Peter K. *Gothic Reflections: Narrative Force in Nineteenth-Century Fiction*. Ithaca: Cornell University Press, 2003.

Gibson, Matthew. *"Dracula" and the Eastern Question: British and French Vampire Narratives of the Nineteenth-Century Near East*. New York: Palgrave Macmillan, 2006.

Greenway, John L. "Seward's Folly: *Dracula* as a Critique of 'Normal Science.'" *Stanford Literature Review* 3 (Fall 1986): 213–230.

Haining, Peter, and Peter Tremayne. *The Un-Dead: The Legend of Bram Stoker and "Dracula."* London: Constable, 1997.

Houston, Gail Turley. From *Dickens to "Dracula": Gothic, Economics, and Victorian Fiction*. New York: Cambridge University Press, 2005.

Hughes, William. *Beyond "Dracula": Bram Stoker's Fiction and Its Cultural Context*. New York: St. Martin's Press, 2000.

Johnson, Allan P. "'Dual Life': The Status of Women in Stoker's *Dracula*." In *Sexuality and Victorian Literature*, edited by Don Richard Cox. Knoxville: University of Tennessee Press, 1984. 20–39.

Leatherdale, Clive. "Social and Political Commentary." In *"Dracula": The Novel and the Legend: A Study of Bram Stoker's Gothic Masterpiece*. Willingborough, Northamptonshire, England: The Aquarian Press, 1985. 206–222.

Messent, Peter, ed. *Literature of the Occult: A Collection of Critical Essays*. Englewood Cliffs, N.J.: Prentice-Hall, 1981.

Miller, Elizabeth. *Dracula*. New York: Parkstone Press, 2000.

Pick, Daniel. "'Terrors of the night': *Dracula* and 'Degeneration' in the Late Nineteenth Century." *Critical Quarterly* 30, no. 4 (1988): 71–87.

Senf, Carol. "*Dracula*: Stoker's Response to the New Woman." *Victorian Studies* 25 (1982): 33–49.

_____, ed. *The Critical Response to Bram Stoker*. Westport, Conn.: Greenwood Press, 1993.

Showalter, Elaine. "Blood Sells: Vampire Fever and Anxieties for the *Fin de Siècle*." *Times Literary Supplement* (January 8, 1993): 14.

Smith, Andrew, and William Hughes, eds. *Empire and the Gothic: The Politics of Genre*. New York: Palgrave Macmillan, 2003.

Spencer, Kathleen L. "Purity and Danger: *Dracula*, the Urban Gothic, and the Late Victorian Degeneracy Crisis." *ELH* 59 (1992): 197–225.

Varnado, S. L. "The Daemonic in *Dracula*." In *Haunted Presence: The Numinous in Gothic Fiction*. Tuscaloosa: University of Alabama Press, 1987. 95–114.

Weissman, Judith. "Women as Vampires: *Dracula* as a Victorian Novel." *Midwest Quarterly* 18 (1977): 392–405.

CRITICAL INSIGHTS

About the Editor _____

Jack Lynch is Associate Professor of English at Rutgers University in Newark, New Jersey. He has published both scholarly and popular books and essays, mostly on British and American culture in the long eighteenth century. He is the author of *The Age of Elizabeth in the Age of Johnson* (Cambridge University Press, 2003), *Becoming Shakespeare: The Unlikely Afterlife That Turned a Provincial Playwright into the Bard* (Walker & Co., 2007), and *Deception and Detection in Eighteenth-Century Britain* (Ashgate Publishing, 2008). He is also the editor of *The Age of Johnson: A Scholarly Annual* and co-editor of *Anniversary Essays on Johnson's Dictionary* (Cambridge University Press, 2005). His essays and reviews have appeared in scholarly forums such as *Eighteenth-Century Life*, *The Review of English Studies*, and *Studies in Philology*, as well as in *The American Scholar*, *The New York Times*, and the *Los Angeles Times*.

About *The Paris Review* _____

The Paris Review is America's preeminent literary quarterly, dedicated to discovering and publishing the best new voices in fiction, nonfiction, and poetry. The magazine was founded in Paris in 1953 by the young American writers Peter Matthiessen and Doc Humes, and edited there and in New York for its first fifty years by George Plimpton. Over the decades, the *Review* has introduced readers to the earliest writings of Jack Kerouac, Philip Roth, T. C. Boyle, V. S. Naipaul, Ha Jin, Jay McInerney, and Mona Simpson, and published numerous now classic works, including Roth's *Goodbye, Columbus*, Donald Barthelme's *Alice*, Jim Carroll's *Basketball Diaries*, and selections from Samuel Beckett's *Molloy* (his first publication in English). The first chapter of Jeffrey Eugenides's *The Virgin Suicides* appeared in the *Review*'s pages, as well as stories by Edward P. Jones, Rick Moody, David Foster Wallace, Denis Johnson, Jim Shepard, Jim Crace, Lorrie Moore, Jeanette Winterson, and Ann Patchett.

The Paris Review's renowned Writers at Work series of interviews, whose early installments include legendary conversations with E. M. Forster, William Faulkner, and Ernest Hemingway, is one of the landmarks of world literature. The interviews received a George Polk award and were nominated for a Pulitzer Prize. Among the more than three hundred interviewees are Robert Frost, Marianne Moore, W. H. Auden, Elizabeth Bishop, Susan Sontag, and Toni Morrison. Recent issues feature conversations with Salman Rushdie, Joan Didion, Stephen King, Norman Mailer, Kazuo Ishiguro and Umberto Eco. (A complete list of the interviews is available at www.theparisreview.org.) In November 2008, Picador will publish the third of a four-volume series of anthologies of *Paris Review* interviews. The first two volumes have received acclaim. *The New York Times* called the Writers at Work series "the most remarkable and extensive interviewing project we possess."

The Paris Review is edited by Philip Gourevitch, who was named to the post in 2005, following the death of George Plimpton two years earlier. Under Gourevitch's leadership, the magazine's international distribution has expanded, paid subscriptions have risen 150 percent, and newsstand distribution has doubled. A new editorial team has published fiction by Andre Aciman, Damon Galgut, Mohsin Hamid, Gish Jen, Richard Price, Said Sayrafiezadeh, and Alistair Morgan. Poetry editors Charles Simic, Meghan O'Rourke, and Dan Chiasson have selected works by Billy Collins, Jesse Ball, Mary Jo Bang, Sharon Olds, and Mary Karr. Writing published in the magazine has been anthologized in *Best American Short Stories* (2006, 2007, and 2008), *Best American Poetry, Best Creative Non-Fiction*, the Pushcart Prize anthology, and *O. Henry Prize Stories*.

The magazine presents two annual awards. The Hadada Award for lifelong contribution to literature has recently been given to William Styron, Joan Didion, Norman Mailer, and Peter Matthiessen in 2008. The Plimpton Prize for Fiction, given to a new voice in fiction brought to national attention in the pages of *The Paris Review*, was presented in 2007 to Benjamin Percy and to Jesse Ball in 2008.

The Paris Review won the 2007 National Magazine Award in photojournalism, and the *Los Angeles Times* recently called *The Paris Review* "an American treasure with true international reach."

Since 1999 *The Paris Review* has been published by The Paris Review Foundation, Inc., a not-for-profit 501(c)(3) organization.

The Paris Review is available in digital form to libraries worldwide in selected academic databases exclusively from EBSCO Publishing. Libraries can contact EBSCO at 1-800-653-2726 for details. For more information on *The Paris Review* or to subscribe, please visit: www.theparisreview.org.

Contributors

Jack Lynch is Associate Professor of English at Rutgers University in Newark, New Jersey. He is the author of *The Age of Elizabeth in the Age of Johnson* (2003), *Becoming Shakespeare: The Unlikely Afterlife That Turned a Provincial Playwright into the Bard* (2007), and *Deception and Detection in Eighteenth-Century Britain* (2008). He is also the editor of *The Age of Johnson: A Scholarly Annual*.

Richard Means earned his bachelor of arts degree from Bates College in 2004 and currently works as a web editor. He has published biographies on John Milton, Emily Brontë, Samuel Taylor Coleridge, Nathaniel Hawthorne, and Voltaire.

Juliet Lapidos is an assistant editor at *Slate*. Her writing has appeared in *Slate* and *The New York Observer*, among other publications.

Bridget M. Marshall is an Assistant Professor in the English department at the University of Massachusetts, Lowell, where she teaches courses in American literature, the horror story, the Gothic novel, and disability in literature. She earned her Ph.D. at the University of Massachusetts, Amherst, with a dissertation on legal themes in the Gothic novel. She has recently published articles on a seventeenth-century witch in Hadley, Massachusetts, and on witch-themed tourism in Salem.

Camille-Yvette Welsch is a senior lecturer in English at the Pennsylvania State University. She is the director of Penn State's Summer Creative Writing Conference for high school students and the coordinator of the Red Weather Reading Series. Her work has appeared in *Mid-American Review, Barrow Street, The Writer's Chronicle, The Women's Review of Books*, and *Small Spiral Notebook*.

Matthew J. Bolton is a professor of English at Loyola School in New York City, where he also serves as the Dean of Students. Bolton received his doctor of philosophy in English from The Graduate Center of the City University of New York (CUNY) in 2005. His dissertation at the university was entitled: "Transcending the Self in Robert Browning and T. S. Eliot." Prior to attaining his Ph.D. at CUNY, Bolton also earned a master of philosophy in English (2004) and a master of science in English education (2001). His undergraduate work was done at the State University of New York at Binghamton, where he studied English literature.

Allan Johnson teaches at the University of Leeds, where he is a Bonamy Dobrée Scholar. He is currently working on his dissertation on Alan Hollinghurst.

Beth E. McDonald teaches at the University of Nevada, Las Vegas. She has written *The Vampire as Numinous Experience* (2004) and also has written for the journal *Extrapolation*.

Carrol L. Fry is a professor emeritus at Northwest Missouri State University. He has published articles on eighteenth- and nineteenth-century British literature, film, and American literature. His books include *Charlotte Smith: Popular Novelist* (1980) and *Cinema of the Occult* (2009).

Carla Edwards teaches in the Department of Psychology, Sociology and Counseling at Northwest Missouri State University.

Samuel Lyndon Gladden is Associate Professor and Coordinator of Graduate Studies in English at the University of Northern Iowa. He has published essays in *Victorian Literature and Culture*, *Studies in Romanticism*, and *Victorians Institute Journal*. He is currently working on several book projects, including a forthcoming edition of Wilde's *The Importance of Being Earnest* and a textbook on argument and visual culture. His book *Shelley's Textual Seductions: Plotting Utopia in the Erotic and Political Works* was published in 2002.

Jimmie E. Cain, Jr. teaches in the English department at Middle Tennessee State University, where he is also director of the Writing Center. He has contributed to the text *Dracula: The Shade and the Shadow—A Critical Anthology* (1998) and several journals, including *West Georgia Review*, *Review of Contemporary Fiction*, and *Film Criticism*.

David Glover teaches in the English department at the University of Southampton, England. His books include an edition of Edward Wallace's *The Four Just Men* (1995), *Vampires, Mummies, and Liberals: Bram Stoker and the Politics of Popular Fiction* (1996), an edition of Bram Stoker's *The Jewel of Seven Stars* (1996), and *Genders* (2000). His articles have appeared as chapters in numerous books, and he has contributed essays to journals such as *Gender and History*, *Gothic Studies*, *Victorian Literature and Culture*, and *PMLA*.

Nancy Armstrong is Nancy Duke Lewis Professor of English, Comparative Literature, and Modern Culture and Media at Brown University. She is editor of the journal *NOVEL: A Forum on Fiction* and has published more than one hundred articles on topics concerning feminist theory, eighteenth- and nineteenth-century British Literature, and visual culture. Her books include *Desire and Domestic Fiction: A Political History of the Novel* (1987), *The Imaginary Puritan: Literature, Intellectual Labor, and the Origins of Personal Life* (1992), *Fiction in the Age of Photography: The Legacy of British Realism* (1999), and *How Novels Think: British Fiction and the Limits of Individualism* (2005).

Patricia McKee is Professor of English and Edward Hyde Cox Professor in the Humanities at Dartmouth University. Her works include *Heroic Commitment in Richardson, Eliot, and James* (1986), *Public and Private: Gender, Class, and the British Novel (1764-1878)* (1997), *Producing American Races: Henry James, William Faulkner, Toni Morrison* (1999), and articles in numerous publications.

Acknowledgments

"Bram Stoker" by Richard Means. From "Bram Stoker: Background and Early Life," "Bram Stoker: Early Literary Career," and "Bram Stoker: Writing Dracula" in EBSCO Online Database *Literary Reference Center.* Copyright © 2006 by Great Neck Publishing. Reprinted by permission of Great Neck Publishing.

"The *Paris Review* Perspective" by Juliet Lapidos. Copyright © 2008 by Juliet Lapidos. Special appreciation goes to Christopher Cox and Nathaniel Rich, editors for *The Paris Review.*

"Recreating the World: The Sacred and the Profane in Bram Stoker's *Dracula*" by Beth E. McDonald. From *The Vampire as Numinous Experience: Spiritual Journeys with the Undead in British and American Literature.* Copyright © 2004 Beth E. McDonald by permission of McFarland & Company, Inc., Box 611, Jefferson NC 28640. www.mcfarlandpub.com.

"The New Naturalism: Primal Screams in Abraham Stoker's *Dracula*" by Carrol L. Fry and Carla Edwards. From *Midwest Quarterly* 47, no. 1 (Autumn 2005), pp. 40-54. Copyright ©2005 by Midwest Quarterly. Reprinted by permission of Carla Edwards.

"*Dracula*'s Earnestness: Stoker's Debt to Wilde" by Samuel Lyndon Gladden. From *English Language Notes* 42, no. 4 (June 2005), pp. 62-75. Copyright © 2005 by *English Language Notes.* Reprinted by permission of *English Language Notes.*

"*Dracula*: Righting Old Wrongs and Displacing New Fears" by Jimmie E. Cain, Jr. From *Bram Stoker and Russophobia: Evidence of the British Fear of Russia in "Dracula" and "The Lady of the Shroud."* Copyright © 2006 Jimmie E. Cain, Jr. by permission of McFarland & Company, Inc., Box 611, Jefferson NC 28640. www.mcfarlandpub.com.

"Vampires, Mummies, and Liberals: Questions of Character and Modernity" by David Glover. From *Vampires, Mummies, and Liberals*, pp. 58-81. Copyright © 1996, Duke University Press. All rights reserved. Used by permission of the publisher.

"Feminism, Fiction, and the Utopian Promise of *Dracula*" by Nancy Armstrong. From *differences* 16, no. 1 (Spring 2005), pp. 1-23. Copyright © 2005, Brown University and *differences: A Journal of Feminist Cultural Studies.* All rights reserved. Used by permission of the publisher, Duke University Press.

"Racialization, Capitalism, and Aesthetics in Stoker's *Dracula*" by Patricia McKee. From *Novel: A Forum on Fiction* 36, no. 1 (Fall 2002), pp. 42-60. Copyright © 2002 by Novel Corporation. Reprinted by permission of Novel Corporation.

Index

Lloyd, David, 290, 292, 302

Locke, John, 269

Locks and doors, 81-83

Lombroso, Cesare, 48, 111, 137, 182, 228, 230-231, 238, 240, 248, 250

London, England, 76-79, 83, 144, 147-148, 150, 173, 177, 179, 183-184, 186, 188-189, 193, 197-198, 201, 207, 210, 213, 215-216. *See also* England

London Labour and the London Poor (Mayhew), 104, 279

Loser's myth, 202

Love in Earnest (Nicholson), 157, 167

Lugosi, Bela, 17, 32, 34, 143

Lukács, Georg, 10, 258, 272

Lyceum Theatre (London), 13-16, 32, 38-39, 169

McDonald, Beth E., 6

McKee, Patricia, 11

Macnaghten, Melville, 249

McNally, Raymond T., 110, 137, 211-212

Madwoman in the Attic, The (Gilbert and Gubar), 255

Madwomen, 255

Malapropisms, 77

Male bonding, 139, 148

Man, The (Stoker), 16, 249

Man Who Wrote "Dracula," The (Farson), 51

Marcus, Sharon, 275

Marcuse, Herbert, 258

Marr, Wilhelm, 196

Marriage, 260-261, 273

Marshall, Bridget M., 3, 5

Marx, Karl, 168

Marxism, 11; theory of romance, 50

Masculinity, 244, 254-255, 257, 265, 271

Masculinization, 195

Mass culture, 72, 76, 79, 234

Masterman, Charles, 227

Materialism, 241-242

Maudsley, Henry, 230, 247

May, Leila S., 44

Mayhew, Henry, 104, 279, 282

Men, 56, 62, 64, 68, 175, 195, 204, 209, 215-216, 254-256, 260, 264-265, 271-272, 274; desire, 59; male bonding, 139, 148; sexual behavior of, 148; Western, 285

Mesmer, Franz Anton, 226

Mesmerism, 9

Middle-class society, 231

Mill, John Stuart, 220, 242-243, 250

Miller, Elizabeth, 212

Miller, Jonathan, 250

Miscegenation, 194

Miss Betty (Stoker), 16

Modernism, Romance, and the Fin de Siècle (Daly), 274

Modernist style, 74-75, 79

Modernity, 47, 49, 72, 76, 84, 219-221, 228, 235, 280-284, 287, 292, 300

Modernization, 19

Modest_Witness@Second_Millennium (Haraway), 275

Monarchy, 268

Money, 186-187, 200, 214

Monk, The (Lewis), 4

Monogenesis, 263

Monster (etymology), 19

Monstrosities, 3-4, 8

Moonstone, The (Collins), 223

Moral fitness, 221, 228

Moral insanity, 218, 228

Moral Viking, 212, 237, 244

Moretti, Franco, 29, 40, 50, 184-187, 200, 289, 304

Morris, Quincey (*Dracula*), 58-59, 63,